The Abode of Grace
Bhagawan Nityananda of Ganeshpuri

Sadguru Kedarji

The Bhakta School of Transformation, Inc.
Youngstown, Ohio

The Abode of Grace
Bhagawan Nityananda of Ganeshpuri

Copies of this book may be ordered through booksellers or by contacting:

The Bhakta School of Transformation, Inc.
330-623-7388 Ext 10

NityanandaShaktipatYoga.org

ISBN: 979-8-218-18009-6

Printed in the United States of America

Contents

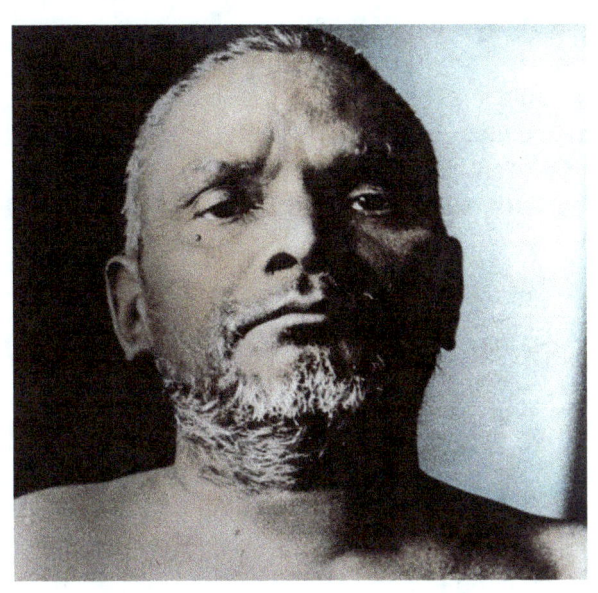

Bhagawan Nityananda of Ganeshpuri

About the Author

Sadguru Kedarji is the Founder of The Bhakta School of Transformation, an Ohio-based not-for-profit public charity devoted to lasting Inner Peace and permanent spiritual transformation. The curriculum offering here is based on Kedaji's 4 Pillars of Joy In Daily Living.

He had an early career in the Performing Arts as an actor and singer in Broadway musicals, plays, movies and television. He went on to study violin and conducting at the Juilliard School of Music and graduated with degrees in performance and composition from the Manhattan School of Music. Later, he studied Eastern and Oriental Medicine, graduated with degrees in both from the Kushi Institute, and had a practice in New York City for many years.

Leading With Love

Sadguru Kedarji helps people embrace the Grace in life's joys and challenges in a way that causes lasting happiness and peace. In a world seemingly mad with greed and corruption, Kedarji has a long track record of helping people affirm and expand the best parts of their lives.

He is a Sadhu in the lineage of the great sage and saint, Bhagawan Nityananda of Ganeshpuri. He imparts the same instruction and leadership he was taught— the same methods used by a line of spiritually proven and powerful masters who have uplifted people's lives for thousands of years.

A Sadhu is one who has made the commitment to live as an ascetic, renouncing the pursuit of worldly pleasures and fantasies to serve the greater good and to work to uplift humanity. In this regard, Kedarji is also known as a Sadguru, meaning true spiritual leader, and a Shaktipat Guru (see below) who leads by example in becoming both wise and well with a powerful, heart-centered approach.

Practical Leadership In A Shaktipat Guru

Kedarji has a reputation for leading without insisting that people follow. This allows students and seekers to come to our approach in their own way. Although 'Sadguru' is an affectionate term used by those who have benefited from his leadership, for Kedarji, the reference to Sadguru is a reference to our lineage of Sadgurus on whose shoulders he stands and takes refuge in. This is the great Shiva lineage that Bhagawan Nityananda of Ganeshpuri also made, of which Kedarji is a part.

Wise, Happy and Well

Many of Kedarji's students say that, through his leadership, he has transformed their lives in profound ways not experienced in other modalities or on other paths.

His students blossom and uncover hidden strengths through a well-integrated and time-tested approach. Through his leadership, it's possible for anyone and everyone to experience life's magic in a way that they come to know their true nature and attain a state of lasting happiness, peace and joy.

With his 4 Pillars of Joy In Daily Living as the foundation (the Spiritual Power, Improved Mental State, Emotional Resilience and Vibrant Health), he combines the power of Grace of his spiritual lineage with the time-honored, Siddha Science of the Yoga of the Siddhas. This powerful combination includes his skill as a Shaktipat Meditation master.

Authentic Shaktipat Guru – Shaktipat Meditation Master

Sadguru Kedarji is a Shaktipat Guru. He has been vested with the power and authority to fully awaken and nurture the dormant spiritual awareness known as Kundalini. Specifically, this awakening occurs by way of the transmission of the Grace-bestowing power inherent in the Blessing of Shaktipat. In particular, you will find that Sadguru Kedarji is a recognized and very skilled spiritual leader and Shaktipat Meditation Master. Additionally, his is the ability to lead you on the journey to the realization of your true nature or Self-Realization. Indeed, this is a journey in which you retrace your steps back to God.

Author/Producer

Sadguru Kedarji is the author of several books and courses, including:

- Vibration of Divine Consciousness. A Spiritual Autobiography.
- The Verses On Witness Consciousness.
- How To Be Fearless, Happy and Resilient In The Age of Noise and Distractions. (a video home-study course and weekend retreat).
- The Sutras On The 5-Fold Act of Divine Consciousness.
- Live Strong and Be Happy. Learn The Daily Rituals of The Most Spiritually-Powerful, Happiest and Healthiest People On The Planet.

Spiritual Journey

Sadguru Kedarji began his quest to understand and fully imbibe Yoga Science at an early age. Feeling incomplete, Kedarji began an intense spiritual journey that took him to India and Asia. Soon after, he experienced an initiation, an awakening into the power of true Meditation, Chanting and Contemplation that formed the foundation for putting all the pieces together.

Due to this event and ongoing application of the methods taught connected to it, Kedarji was able to fully apply the science behind well-being that is based on the Spiritual Power. He calls it the energy substratum of everything. His direct, unfolding experience of this power is the basis for the integration of his 4 Pillars of Joy In Daily Living embodied in his unique approach; An approach that combines Siddha Science and the science of a holistic lifestyle of health and well-being with the transmission of Grace that he extends as a God-realized, Shaktipat Guru.

Sadguru Kedarji

Acknowledgements

We extend our heartfelt thanks to Niranjan Suvarna, son of M.D. Suvarna. Special permission has been granted by Niranjan Suvarna, Foto Corner, Khar West, Mumbai, for use of all pictures in this book.

Special thanks also goes to Professor Shivananda Kamath (now deceased), and Madhava Hegde (now deceased), descendants in the line of Bhagawan Nityananda of Ganeshpuri, for their contributions to facts and stories presented here about Bhagawan Nityananda's existence on Earth.

I sing and I dance in the glory of my Shri Gurudev. Words cannot describe the Blessings of Grace showered on me by Gurudev Muktananda Paramahamsa. Such Blessings have transformed my existence here into a paradise of Joy, of which the experience is permanent.

It is through Muktananda that I came to know Bhagawan Nityandanda of Ganeshpuri (Muktananda's Guru and the Master of our lineage in these modern times) intimately in the instructed, inner worship of Bhagawan Nityananda. In this way, Bhagawan Nityananda of Ganeshpuri is the cause and the effect of our Nityananda Shaktipat Yoga offering that is supported by His Grace and the Grace of the Siddha lineage, of which I and our Sangham are a part.

I also offer my heartfelt gratitude to my staff at The Bhakta School of Transformation for their help in proofreading and finalizing this manuscript. Gratitude is also offered to our Board of Directors; Deana Tareshawty, Kambra McConnel, Shanti Harkness, Ben Tucker and Sarah Porter, for their support.

May all be Joyful in the knowledge of Nityananda – the eternal Bliss of the Absolute!

~ Kedarji

Introduction

Bhagawan Nityananda of Ganeshpuri is the Avadhut and Supreme Guru of my lineage in this modern age, a descendant of Lord Shiva himself. Swami Muktananda Paramahamsa was a very great servant and Disciple of Bhagawan Nityananda. After initiating Muktananda through Shaktipat and leading him in the completion of his Sadhana, Bhagawan Nityananda had three rooms built for Muktananda's dwelling place in Ganeshpuri, just a short distance away from his own ashram in Ganeshpuri. Today, that place has become a thriving ashram known as Gurudev Siddha Peeth.

Gurudev Siddha Peeth Ashram – Ganeshpuri, India

By the Grace and at the command of Bhagawan Nityananda, Muktananda Baba toured the world three times, bringing Bhagawan Nityananda's Siddha Yoga to the world. Muktananda became known as a Jagadguru (world Guru) and his mission rescued and freed many souls, including mine. Muktananda Paramahamsa is considered to be one of the greatest and foremost Disciples of Bhagawan Nityananda of Ganeshpuri.

After initiating me by his Grace through Shaktipat, Paramahamsa Muktananda told me to merge in Bhagawan Nityananda. Bhagawan Nityananda was and is the perfect embodiment of the Shiva-Shakti Principle (God-principle). For more about my initiation and Sadhana led by Paramahamsa Muktananda, you can read Vibration of Divine Consciousness, available here https://www.nityanandashaktipatyoga.org/books-by-sadguru-kedarji/

Everything that takes place in Nityananda Shaktipat Yoga is due to the Grace of my Guru, Muktananda Paramahamsa, and Shri Avadhuta Bhagawan Nityananda. Without their Grace, I would not be able to take a single step. And Bhagawan Nityananda's Love Is So Beautiful that nothing else matters. Shri Nityananda Baba is the flame that keeps the Shakti power of our lineage alive in the transmission of Grace that is experienced by so many Nityananda Shaktipat Yoga devotees.

The Grace-bestowing power that flows through Kedarji does so by the Will, Grace and Blessings of Muktananda Paramahamsa and Bhagawan Nityananda of Ganeshpuri. Just as a light bulb cannot illumine anything without power, Kedarji could offer nothing without their Grace. It was Bhagawan Nityananda who took me to Lord Shiva's abode and I am certain that he must have convinced Lord Shiva to bless my life and, this, my Guruseva offering.

Bhagawan Nityananda burned away the last vestiges of my identity and took up residence in me. In this way, Shri Nityananda also made a permanent abode within me for Lord Shiva to enter into and reside. "Sadguru Kedarji" is just a name, a label for this form. Truly, my real identity is bound up in Him.

Muktananda Paramahamsa

*I consider you all sisters and brothers in the family of
my Nityananda Baba. You are all pure souls. You were
born pure. Your perfection is already with you. Each of
you is a flame of that pure Self. Being of the family of
Nityananda like me, you have joined me to do his work.
You are me and I am you.*

*Do not get involved in "mine and thine," "this is small
and this is big," "this is yours and this is mine." Do not
create such divisions. Keep working without ego or pride.
If the feeling of "mine and thine," "small and big,"
arises in you, and the desire to raise someone up and
bring another down, then you can be sure that you are
falling.*

> Muktananda Paramahamsa
> Bhagawan Nityananda of Ganeshpuri

Muktananda's last tour to the West took place in the
summer of 1981. Three significant events occurred for me
just before Baba left to return to India that Fall.

Inwardly, I had been asking Baba for direction for

my life and some insight into what the future held for me. I had also asked to become his disciple. That summer, I took almost every intensive Shri Gurudev gave. These intensives were one of the ways in which Baba gave Shaktipat.

During one of these intensives, Baba started past me while exiting the hall. He stopped, turned to me and said, "Again? Again here?" He then starred at me intensely. As he continued to speak, our eyes locked and I heard, from inside myself, "Just meditate on my Guru, Bhagawan Nityananda, and you will attain everything." Baba then smiled at me and nodded his head, raising his eyebrows as if to say, "Did you hear me!?" Baba also told me that I would attain Moksha, Liberation in this very life.

The second event occurred right after I had this encounter. Gurudev held a private program for leaders of the African-American community. I was invited to attend this program by one of Baba's swamis who, at the time, assisted Baba in teaching many of the courses. Just before the start of this program, this swami said, "You know, there's a great sutra that I find makes a beautiful meditation on Shiva. It is *Na Shivam Vidyate Qua Chit*, which means; *Nothing exists that is not Shiva.* For some reason I am told to share this with you."

That morning I attended the private program. Baba gave Darshan at the end of this program and we were all invited to receive Baba's blessing. There was Gurudev sitting in his chair cross-legged, with his feet folded up on his legs. He had his peacock feathers and he was bopping people as usual. As I waited in the Darshan line to be received by Baba, inwardly, I asked for confirmation of what he had told me the day before; that I would go across in this life. I also asked for confirmation that he would take me as his disciple.

Inwardly, I asked, if this all were true, for Baba to put his feet on the floor and allow me to embrace them. Then, as I got to the chair and bowed my head, I blurted out, "Na Shivam Vidyate Qua Chit." Baba smiled at me and immediately put his feet down on the floor. I then embraced his feet for several minutes!

The third event took place when I asked Baba for a spiritual name. First, he handed me a crystal statue of Lord Ganesh, the deity who removes all obstacles on the path to Liberation. Then he gave me the name Kedar. Kedar is a reference to *Kedara Shiva*, the expression of Lord Shiva as he arises from meditation to give Blessings, to grant Grace. In giving me this name, Gurudev knew much more about where I was headed than even I.

Kedara Shiva

Muktananda Paramahamsa passed in 1982 on the full moon of Lord Krishna's birthday. I say Baba "passed" rather than "died" because Baba took *Mahasamadhi*. A Liberated Being does not take another birth. Mahasamadhi occurs when the Prana (life force) rises up the Sushumna Nadi (subtle body) one last time and merges in the Sahasrar. For Liberated beings, the Prana remains in the Sahasrar at the moment of dropping the body, rather than leaving the body and taking the Sushumna with it, to be reborn again in another form.

Baba understood that, because each of us is Shiva, because each of us is God, that limitless Consciousness that also takes the form of the body, we never die. It is only the body that we cast off. Death does not really exist. So, Baba consciously merged his Prana into Paramshiva (the formless Absolute) for the last time, and willfully dropped his body as Siddhas do.

In the path of the Siddhas, the passing of a great saint is a time for celebration and the intense renewal of spiritual practice. Disciples of a great saint like Baba experience their Master entering them fully at the time of the Master's passing. And this is the way it was for many of us when Baba left. In fact, devotee and disciple alike had the same experience; that Baba had never really left, that he has continued to do his work by entering each and every one of us fully.

The evening that Baba took Mahasamadhi I had a dream in which he appeared to me. In this dream, he told me to walk with him and I found myself following Baba down a path and around the bank of a huge Blue lake. He was pointing to the lake and the horizon and giving me instruction.

We walked and then stopped to sit by the lake and then we got up and walked again. This dream went on for quite some time. It was cut short by a phone call that woke me from my dream. The call was from a fellow disciple who called to tell me that Baba had just taken Mahasamadhi. I was told Baba had passed, but this was not the last time I saw him.

The entire nature of my Sadhana changed when my Gurudev took Mahasamadhi. I experienced a profound shift inside and I felt as if I had turned a corner and shed "many skins," never to turn back again. My Meditation practice became much more intense. For the first time ever, I developed a strong desire to study the scriptures and sacred texts of Shaivism and Vedanta. Baba appeared to me often in those days in most of my meditations. In this way, my relationship with Baba intensified.

Then, one day, Baba reminded me of what he had told me before taking Mahasamadhi, to meditate on Bhagawan Nityananda of Ganeshpuri. So, I began doing so. I started to develop a strong inner relationship with Bhagawan Nityananda (Bade Baba, as he was affectionately called – meaning 'Big Baba'). Baba had told me to meditate on Bhagawan Nityananda and now this Meditation was becoming spontaneous. This shift in my inner experience was very significant.

Two years after Baba left his body I traveled to Ganeshpuri, India to participate in his annual Mahasamadhi celebration at the Ganeshpuri ashram. Thousands of people had come together from all over the world to celebrate his life and work. During this celebration, there was a Yajna (fire ceremony) presided over by Brahmin priests. This Yajna went on for 16 days, with chanting and oblations (offerings) being made to the fire.

While meditating in front of the fire, I saw Bhagawan Nityananda standing in the flames. He spoke to me, giving me the command to begin offering the work I now volunteer through Nityananda Shaktipat Yoga. Bhagawan Nityananda then stepped out of the fire, touched me on the head and then disappeared. At first, I ignored this vision, thinking that it must have been an hallucination of some kind. Bade Baba had never appeared to me in such a vivid way as this.

But I did start intense meditation on Bhagawan Nityananda. During this and subsequent trips to the Ganeshpuri ashram, I spent a lot of time in Bhagawan Nityananda's Mahasamadhi shrine in the village of Ganeshpuri. I made many offerings to Bade Baba's Murti there and spent many hours meditating in the shrine. As a result of this pilgrimage, I started to have even more profound experiences during chanting and Meditation.

Mahasamadhi Shrine of Bhagawan Nityananda
Village of Ganeshpuri

During this period of my Sadhana, I felt that events in my life had sped up. It was as if things that were to happen were now happening in a hurry. Whatever needed to be completed was being completed in triple time. For example, I had several astrological readings during this period.

In these readings I was told about relationships and events that were not "scheduled" to happen until very late in my life or in a future life. Yet these events and relationships were happening right there during that time. Relationships were starting and culminating very quickly. I was meeting people who I was not to meet until I was an old man. That which was predicted to occur near my death had just happened!

I later came to realize that many of my karmas were being burned. It was as if those things that I needed to experience, those things that may have become obstacles to my Liberation, were either happening and being completed or had been burned from my being.

I felt as if I was living many lifetimes in a very

short period. The Guru does burn many of your karmas, those that cause you to conceal God from yourself. And this is what was happening to me. My perception of time changed entirely during this period. I felt the Universe was unfolding inside me. All this was a result of my pilgrimages to Bhagawan Nityananda's Mahasamadhi shrine and my meditations on him.

Shortly after this period, I had several experiences in Meditation that not only changed the quality of my Sadhana, but also changed the entire course of my destiny. I am going to share one of those experiences here, just as I wrote it in my journal.

* * *

I am meditating in the Bhagawan Nityananda temple. I open my eyes and look at the Murti of Bhagawan. Suddenly, Bhagawan Nityananda has come out of the Murti. He walks toward me and is now dancing around me in a circle. He is laughing and singing ecstatically, while dancing around me. He stops in front of me and puts his hands on my head. He then runs his hands down over my face. Bhagawan Nityananda pauses there, his big hands on my face and his long fingers stretching to the top of my head.

He then starts dancing around me and singing once again. After he finishes singing and dancing around me, he climbs back into the Murti. But he has entered me also! Bhagawan Nityananda has taken up residence in me! Now I am having an inner vision of Bhagawan Nityananda and the Siddhas of our lineage throwing flower petals on me. They are garlanding me with flowers.

* * *

There were other, similar, experiences as well. With each experience, with each vision and message, I dove deeper into my own heart. I discovered states of indescribable Joy that I did not believe could be experienced by a human being. My longing for God and the Guru increased. My state of Devotion had risen to the point where I really didn't care whether Liberation was at hand or not. I had no thoughts of siddhahood or enlightenment. I only wanted to drink the nectar of this Supreme Love, this Joy, over and over again.

This entire experience nurtured the longing in me to worship the feet of the Guru and to experience the waves of Love and Bliss that became mine as I merged into my Guru and into God. I was becoming a mad lover of God. This state of ecstasy was all that I lived for.

It was with this experience and expanded vision that I began performing many additional years of Seva in the ashram. I would offer Seva and chant. Then more Seva, chant and meditate again. Time seemed to stand still. I started to see God in everyone. I started to recognize my Guru's Shakti everywhere. When I meditated on the form of Bhagawan Nityananda, my Shri Gurudev Muktananda's form appeared to me inside. Then I would meditate on Muktananda Baba's form. I was awash in ecstasy in doing so. Then Lord Shiva's form appeared to me and I would meditate on Shivaji's form and disappear in the ocean of Joy. So, my experience became that of the three in 1, Bhagawan Nityananda, Gurudev Muktananda and Lord Shiva. I did become mad, but not in the way you may think. This madness I could not attempt to describe. *Om Guru Om!*

I am very fortunate to have had the privilege of interacting with several of Bhagawan Nityananda's elder disciples. My own Shri Gurudev was a humble and faithful servant of Shri Nityananda who carried on the lineage by spreading His love and Shakti to millions of people.

These servants of the great sage Bhagawan Nityananda of Ganeshpuri have shared their experiences of the Master and their eyewitness accounts of His offering on the planet. These experience shares and stories are posted at www.bhagawannityananda.org

People reading this website have reported receiving Bhagawan Nityananda's Grace in dreams and Meditation.
No book about Bhagawan Nityananda would be complete without sharing some of the history of his Divine presence here on Earth. To that end, I offer this work by sharing some of the insights, principles and stories of Bhagawan Nityananda. May all who read these words be uplifted and filled with God's Grace and the All-Pervasive Love of Bhagawan Nityananda of Ganeshpuri.

~ Kedarji

Chapter 1
Bhagawan Nityananda of Ganeshpuri

Salutations to Nityananda, the Guru, who rescues his disciples from transmigration, who has assumed a body for the needs of devotees, whose nature is Consciousness and Being.

Free of desires, free of expectations, free of all defects independent and fearless – to that Nityananda, I bow.

Free of possessiveness, free of egoism, regarding as the same a clod, a stone, and gold, even-minded in happiness and sorrow, all-enduring – to that avadhut indeed, I bow.

From the Avadhuta Stotram

Bhakti means intense longing for and love for the Master and His teachings. This Bhakti is also known as Supreme Devotion and Surrender to God and to the Master. Bhakti also means Dharma. Dharma is the act of loving Truth more than mundane life itself. Bhagawan Nityananda was the very embodiment of this Dharma, this Bhakti.

In *Bhakti* are all the other attainments. The journey to God-realization is the process of Liberation from the ignorance that has kept you separate from God. Bhakti is the easiest and quickest way to make this journey. With Bhakti, it is your intense desire and longing for the Guru and His instruction that does all the work. It is this intensity that causes God to come looking for you.

There are many thousands of people on every continent on the globe who practice this Bhakti for Bhagawan Nityananda. Even though he is no longer in the body, people of every race, color and creed who worship

1

his form share that they experience him in Meditation and in dreams.

Many who did not know him in his physical form share that He has healed them from illness in a dream or vision. There are those, even today, who receive Shaktipat (Kundalini awakening) just by meditating on a picture of Bhagawan Nityananda.

Those who gather in his name to celebrate his Divine Presence in Chanting, Meditation, Prayer and the taking of Prasad, all share that the presence of Bhagawan Nityananda is clear and palpable. Truly speaking, he has never left. He dwells in perpetuity, in the hearts of those who love him and remember him daily. This is true Bhakti.

There was a devotee named Padmanabh S. Prabhu from Murdeshwar (in India). He was known to most as Murdeshwar Mama. Mama means Uncle. In India, it is customary to call an elderly gentleman "Mama."

Lord Vishnu is the deity manifested by Lord Shiva who also shares equal status with Shiva. Lord Vishnu is often shown reclining on a snake with a hundred heads. The snake is known as Shesha. In that reclining pose on top of Shesha, Vishnu is called Sheshashayana Vishnu (Shayana means sleeping or resting).

Murdeshwar Mama once made a statue of Bhagawan Nityananda in this Sheshashayana pose. He then took the statue to Ganeshpuri to present it to Nityananda Baba. Bhagawan Nityananda was living in the old ashram then. When Murdeshwar Mama arrived, he placed the statue in front of Baba and bowed before him for his approval. Baba Nityananda was in a very jovial mood and began to speak about this Sheshashayana form of Vishnu.

This form of Vishnu is also known as Ananta (The Endless One). In Karnataka, God is also worshiped as this endless one. Beginning on the fourth day of the month of Bhadrapad (from the Hindu calendar), Lord Ganesh (also known as Ganapati) is worshipped. This month of Bhadrapad is also called Ganesh Chaturthi. In India, Lord

Ganesh is worshipped during Bhadrapad often by making a clay murti (statue) of Ganapati and then meditating on, praying and chanting to it as a means of cultivating intense devotion for God. Some keep their Murti for 1, 5 or 10 days. Then they immerse the Ganesh Murti in a river or the ocean.

The 14th day of Bhadrapad is called Ananta Chaturdashi. In Karnataka the Konkani speaking Brahmins celebrate this day as a festival of Lord Ananta. Now, Murdeshwar Mama was a Konkani Brahmin. When Bhagawan Nityananda began speaking about the Sheshashayana form of Vishnu, he also spoke of Lord Ananta and began describing the significance of Lord Ananta. Baba also described how one should worship him and what offering should be made.

According to Baba, "One should offer a 14-course lunch to God Ananta." Lord Ananta becomes happy and satisfied with your Devotion and Surrender when this is done. Baba then asked Murdeshwar Mama, "Will you give Him this lunch?"

Mama was a poor man. So he quickly responded, "No Bhagawan. I cannot afford to give Him this fourteen course lunch." As soon as he said this, Bhagawan Nityananda fell silent. Until that point in the conversation, Baba was in a great mood. Murdeshwar Mama realized his mistake but he thought it was too late. It is very rare that Baba gave someone a chance to serve Him in this way.

What Murdeshwar Mama could have said was, "By Your Grace, O Deva, I shall do as you say. By your will alone, I will be able to offer you this." Instead, Mama made the mistake of saying, "No," and many believed that Baba only gives this kind of privilege once to a disciple. So, Mama felt he had missed his one and only chance. Having realized this, Murdeshwar Mama fell at Bhagawan's feet crying and begging his forgiveness. With great humility, Murdeshwar Mama then said, "O Dear Deva. I shall offer you this lunch and you shall be my guest as Lord Ananta. Baba just said "Humph," which was his typical way of saying "Yes."

Ever since that day, Murdeshwar Mama celebrated Ananta Chaturdashi in Ganeshpuri and offered food to all the devotees in attendance. Even today, this festival is celebrated by his daughters (as he had no sons) and those disciples of Bhagawan Nityananda who know that Baba promised Murdeshwar Mama that he would attend this lunch.

Till this day, in Ganeshpuri and Murdeshwar, they attend and partake of the lunch as Prasad (blessed food). Each year on Ananta Chaturdashi, devotees of Bhagawan Nityananda do experience Baba's Divine Presence at this lunch and take this celebration as a great privilege to be with Baba and to have lunch with him.

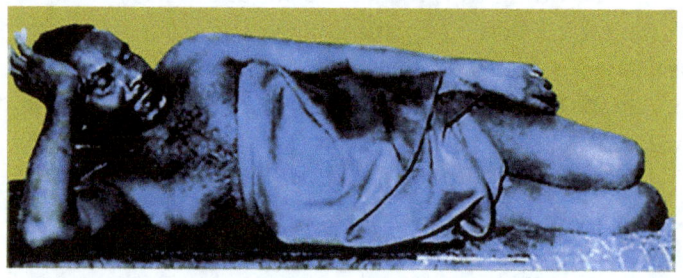

Bhagawan Nityananda In Vishnu Sheshayana Pose

Devotion and Surrender

na kasthe vidyate devo na pasane na kardame /
bhavesu vartate devas-tasmad-bhavam na samtyajet //

The deity worshipped through the image does not reside in the wood or stone or clay of which the image is made, but in the feeling of the worshiper. For this reason the feeling of devotion must never be given up.

It is said that God exists in your feeling. It is the cultivation of this feeling of Love and Devotion for the

Master and for God that is at the heart of all spiritual transformation. Devotion is the nectar of Supreme Awareness. It is that which causes God to come looking for you.

There are many stories of the mad lovers of God, those disciples who, through their own mad love for their Guru, drank the nectar of Self-Awareness constantly. Devotion is the fire that spiritual practice is cooked in. For the yogi, this devotion takes the form of intense longing for and Love for the Master. Directing all of one's feeling toward God, and especially the feeling of Love; This is the bridge by which one crosses over the bondage of this worldly existence. This is the Truth.

Listen! Your spiritual attainment will always be equal to the level of intensity of your feeling. Progress on the spiritual path is completely dependent on the intensity of your Faith, the intensity of your Devotion and the intensity of your identification with the Master. You become what you think on the most.
In the same way, the greater your intensity of identification with your chosen Guru, the more of the Guru's power (the Grace-bestowing power of God) you will absorb into yourself.

Bhagawan Nityananda was the personification of Bhakti, this Devotion that makes one mad with Love for God. He gave so much to so many. Baba Nityananda granted people's desires for objects (people, places and things), healed their illnesses and granted them the fulfillment of their dreams. Baba gave people what they wanted in the hope that they would want what he had to give. In this way, he was so compassionate, especially toward the poor and the indigent.

But what he really had to offer, his most worthy gift, could not be found in the fulfillment of any limited desire or materialistic gain that most sought his Darshan for. His greatest offering to his disciples was the guarantee of God-realization. It is this Liberation that he was ready to bestow upon anyone who would be a true disciple by cultivating an intense longing for him in their own hearts. What many did not realize is that, with this Devotion in their hearts, he would have gone to the edge of the Universe looking for them.

In the Bhakti tradition, there is a highly revered Saint known as Pundalik. Pundalik has come to be known as a symbol for Supreme, Unconditional Love. His heart was so open and his Love forgot no one. Pundalik's devotion caused God to go looking for him.

Now, Pundalik lived in Maharashtra and he was not always a Saint. His profession was that of a local goon who used to harass people. He mistreated and abused his own parents and cared little or nothing for anyone, except himself. One day Pundalik met a Saint who initiated him into the path of Bhakti Yoga. Pundalik began his spiritual practice but was unable to change his evil ways. He could not still his mind and was not able to experience any inner peace.

So, he went back to his Guru, the Saint who had initiated him, and asked for further instruction. His Guru told him to serve his parents and assured him that, in serving his parents wholeheartedly, with complete unconditional love and surrender, he would attain eternal peace. Pundalik followed the Saint's command and began to serve his parent's every need. He looked after them and nursed them. Through his service to his parents, Pundalik learned the art of Devotion and caused Lord Vitthal to come looking for him.

Lord Vishnu is a manifestation of Lord Shiva. One of Vishnu's incarnations on this Earth plane is Lord Krishna. Many believe Bhagawan Nityananda to be a reincarnation of Lord Krishna (others say Lord Shiva). Baba often spoke about Krishna when, in a meditative trance, he said "Uncle Arjuna, come here. Listen to what Grandfather Krishna has to say," as he dictated the verses of the Chidakasha Gita to Tulsi Amma.

In Pandarpur, many have had the vision of Lord Vitthal. Vitthal is the manifestation of Lord Krishna (also known as Krishna standing on a brick) who appeared to the poor people of the region of Pandarpur (and elsewhere), often with the goddess Lakshmi, the greatest Devi Vishnu's consort.

Lord Krishna was deeply moved by Pundalik's total Devotion for his parents. The goddess Lakshmi asked Krishna "My dear Lord, who is your greatest disciple in all the Earth?" Krishna replied, "Of course, it is Bhakta Pundalik. He is very dear to me. Let us go and visit him tonight." Both Krishna and Lakshmi went to Pundalik's house, appearing there as Lord Vitthal and Rakhumai. It was late at night and Pundalik was busy massaging the legs of his parents. While doing so, in his mind, Pundalik was also composing and singing devotional songs to Lord Vitthal. In this way, while serving his parents, he constantly remembered the Lord. His Seva to his parents had become worship of God.

In the middle of that night, Lord Vitthal knocked on Pundalik's door, intending to give him final Liberation and to take him to Vaikunth (Vishnu's abode). Pundalik asked "Who is it?" Krishna replied, "It is I, your beloved Vitthal. Come. Let's go. The time has come for you to join me in Vaikunth. Your liberation is at hand. Drop your body now. I am here to take you and I cannot go without you."

Pundalik got very excited. All his life he had waited for this moment to come. He had spent years longing to merge with the Absolute and he really wanted to be free from this cycle of birth and death. Even the greatest of renunciants do not get such a chance for God-realization, even after thousands of years of penance. Now, here was Parabrahma, God himself, standing at Pundalik's doorstep to take him across. He was going to allow Pundalik to merge in Him.

Pundalik thought to himself, "If I go to meet Him now I will be Liberated. I will merge with Him. But how will those who do not know Him experience His Grace? I can't keep His Love for just myself. I should share His Love with others. I want His Divine Love to spread to everyone. I must do my part. I cannot leave now." So, Pundalik said to Lord Vitthal, "O Vitthal! I am very busy serving my parents and they are still awake. Let them fall asleep and then I shall join you." After saying this, he threw two bricks in the doorway for Vitthal and Rakhumai to rest on.

It is said that, still today, Lord Vitthal is infinitely awaiting His Bhakta (devoted servant) Pundalik. Through his love and service to his parents, Bhakta Pundalik brought the Lord of the Universe to that region. Lord Vitthal appears to his devotees in visions, even today, still standing on a brick. The Lord is forever awaiting his true disciples, making Himself available to all those who cultivate Devotion and Surrender in their own hearts. He is standing on the brick with both hands resting on His hips. This is due to the Supreme Love of His disciple, Bhakta Pundalik.

Lord Vitthal

Who Will Become Like That Pundalik?

Sri Bhagawan Nityananda of Ganeshpuri was a Janma Siddha, a being who was born God-realized. He manifested himself on this planet out of Love and Compassion for the suffering of those who are ignorant of the Truth. He did not have to come here. He did not have to take a physical form. He did so out of Love for those seeking God. Bhagawan Nityananda spent his entire life serving the needs of his devotees, very much in the same way Pundalik served his parents. Only he became mother, father, brother, sister, healer, caretaker and Guru to thousands of people all across the globe.

His powers were that of the Absolute, of God himself. Yet he kept nothing for himself. He remained in that one loincloth and shawl, sleeping on that same concrete parapet, completely devoid of any desire for materialistic gain. When his body wore out, he had the power to heal it and remain here in physical form. Instead, he left us with a very important teaching, one that, by remembering it, causes Him to instantly manifest in the heart of a true mad lover of God.

It was the 8th of August, 1961. Bhagawan Nityananda was asleep in the main hall of the Bangalore Walla Building in Ganeshpuri. It was about 4am in the morning. On the street just outside of the Bangalore Walla Building, was a small beverage stand run by a devotee who suffered from a lifelong skin disease. Day in and day out, this man served coffee and tea to those coming and going to the ashram to have Bhagawan Nityananda's Darshan. For years, he had one secret desire -- that a cup of coffee that he made would be served to Baba Nityananda.

One of Baba's lifelong devotees was a man named Madhava Hegde. Hegde had regular access to Bhagawan Nityananda. On this morning of August 8th, between 4-6am, Madhava Hegde (also known as Engineer Hegde) told the beverage stand owner to make a strong cup of coffee for Baba. Knowing that this might be his only chance to have his secret desire fulfilled, the beverage stand owner made the best coffee of his life, excited that Bhagawan would, at last, drink his coffee. He knew that, since Madhava Hegde was one of Baba's long-time devotees, his coffee would surely reach Baba.

Hegde took the cup of coffee and entered the room where Bhagawan was resting. Baba noticed Madhava Hegde and acknowledged him. Hegde then gave Baba some of the coffee to drink. The wish of the beverage stand owner was finally fulfilled.

As Madhava Hegde watched Bhagawan Nityananda carefully, he understood in his heart, that Bhagawan Nityananda was about to take Mahasamadhi (leave his body for the last time). With tears in his eyes Hegde said, "Oh Dear Deva, can't you postpone giving up your body?" Baba replied, "Yes, it can be postponed if you bring at least one Bhakta like Pundalik. Only one who is like Pundalik can postpone my leaving." (What Bhagawan Nityananda meant is, if even one true disciple, if even one mad lover of God who is willing to sacrifice everything to love and serve Him for love's sake alone, would come and ask Him to stay, He would remain in His physical form). In those days many of the people who came for Baba's Darshan were only interested in His blessings for some materialistic gain. Few came out of Shuddha Prem (pure love).

Again, Bhagawan Nityananda assured Madhava Hegde that he would postpone leaving his body if even one disciple like Pundalik would come and ask him to do so. Then he demanded that such a person be brought to him. Baba then asked Engineer Hegde "Are you like Pundalik?" Madhava Hegde said "No, Deva. I cannot make that tall a claim. I am a worldly man." Hegde then wept like a child.

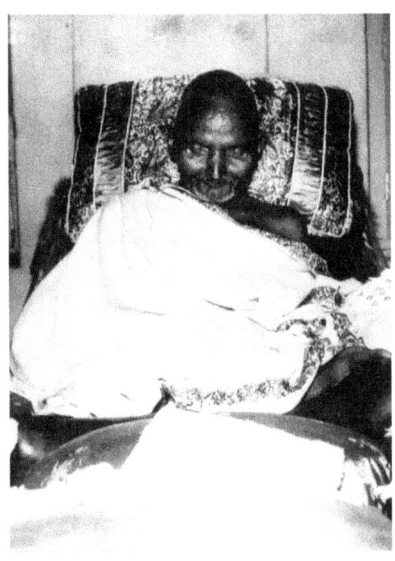

Bhagawan Nityananda Mahasamadhi

Bhakti

Bhagawan Nityananda is also just like Lord Vitthal. Lord Vitthal often appears to people in the form of a cowherd, dark in color wearing a loincloth, a coarse black blanket on his shoulder and a stick in his hand. Bhagawan Nityananda also wore a loincloth and, in earlier days, had a blanket on his shoulder. Baba came to the rescue of his devotees at the time of their suffering. But to realize Him all one needed to offer him was Love.

Bhakti is the easiest way to know and merge with God. The Lord is waiting for you. With Bhakti, with this burning desire and complete longing for the Master, you cause God to come looking for you. In Ganeshpuri, the Lord is waiting for you in the form of Bhagawan Nityananda. Even today you can go and feel His Divine presence there.

On the celebration of Gurupurnima (the day that

disciples celebrate and glorify the Guru) people are allowed into His Mahasamadhi shrine. They hug the Murti of Him and wet His feet with the tears of their Love. Many have observed the ecstasy that wells up inside these devotees as their eyes fill with tears. The whole atmosphere becomes full of Love, and one can sense that Baba's eyes get equally filled with Love.

Chapter 2
A History of His Existence Here

Shri Bhagawan Nityananda is said to have been an incarnation of Lord Shiva. Still others say he was an incarnation of Lord Vishnu. And others claim that he was the very incarnation of Lord Krishna. Is it any wonder that, when people pressed Bade Baba about such details, he responded by saying "You want me to tell you about myself? How is that possible when I have realized that I am in everything and there is nothing around me in which I don't find my own Self?" He went on to say that his family is those who love God and work to serve God.

There are many stories about how Bhagawan Nityananda arrived on this Earth plane. When people made attempts to verify these stories, Bade Baba usually admonished them, stating that such details are important only to curiosity-seekers. And yet, on one occasion, in response to questions about his birth, he was heard to say, "Two crows came and went."

After arriving here on this Earth plane, Bhagawan Nityananda spent several years in the South Kanara district in Quilandy. From there, he moved about quite a bit (mostly on foot and by train), making his way deep into the Himalayas and staying for a time in places such as Quilandy, Shri Lanka, Burma, Kanhangad, Kumbla, Gokarna, Udipi, Calicut, Mangalore, Manjeshwar, coastal Karnataka and Vajreshwari.

The Puja and Temple At Quilandy

The Three Devi Temple In Vajeshwari

Later he settled in Ganeshpuri, at the foot of the majestic Mandakini Mountain near the Bhimeshwar temple, surrounded by rolling hills, lush fields and hot springs. At the time he first went to Ganeshpuri it was still a jungle, practically uninhabitable.

It is said that around 1897-1900, in late November or early December, an elderly woman was out picking flowers and collecting wood in the dense jungle near Quilandy, now called Guruvan. As she approached a nearby tree, she heard two crows cawing loudly. It was as if the crows were purposely making a ruckus to get her attention. So, she followed the cawing of the crows and found herself standing in front of a bush. Under that bush was a baby boy wrapped in a white cloth.

The woman picked the child up and took the baby boy to the safety of her home. Having a large family of her own, she decided she would have to give the child away. In her village, there was a woman named Unniamma who was not able to bear a child. She knew Unniamma's mother and decided to take the baby to her, believing that the daughter would adopt the child. The next day she took the baby boy to the village and Unniamma's mother accepted the baby on her daughter's behalf.

The Jungle Where Bhagawan Nityananda
Was Found By Unniamma – The Tent
Structure Marks the Spot Where He Arrived

Unniamma worked in Pantalayini near Calicut, in a region called Koilande. She cleaned the local temples and also worked as a housekeeper in the household of a local attorney, Ishwar Iyer. The following morning her mother went to Pantalayini to present the baby to Unniamma, who, full of joy, adopted the boy. She named him Ram.

Unniamma died when Ram was very young, leaving him to be cared for by Ishwar Iyer. Ishwar Iyer was well known in Quilandy for his work as a lawyer and he was also very religious. His chosen deity was Surya Narayana (the Sun God), and Iyer diligently engaged in worship throughout each and every day. He also introduced the young Ram to many scriptures and the study of sacred texts on which discourses were given in his home. In this way Ram was exposed to these teachings at a very early age and took Iyer as his Guru.

Late in his life, Ishwar Iyer decided to make pilgrimages to several holy shrines. He took the young Ram with him. After visiting several shrines, they reached Kashi. Ram was about age 10 at the time. Just as Ishwar Iyer decided it was time for them to return home, Ram told him that it was time for them to part. He told Ishwar Iyer that he wanted to spend time in the Himalayas and that he would return to him at the appropriate time.

Shocked and dismayed, Ishwar Iyer tried to change Ram's mind, but to no avail. He then left Ram and returned home. The young Ram then spent several years in the Himalayas, travelling on foot and meditating in the holy caves there.

When Ram returned to Quilandy several years later at age 16, Ishwar Iyer had taken ill and was on his deathbed. Just before passing, he told Ram that he wanted to see the Sun God, Lord Surya, in all his splendor and he asked Ram to grant him that boon. Then he had a profound vision of Surya Narayana. In ecstasy, the old man exclaimed "You have brought Ananda (Bliss) to me. You are Nityananda! May you be Nityananda to all!" This is how Bhagawan Nityananda got this name, that he later said was not a name, but a state (it means the Eternal Bliss of the Absolute).

After visiting other places, including Shri Lanka and Burma, Bhagawan Nityananda returned to Quilandy

again. By this time he was already known as a great
Kundalini Yogi and Avadhoot. From Quilandy he went to
Kanyakumari, Calicut, Tellicherry, Cannanore and
Kanhangad. He then appeared in Kumbla.

It is during this time that he started to attract large
crowds of people. He performed miracles, healing the sick
and alleviating the suffering of the masses. He also
stopped trains, slept comfortably on a rope tied between
two windows and was found levitating in a barn. In
villages where people had no drinking water, Bhagawan
Nityananda created wells with running water, in places
where there was no sign of water. These wells have never
run dry, despite the fact that they are not attached to any
water sources. He attributed these miracles to God and the
faith of his devotees.

*The Well Bhagawan Nityananda
Installed at Gokarna*

Even though Bhagawan Nityananda was welcomed by the masses wherever he went, there were those who were jealous of him and wanted to see him dead. Several attempts were made on his life. One such incident happened in Manjeshwar where a man tried to poison him with a rolled tobacco leaf. There was also an incident in another village where a local goon attempted to have him run over by a train. Other people attempted a knife attack. None of these attempts were successful and the perpetrators soon found themselves sick or dying in a local hospital of a serious illness.

In Mangalore, Tulasi Amma met Bhagawan Nityananda and became his devoted disciple. This led to the events in which the Chidakasha Gita was recorded for posterity. Bhagawan Nityananda has many devotees in Mangalore and there are four Ashrams there established in his name.

Tulsi Amma

Bade Baba spent time in Mulki, Padubidri, Bantwal and then Udipi. In Udipi he was often seen in and around the famous Shri Krishna temple. At first, he was not always welcome there. The priests of the temple thought him to be a mad man and attempted to scare him away by arranging to have him stoned. As the hired hands threw stones at Bhagawan Nityananda, the stones disappeared before hitting him, or sometimes they turned into sweet meats before landing on the ground. Many of these same stones were then found around the feet of the Krishna Murthi in the temple.

Over time, people from all over India flocked to Udipi to receive Bade Baba's blessings. He healed many of the sick and dying and gave special attention and love to the poor and indigent there.

Bhagawan Nityananda then moved on to Kanhangad where he spent more than 25 years. He selected Kanhangad as the seat for his mother Ashram, stating that the Kanhangad Ashram is a University for sages and that, one day, sages from abroad will occupy the Ashram and make it a hub for spiritual pursuit.

The Kanhangad Ashram

Entrance to Kanhangad Ashram Meditation Hall

Inside Kanhangad Ashram Meditation Hall

He cleared the land around an old fort there with his bare hands and also participated in the building of the Ashram that is now located on a rocky hill. Bhagawan Nityananda spent many days lying on a huge rock there in the hot sun, deep in the trance of meditation. Later, with his own hands, he carved away the stone from inside of that rock to build the famous meditation caves that are still located there under the Kanhangad Ashram.

The Meditation Caves at Kanhangad Ashram

With respect to the construction of the Kanhangad Ashram, there is a wonderful story. At that time, the British still occupied India. As the caves were being completed and construction on the Ashram began, workers from the village were hired. There was no money to pay wages but Bade Baba manifested the workers' wages in miraculous ways. Sometimes he would take the exact amount needed from his loincloth. At other times he told the workers to collect their wages from underneath a tree or rock. Each time the exact amount to pay each worker (not a penny more or less) was manifested. This was so startling that some observers believed the money was either counterfeit or stolen.

Some local officials filed a complaint with the district collector's office run by the British. They said that there was a mad, naked sadhu encroaching on government land and using stolen money to pay laborers. The British sent a Captain Gawne to investigate. When the Captain arrived, Bhagawan Nityananda was nowhere to be found. After making many demands for his whereabouts, Bade Baba appeared from one of the caves. The Captain asked him about the construction going on. To everyone's surprise, Bade Baba responded in English! As the two spoke, Captain Gawne was very taken with Bade Baba's presence.

When Captain Gawne asked about where the money was coming from to pay the workers' wages, Bade Baba took him, along with the local officials, to Guruvan where there was a swampy area covered with water. He then told them that he was paying the workers from a bag of money at the bottom of the swamp and that they were welcome to dive into the water to verify that the bag of money was there.

Seeing the very large alligator and other wild animals that were there, none dared to take him up on his offer. Indeed Bhagawan Nityananda had pulled a bag of money out of the water to pay the workers with.

Captain Gawne then instructed the local officials not to disturb the construction of the caves and the Ashram. In fact, he told the people there that they should be helping Bhagawan Nityananda to complete the construction and that no one should bother him. The Captain then left the Ashram to go back to the Kanhangad train station.

On his way back, at the point where the Ashram road joins the main road, to his complete surprise, Captain Gawne saw a street sign that read "Gawne Road" posted on the corner. Bade Baba had named the road after the collector to commemorate his visit. Today, the Ashram road still bears the name "Gawne Road."

Bhagawan Nityananda spent several years in Guruvan, located about 5 kilometers east of Kanhangad. In those days Guruvan was a jungle inhabited by wild animals and poisonous snakes. There was no water. One day Bade Baba struck a rock with his hand and water started to gush out of the barren rocky hillside. Water has been flowing from that place ever since. This water is now a stream that forms into a pool. It was named "Papanashini Ganga" by Bade Baba. Many go to this place to bathe, as it is considered to be as holy as the Ganges.

Papanashini Ganga

Bhagawan Nityananda said that, in the past, many
Siddhas had come to live in Guruvan and took
Mahasamadhi there. For this reason, he created a circle of
eight stone pillars/lingams signifying the Ashta Siddhis.
Guruvan is rightly considered a Thapobhumi. Later,
Swami Janananda Baba, the one who Bhagawan
Nityananda had appointed to run the Ashram and all
administrative and financial affairs, cleared the land at
Guruvan and turned it into a beautiful garden with a temple
and rest house.

Ashta Siddhi Lingas - Guruvan

After completing construction of the caves and the Kanhangad Ashram, Bhagawan Nityananda set off on tour, leaving the Ashram to be further developed and run by Swami Janananda. Nityananda Baba then visited most of the holy Shrines in India. Later he was seen in Mumbai, Akroli and Vajreshwari, before settling in Ganeshpuri, where he spent the remainder of his years before taking Mahasamadhi there on August 8, 1961.

Chapter 3
Service to Shri Gurudev

Seva. The Mystical Spiritual Practice

Of all the mystical experiences disciples share from performing Seva (selfless service), the one spoken about the most is the experience of being overcome with Love for God. Jnaneshwar Maharaj, Mirabai and Saint Tukaram Maharaj are examples of Siddhas who caused God to go looking for them, through their devoted service to him, born of this Love.

In order to attain this Shudha Prem, this pure Love for God and humanity who should you serve? God or the Guru? The poet Saint Kabir faced this very dilemma. One day both God and his Guru manifested in front of him. Kabir was confused. Who should he honor first, his Guru or God? What protocol should he follow? Kabir understood that it was because of his Guru that he had the privilege and ability to attain the state of Liberation, to merge his individual identity in God. But, at the same time, God was his ultimate Goal. What to do!?

Swami Sadananda was a Guru in the lineage of Bhagawan Nityananda. He is also known as Padiyar Swami (his pre-monastic family name was Padiyar). Sadananda Swami once answered this dilemma by describing what it takes to serve God by serving the Guru. He shared that the Guru is the very reflection of God. So serve your Guru first, he would say.

To do so you have to be very, very alert. You should understand the body language of your Guru. Without having to be told, you should be able to, not only discern, but also to deliver what the Sadguru desires. The Guru wants nothing and there is nothing that you can ever give him/her. The purpose of your Seva to the Guru is to

cultivate Devotion, Surrender, Unconditional Love and Joy
in your own heart. You do it to make yourself happy and
spiritually strong.

Swami Sadananda

The Guru's love for you does not change because
you have served him or not served him. He is always
content in his love for his devotees and disciples. The Guru
is like the Ocean; Always available to you, irrespective of
the stance that you take. He is also like a mirror. Whatever
Bhava or attitude (intention, feelings, emotions) you
approach the Guru with, will be reflected back to you in the
same way. This happens spontaneously, so that you can
see where you're really at. The Guru is available yet he is
also beyond reach. Only your pure Love alone can win the
Guru. Then you have him as your very own.

More Great Servants of Bhagawan Nityananda of Ganeshpuri

When it came to serving Bhagawan Nityananda, the emphasis was on being present with Him. Being present means being aware. Over the years, we have lost the art of being present. How many of us are aware of who else is around us when we are in an elevator? Are we aware of who sits next to us on a bus or train, even when our trip takes several hours? The truth is, most times, we are not even aware of ourselves, only the chatter in our minds!!

Serving Bhagawan Nityananda demanded this very quality of being present. He never demanded anything. But if you wanted the opportunity to serve him, you had to be "tuned in" to his needs and his intention. Some of Baba's close disciples were very good at this, so good that they had turned it into an Art. They would offer him water, his lunch or snacks at precisely the moment he wanted them, without asking. And if Bhagawan was displeased because he had been disturbed while immersed in deep meditation, they learned from that too.

Serving Baba meant you had to be very attentive, very alert. At the same time, disciples could never take credit for or have pride in serving Him. In other words, as a disciple of Bhagawan Nityananda, you could not claim yourself to be a close disciple just because you had the privilege to serve Him. He did not want his disciples to become egotistic in this way and he had an uncanny ability to know when this had happened.

How Baba came to know that a disciple had become egotistic in this manner was a mystery. If Baba knew that you were babbling about your experience of serving him (as if you were better than anyone else for having served him), you immediately lost the privilege to serve him. Serving Bhagawan Nityananda demanded total humility. It also demanded austerity and presence of mind.

In the old days, Ganeshpuri, India was nothing but a jungle and the climate was extreme. In winter, disciples visiting Baba's Ashram sometimes had to sleep on the floor without any blanket or warm cloths. In the middle of the night Baba used to ask, "Is it very cold?" How you answered such a question was equally important as the question itself.

If you answered something like "The floor is a little cold but the weather is not too bad," immediately Baba understood that you wanted to be there with him and you did not want to complain. He would then throw a blanket and warm cloths at you so that you could be more comfortable. But Bhagawan remained in his loincloth, unmindful of the weather.

He used to ask, "Are you hungry?" Again, not wanting to complain, sometimes a disciple would answer, "O Baba, I had some snacks a while ago." This meant, "Yes. I am hungry." Then Baba would say, "There is some bread there in that box." Sometimes when you opened the box, you would find old, stale or moldy bread. Baba would then offer some hot and spicy pickles to eat with that bread. Hunger makes you eat, even when the food doesn't look so great. But, in Baba's presence, everything turned tasty.

Bhagawan Nityananda also used to offer black coffee to his disciples, with a little fat added to it when there was no milk available. At the same time, he tended to you with loving care, as if he were your mother, and you his child.

Once Captain Hatangdi hurt his toe and it was bleeding profusely. All of a sudden Baba came into his room and, without saying a word, Baba poured sandalwood oil over the wound. Sandalwood oil is very soothing. Baba often knew his disciples' suffering and came to their aid in this way, without being told the circumstance.

At times, one could see Baba sitting out in the open for hours, as if waiting for someone. After some time passed, a group of devotees would arrive and then Baba would go inside to his room. At that very moment it began to rain heavily. It was as if Baba held back the rains until the devotees had arrived and were safe in the Ashram.

To Bhagawan Nityananda all were equal, all were God. He only saw God in everyone. Baba also had a special love and patience for those devotees who were weak of mind and heart or difficult in their behavior. The Guru lovingly serves those who are weak, needy and down-trodden.

Another example is that of Jnaneshwar Maharaj. Jnaneshwar called his Guru, "Mauli," meaning mother. The true mother is supreme because she is one who loves all her relations without any selfish motive. A mother is the embodiment of Shudha Prem, pure Love. In fact, due to the Supreme Love that he showed for his disciples, Jnaneshwar is lovingly called Jnaneshwarmauli.

Serving the Guru is a privilege very few get. One who serves his/her Guru, with Love and Devotion, becomes a Karma Yogi (a yogi who is dedicated to service). Serving a Siddha Guru is the same as serving God because the Guru is the very embodiment of God in a physical form. Bhagawan Nityananda says, "The Guru is God and is also the form of your worship of God."

God is Brahma, Vishnu and Rudra because God Creates, Sustains and Destroys. The Guru also has these three qualities and one additional quality that is most important. The Guru is the Grace-bestowing power of God. This Grace-bestowing power operates at the will of a Siddha Guru. In the Shri Guru Gita Shivaji utters, "God can save you from men or women. Shiva can save you from the wrath of the Devas (demigods). The Guru can even save you from Shiva's wrath. But there is no one who can save you from the Guru's wrath."

The Siddha Guru is Shiva and Shiva is the Siddha Guru. How do you serve such a Guru? Bhagawan Nityananda says, "Sradha. Have Sradha (faith) in the Guru. No penance, yaga, sacrifice or prayers are required. Pure Faith alone is enough for the Guru to give you salvation."

Plucking a hair from his head and pointing at its

root, Baba said to his disciple, Babu Rao Khade of Sion, "Even Faith that is equal to the size of this root is enough." But, for your Faith to work, it has to be pure and unconditional.

Tulsi Amma

Of all the disciples of Bhagawan Nityananda, Tulsi Amma was a class apart. Bhagawan Nityananda himself declared her to be "One who has seen the Sun," meaning that she had realized the eternal Bliss of the Absolute, that she had gone across. If this is how Bade Baba described her, any words that I use here pale in comparison. It is Tulsi Amma who recorded Bhagawan Nityananda's words whenever he spoke, while in deep in Meditation. These utterances were compiled in a work called the Chidakasha Gita.

The name "Chidakasha Gita" was approved by Bade Baba and the work was originally written in Kanada. It is because of Tulsi Amma that we have the teachings of Bhagawan Nityananda available to us in this way. The original Chidakasha Gita was translated into English, unedited, by Mr. Mangalore Sanjiva Kamath of Mahim, Mumbai. He was a great devotee of Baba. *You will find the entire Chidakasha Gita, with my commentary on the verses, at the end of this book.*

Very little is known about Tulsi Amma and those who know about her are no more. Although she wrote several books, she never mentioned her name as author of those books nor did she reveal anything about herself. I am sharing what I remember from the discussions that I heard from disciples of Bhagawan Nityananda, and from her book of Bhajans entitled Atmaspuran (inspiration from the soul).

Tulsi Amma

Tulsi Amma was from Mangalore in South India
and must have met Bhagawan Nityananda in early 1920.
She was a young widow at the time. In those days life for a
widow in India was very difficult and painful. In that pain
she turned to God. She belonged to the community of
Gowda Saraswat Brahmins and became a monk. This
enabled her to wear janava (holy thread) and perform
Sandhya Vandana, the ritual usually only performed by
Brahmin men. She wore a white sari as a widow is
supposed to wear and she kept her head covered. She was
fluent in the Konkani, Kanada and Marathi dialects.

Tulsi Amma was also known as Anandi. She met
Bhagawan Nityananda in Mangalore. Bhagawan
Nityananda lived in the Avadhuta state, completely
absorbed in his own being. He lived a carefree life like a
small child. It was often necessary to take care of him just
as one takes care of a small child.

Tulsi Amma had rented a house from Basti
Shanbaug in Mangalore. Being a young widow, she had to
lead a very austere life, as was the societal norm of the
time. Meeting Bhagawan Nityananda caused a complete
transformation in her. She became intensely devoted to

Bade Baba and, through her renunciation, attained the state of elated dispassion. By His Grace, her intense devotion and surrender gave rise to the constant, uninterrupted experience of Supreme Love within her own being.

Tulsi Amma began to express her profound spiritual experiences by composing several Bhajans (devotional songs). These were compiled in her book, Atmaspuran. Bade Baba really loved these Bhajans. The Bhajans open with Gurustavan, a song-sermon to the glory of Bhagawan Nityananda that was later recorded by Professor K. Shivananda Kamath of Kanhangad. This recording is part of a video of the Kanhangad meditation caves. You can view the video at
https://bhagawannityananda.org/song-of-praise/
This is the first time in recent memory that anyone has paid homage to Tulsi Amma for her contribution in bringing the instruction of Bhagawan Nityananda to us.

If you carefully observe in the video where a lotus is shown with the reflection of the Sun in a pond (outside the Kanhangad Ashram), you will see an image of Bade Baba. Actually it is the reflection of the sun in the pond which appears like Bhagawan Nityananda's face.

In her Gurustavan, Tulsi Amma describes Bhagawan Nityananda as the eternal Bliss of the Absolute that is comparable to none. In her Bhajans she describes the practice and experience of Gurukripa, the way in which a disciple attracts the Guru's Grace into his/her life through complete surrender and devotion to the Master.

Tulsi Amma suffered a great deal during her life. But she understood her suffering as her Karma from many past lives. In the pain of her suffering, she sought her Guru and developed unconditional love for him. Although she had to take many births to wash off the effects of her past Karma, she never compromised her love for her Guru. She asked only for Liberation, for her Nityananda's state and never demanded relief from her suffering.

Unconditional Love, Unconditional Surrender and non-attachment to pain or pleasure are some of the principles she spread through her own life. Her Bhajans were first published by Shri Ramkrishna Shenoy (brother of Sitaram Shenoy) on March 7, 1940, on Mahashivaratri. They were reprinted on Gurupurnima day of 2000 by Ratnakar Shenoy (son of Sitaram).

Tulsi Amma established a small Ashram in Managooda, Mangalore. It is known as Ananda Ashram. There in the Ashram she placed a set of small golden padukas. She had two identical sets of these golden sandals made, along with a golden throne and silver puja articles. One set of padukas she offered to Bhagawan Nityananda. Baba gave the sandals to Raghunath Shenoy at Bhramawar, Karnataka. This was during the World War.

Bhagawan Nityananda did not teach or recommend Pranayama to everybody. Of the few of his devotees, it was Tulsi Amma who was initiated into the techniques of Pranayama. She acquired great spiritual power through the practice of Pranayama as taught by Bade Baba.

Bhajans of the Divine Mother

Tulsi Amma wrote several Bhajans that give a glimpse into her past lives. I have made an effort to translate one particular Bhajan in which she describes how she had met Bhagawan Nityananda in a past life, and how they are now eternally connected. It is given below.

Translated Tulsi Amma Bhajan

In my previous birth I was born as a cruel animal. For my survival I used to kill any living being that I came across in the jungle. I killed mothers and poor orphaned babes. And sometimes I killed these babies to quench my hunger. I sometimes killed a husband and destroyed a happy family. In this way, by hurting many, I used to rule the jungle. I was very proud of my cruel deeds. My heinous acts were famous and people avoided the jungle due to my reputation. Noticing me at a distance people ran to save their lives and

I, without any concern for weak and small, ran amuck killing whomsoever I came across.

I saw a beautiful deer and killed her instantly, leaving her four calves orphaned. One day a king and his army entered the jungle on a hunting spree. Noticing me the King chased after me with his bow and arrow. His retinue stayed behind. So, he was separated from his men. Several arrows were aimed at me but all in vain. Finding him alone I roared in anger and pounced on him. I killed him in one stroke. I then killed all his men.

Several days passed with me actively involved in this pastime of killing. Then one day a serene looking Yogi entered the jungle. Absorbed in the Atman, he unexpectedly crossed my path. Obsessed by killing harmless people, I ran up to him with an aim to kill him. Noticing my beastly ignorance, this Yogi smiled and opened his eyes. He said to me, "Just give a thought to who you and I are. Know that it is One subtle essence in both of us. Everything that is seen is illusion. Just be aware of your origin. On knowing it you will have no reason for ego. Then there shall be no cycle of birth and death."

Hearing these words of supreme wisdom, there was instant silence within me. From a cruel angry monster, I was transformed into a creature meeker than a dog and I entered into deep thinking. On hearing these enlightened words, I repented for my past actions. I wanted this Yogi's Grace and I surrendered at his feet. The encounter with this Sage bore spontaneous fruit, melting away my cruel nature.

How can evil stand against divine power? He who was the fountainhead of infinite peace, bestowed his Grace on me. By the very touch of his divine feet, all of my base nature disappeared. With great humility I surrendered to him. With the dawn of knowledge, my ignorance vanished. He understood my thought process that resulted from this transformation. The Endless One assured me,

"The effect of your deeds (Karmas) has to be borne by you. Indeed you will have to take another birth. You will be born in a rich family. But do not get entangled in worldly matters. Merge your mind and being in this Endless One and attain eternal peace. Live in the world doing your ordained duties and, by discrimination, realize that this world is just an illusion. In service of all you shall realize the ultimate truth. Do not ever worry for you shall be ever protected by Shri Hari (God)."

Assuring me in this way, he placed his divine hand on my head. No sooner had his hand touched my head than a most astonishing thing occurred. Tears started flowing from my eyes, and the monster that I was, fell at his divine feet. Soon my soul left my body and with it went what was ordained by the Yogi. I took a birth as a helpless woman to suffer my Prarabdha Karma, the effects of my past deeds.

It just so happened that the king who I had killed became my husband in this life. He was a great support in my spiritual journey. His name was Shankar. My son was called Gangadhar. There were four other short-lived children. Sixth was a beautiful daughter. She was the deer whom I had killed. There was a sister named Devaki, who took care of me. The army of the King that I wiped out were born again and, though they appeared as friends, troubled me in every possible way. I have a dear brother called Anandu. I ever bow to him, my Nityananda. He alone has compassion for me. There is one eternal bond between us.

Karma and Past Lives

Karma is created when experience is "objectified," when one forgets where the experience is really occurring and attributes what is being experienced to the body or people, places and things outside of oneself. Whether the action be virtuous or evil, with this very limited view of one's essence, a person sets in motion a never-ending cycle of birth and death, caught up in the same recurring life lessons, and returning to this world again and again to experience the fruits of past actions.

It is Karma that causes one to sink. It is also Karma that causes one to rise. After accruing the merits of virtuous actions, over a period of many lifetimes, a person becomes worthy of a Sadguru. Through devotion to the Guru and to God, supported by spiritual practice, a person finally merges with his/her own Divinity inside.

At final Liberation, when the ego has been completely destroyed and the yogi's experience is that of Purnaham Vimarsha, there is no more Karma Mala. Anava Mala and Mayiya Mala have also been destroyed. The yogi then dwells in the heart of God and God dwells, permanently unveiled, in the heart of the yogi.

For such a person, although he/she may continue to perform actions, no more Karmas are created. Ever abiding in Purnahanta, the yogi becomes the Guru, that Shiva, and is no longer concerned with grabbing at people, places and things out of fear of lack. She offers all her actions to God and accepts what comes to her unsought, as a result of this attitude of offering. In this way, the yogi remains ever steady in the rapture of Chit Shakti.

Every one of us has a birth reason, the reason we have returned to this earth. This reason is, for each of us, our Prarabdha Karma; that Karma that cannot be burned and must be suffered, whether pleasurable or painful. This Prarabdha Karma is actually our own Superimposition of impressions from a past lifetime that has been already set into motion and, therefore, must be experienced.

All beings, including Siddhas, must suffer through Prarabdha Karma (the Karma that has commenced to bear fruit). This type of Karma cannot even be burned away by the Guru. However, for those who are spiritually aware, this Prarabdha, the birth reason, can become a Labor of Love, leading one directly to God by becoming the reason one stays in the body to serve and uplift others.

Tulsi Ammaji understood this. We are told that she accepted her suffering as God's Grace and took full responsibility for every event and circumstance in her life. In this way, her suffering became her path to Liberation.

Padiyar Swami

There great Siddha called Swami Sadananda of Kanhangad used to say, "You do not have to do anything except do your duty first. Strive for excellence. The key word is Ulgas." In Konkani this means constant remembrance, constant chanting, being present and being aware by allowing your mind to become completely absorbed within.

This can be accomplished easily through Japa and Chanting. This is an excellent means to attract the Grace of the Guru to you. It is the means of "stealing" the Guru's Shakti and absorbing it into yourself. The Siddha Guru then guides you at the pace that your capacity and personality will allow, and in a very safe manner, so that you reach the other shore permanently.

Mr. Padiyar (before he was given the name "swami") had come to Mumbai from Karnataka. Since he was from the community called Gowda Saraswat Brahmins (G.S.B.), he checked in at Sitaram Shenoy's hotel in Mumbai. All the youth from the G.S.B. community who came to Mumbai in search of work were welcomed at Sitaram's place. They slept in his gymnasium at night and went searching for jobs during the day. They were fed all their meals in the hotel until they found a job.

Sitaram Shenoy

Padiyar was one such youth whom Sitaram took a liking. It was obvious to Sitaram that Padiyar had to be introduced to Baba Nityananda. Mr. Padiyar made repeated visits to Bhagawan Nityananda during Bade Baba's stay in Mumbai (early 1930s) and later at Baba's Ganeshpuri Ashram. These visits slowly transformed Padiyar into a devoted disciple. He soon gave up his search for a career and started spending more time in Ganeshpuri with Bade Baba.

Bhagawan Nityananda did not give formal public programs nor did he demonstrate any particular set of spiritual practices like other Gurus who conduct classes. In those days, people received Shaktipat from Baba just by being in His presence and remaining open to His Grace.

Often he lay down on his side facing a wall with his back turned to the congregation. Thousands of people experienced God's Grace through him in this way. He was like the ocean. The ocean doesn't come looking for you. You have to go to the ocean and, depending on the size of the vessel you are carrying, that's the amount of water you're able to take away with you.

This is the way it was with Bade Baba. He was always available to everyone without any disparity. Those who came looking for their mundane desires to be fulfilled were often disappointed. In Baba's presence all you needed to do was to be aware and remain open to receive His Grace. The rest just happened automatically. All Bhagawan Nityananda wanted was your love and devotion. In exchange for this He took you to the height of ecstasy, complete absorption in Shiva Consciousness.

One day Padiyar had become very frustrated with his lack of spiritual progress. He felt nothing was happening for him. So, in a state of frustration he told Bhagawan Nityananda, "I am leaving for good." Bade Baba asked, "Where to and for what?" This simple question resounded in Padiyar's being like a mantra.

Where to? Yes, where will you go? If you want God and you cannot attain His state here at the very seat of Grace, where else can you find it? What will you accomplish by going elsewhere? Why put it off for later? Your time is here and now so why postpone it by leaving?

If in the company of a Maha Siddha you cannot attain peace, where else will you find it? These were the questions that reverberated inside Padiyar's being. So, he decided to stay. Later, he was renamed Sadananda Swami by Swami Janananda Baba of Kanhangad, one of Bhagawan Nityananda's closest disciples.

A New Lease On Life

Jivdan means being afforded a "new lease on life." A Siddha Guru has the power to wash one's karmas away. A saint of the stature of Bhagawan Nityananda does it so naturally that it just happens. By just being in his presence one's past karma is washed off. That is the power of a Janma Siddha. I have direct knowledge and experience of four instances where Bhagawan Nityananda has given this new lease on life to those who served him.

In the first instance it was the son of Engineer Hegde (also known as Madhav Hegde of Mangalore). Hegde was one of the oldest disciples of Bade Baba. He met Sitaram Shenoy, who then brought him to Bade Baba. Because of his great devotion for Bhagawan Nityananda, Engineer Hegde used to travel to the Ganeshpuri Ashram of Bade Baba whenever he had time off and during most holidays.

Hegde's father, being a staunch Brahmin from Gowda Saraswat Brahmin community, had his own community Guru and did not appreciate his son's devotion for Bade Baba. He used to ridicule Madhav insisting, "Your guru does not have the ability to buy a piece of loin cloth worth one anna (six paise). What a guru!"

Now, Engineer Hegde had a son also named Nityananda. During a visit to Ganeshpuri, Engineer Hegde's son was bathing with his grandfather in the kunda (hot spring) near the great Bhimeshwar temple. Suddenly the child slipped below the surface of the water and, before anyone noticed, the boy drowned. His body was removed and Madhav Hegde, along with his wife, took the body to Bade Baba.

The mother was inconsolable. The child's body was placed at the feet of Bhagawan Nityananda and the incident was narrated to him. Bade Baba ordered everyone to leave the room and told one of the attendants to place the body in a gunny bag.

After some time, Bhagawan Nityananda called for the parents. When they entered the room, their son was alive and playing. The grandfather who, until then, ridiculed Bade Baba, fell at his feet in surrender. Bhagawan Nityananda told him, "Bhimeshwar (the deity of Bhimeshwar Temple) is concerned about his reputation. If the child were to die, Lord Bhimeshwar would have lost his image in the eyes of his devotees." Engineer Hegde's son lived to be forty-two.

There was a woman named Gulabi. She too was a great devotee of Bhagawan Nityananda. One day she decided to visit Baba at His Kanhangad Ashram. She left Brahmawar for Kanhangad with her young child and a caretaker. It was dark by the time they reached Kanhangad. During this time there were no lights or torches. So one had to walk in complete darkness. With her baby in her arms, Gulabi walked from the train station to the rock Ashram with the caretaker.

Near the Ashram there was a pond of water. Not being able to see the pond in the dark, Gulabi, with her baby in hand, fell into the pond. The caretaker did not notice and kept walking. Gulabi was frightened. The death of her child, along with her certain death, was too much to bear. She cried out to Bhagawan Nityananda for help.

Just as she called out Bhagawan's name, a huge hand from nowhere just lifted her, along with the baby, out of the pond and transported them to the gate of the Ashram. The moment she entered the gate, Bhagawan Nityananda laughed and said, "So you had a dip in the Ganga?" All-knowing Bade Baba had rescued her.

There was a devotee called Krishnabai. She has been mentioned in several books written about Bhagawan Nityananda. Her son, Mr. Mangalori, is presently living in Talmikiwadi, Girgaon, Mumbai. He too is a great disciple of Bhagawan Nityananda.

Mr. Mangalori lived on the third floor of a building that had an open gallery in it. In one corner of this gallery were stacked many cotton mattresses. One day, Mr. Mangalori's son was hanging out of an open window in this gallery. The boy lost his balance and fell out the window. At that height, death was a certainty. Now, miraculously, a couple of mattresses also fell with the child, beating him to the ground. The boy fell safely on those mattresses and did not get a scratch on him. He got up and climbed the stairs back to his house.

The family who witnessed the child fall out of the window was wonder-struck. In their next visit to Ganeshpuri, Bhagawan, in Konkani Gurbanji, began to tease the child, "So how was your experience in flying like a sparrow." Nobody had related the incident of the boy's falling to Bhagawan. Being all-pervasive, Bade Baba knew of it because it was he who had saved the child by making the mattresses fall to break his fall. The Bhramaupdesh (the Thread Ceremony) of this child was performed by Bhagawan Nityananda and the Kanmantra (Mantra initiation given by reciting the mantra in the ears) was also given to him by Bade Baba himself.

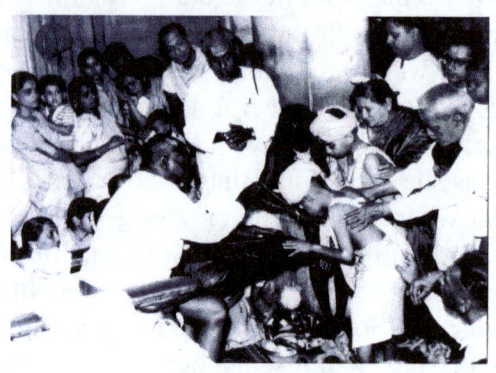

Krishnabai's Bhramaupdesh

Sadananda Swami's Samadhi

On the 15th of June 2007, on the last day of the Adhikh Mas, also known as the month Purshotam in the Hindu calendar, Padiyar Swami, also known as Swami Sadananda, took Samadhi after a brief illness. One of the few remaining elder disciples of Bhagawan Nityananda thus passed away.

After serving Bhagawan Nityananda for many years, Bade Baba gave him the direct command to settle at Kanhangad. That was in 1961, just before Bhagawan Nityananda took Mahasamadhi. Bade Baba had instructed Sadananda Baba to remain at Kanhangad and perform suvichar. He did exactly that for the last of his 46 years here. To every devotee visiting him he spoke of Bade Baba and shared his experiences. He was full of Bhagawan

Nityananda's Grace. Due to his long association with many other devotees, he also experienced, first-hand, the miracle of Bade Baba's Grace in the lives of so many others.

Sadananda Swami set a perfect example of how to follow Guruvakya (devotion to the Guru's word and instruction). He was an extraordinary man with tremendous faith. His tomb is built in Gopal Sadan, Kushal Nagar, Kanhangad, North Kerala. It is exactly opposite the round table built by Bade Baba to commensurate the Round Table Conference held by Mahatma Gandhi with the British Government. In the same compound of Kushal Nagar is a well in which Bade Baba has thrown many Shaligrams (dark oval stones) that are considered very powerful. One should bathe in the water drawn from this well.

Kuti Ram

There were several Disciples of Bade Baba who dedicated their lives at the Lotus Feet of Gurudeva and became His full-time attendants. Appana, Panwalla Mama, Lokhanna, Kuti Ram and Gopal Anna are some. Appana and Gopal Anna dedicated their entire lives. Lokhanna set up a hotel and became a businessman and Panwalla Mama had a small shop selling betel leaves, cigarettes, biddies, tobacco, etc. next to Kuti Ram's hotel. Kuti Ram was a hotelier who later became a monk. His Samadhi Shrine is behind Kailasa Ashram a bit further than Shaligram Swami's Samadhi Shrine.

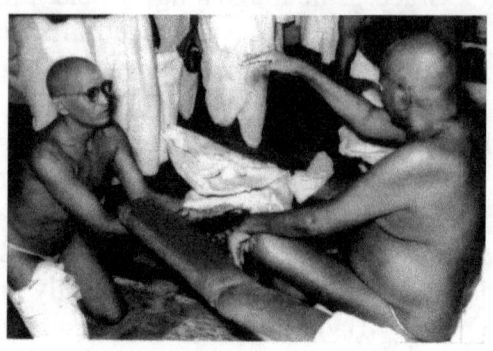

Bhagawan Nityananda Initiating Kuti Ram

Gopal Anna

Among the fulltime attendants of Bhagawan Nityananda, there is one who is held in reverence and great respect. He is Gopal Anna. There is none to measure up to his dedication. He not only served Bade Baba when he was in his gross form, but continued to serve Him even after he passed.

He used to get up at 3:30 in the morning and have his bath. Initially, he lived in Kailasa Ashram. From there he used to come to the Mahasamadhi Shrine of Bhagawan Nityananda and help in performing the puja. He performed every activity with a feeling of deep service, respect and love. After the Arati, he used to come back to Kailasa Ashram, have his breakfast, wash the cloths and coverings of the Murti of Bade Baba and then rest for an hour or so.

Kailasa Ashram

Mahasamadhi Shrine of Bhagawan Nityananda

At 11am, he used to engage in supervising Balbhojan (the feeding of children while chanting God's name). In the early days he used to make weekly visits to Mumbai to make purchases for Balbhojan. He used to personally look after Balbhojan because Bade Baba was always very particular about it being conducted properly.

After all the children were fed, he used to take his lunch and sleep for some time. In the late afternoon he used to meditate and in the evening he used to counsel the local devotees who used to approach him for guidance. He was surrounded by children, young adults and ladies asking for his guidance. While performing this service whole-heartedly, he always remained unattached.

Around 6pm he used to conduct Sanj Arati, the evening puja at Kailasa Ashram. This puja was worth witnessing. He offered it so beautifully that one could feel the presence of Bhagawan Nityananda at that time. After 8 in the evening he used to retire.

Gopal Anna is so great. Like Janananda Swamiji, he is one of the few who not only surrendered to Bade Baba but served Bade Baba all his life. When most of the devotees went back to their old ways after Bhagawan Nityananda took Mahasamadhi, it was Gopal Anna and Janananda Swami who continued to live as if Bade Baba was eternally present. Every activity of theirs was undertaken with that belief and conviction.

Another great quality of Gopal Anna was that he served Nityananda by serving Bhagawan Nityananda's devotees. Gopal Anna used to take care of Balbhojan, feed children, clean the hot springs, guide devotees who sought his advice, treat new devotees with great respect, and he served as a pillar for poor people by supporting them and giving purpose to their lives.

Shri Swami Janananda Baba

Swami Janananda Baba was a disciple of Bhagawan Nityananda and, under the direct command of Bade Baba he looked after Bhagawan Nityananda's Ashram at Kanhangad. Bhagawan Nityananda described him as Dattatreya Avatar. Swami Janananda Baba looked after the Kanhangad Ashram as his Master's Temple and never tried to propagate his own image. He attributed everything to Bhagawan Nityananda and became a true Karma Yogi.

Swami Janananda took birth to set an example of devotion through Seva, as described in the Bhagavad Gita. All his life he worked hard with total devotion to his Guru. He also kept all his spiritual power subdued and never tried

to make a name for himself. He always kept the name of
Bhagawan Nityananda in the forefront of whatever he did.
Janananda Baba had no attachment to name, fame or
worldly possessions. He lived his entire life saying, "Thy
will be done."

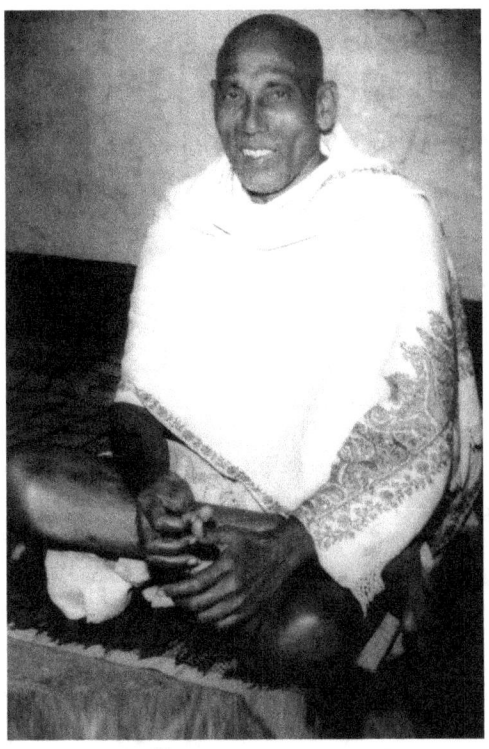

Swami Janananda Baba

Bhagawan Nityananda's love for Swami Janananda
Baba was very great. It was to Janananda Baba who
Bhagawan recommended severe penance by ordering him
to go to the Himalayas and Nasik. Near Nasik, at
Gangapur, the place known for Lord Dattatreya, Bhagawan
made Swami Janananda perform an Anushtan (special
puja). When Swami Janananda visited Ganeshpuri,

Bhagawan Nityananda asked devotees to receive him with great honor and humility.

The greatness of Swami Janananda was in his unconditional surrender to Bhagawan Nityananda. His surrender was so complete that Bhagawan Nityananda named him Datta Avatar.

Bade Baba used to say, "Janananda goes into samadhi. When you perform puja to him, he enters into the Self. When you offer puja to him in that state it is like making an offering to Brahman." Bhagawan Nityananda told Baburao Khade this. Janananda was seen entering into deep trance when the devotees from Sion performed his Padpuja (ritual bathing of a holy person's feet) and Arati. Such events were full of joy.

Janananda Baba remained in a state of complete Samadhi for several hours until the entire Puja was complete. His eyes would roll up into his head and he remained absolutely still.

Swami Janananda Puja

Swami Janananda Baba commanded respect as a senior disciple of Bhagawan Nityananda. Before taking Mahasamadhi, Janananda Baba visited Mumbai in 1982. He was personally received by Swami Muktananda at Ganeshpuri. Guns were fired in his honor and Muktananda Baba took him to his Ashram. There he washed the feet of

Janananda Baba, took the Pada Tirtha himself first, and then distributed it to all his disciples.

He then gave his personal car to take Swami Janananda to Ganeshpuri. He frequently visited there to inquire about Janananda's health. On October 2nd, 1982, the day that Swami Janananda Baba left Ganeshpuri for the last time to return to the Kanhangad Ashram, Muktananda Baba took Mahasamadhi.

Swami Madhavananda

Then there was Swami Madhavananda. He was a short, thin caldron of Shakti! Madhavanandaji also served Bhagawan Nityananda, then Paramahamsa Muktananda, and then Muktananda's successors. I had several conversations with Madhavanandaji during the course of performing Seva in the Ganeshpuri Ashram. We spoke about how to become a mad lover of God and how to cultivate the necessary devotion.

Here too, I experienced swamiji as having gone across by my Gurudev's Grace. I remember that he saw all as God, no matter what their behavior or weakness. Later, he took to singing Qawwali (devotional songs). I will always remember his quiet Grace.

Venkappa Anna

Venkappa Anna was another great servant of Bhagawan Nityananda who later also served Muktananda Paramahamsa and his successors. While performing Seva in Ganeshpuri, I used to ride the garbage truck with him. We would collect the Ashram garbage and divide it up into what was disposable and what was for the compost heap. Venkappa was a long time servant of my Guru who oozed Shakti. He had a wonderful temper that was really funny to behold. He used to laugh at himself. That was a great teaching. He was very humble.

Chapter 4
The Crown On the Kanhangad Hill

In the first week of August 1961, several devotees had gathered at Ganeshpuri. The news that Bhagawan Nityananda's health was failing had reached many of his devotees. However, news of this did not reach all his devotees. So, Bade Baba himself appeared to several people and instructed them to come to Ganeshpuri.

Madhav Hegde was in his factory where he was working as Senior Engineer. Suddenly Bhagawan Nityananda appeared in front of him and ordered him to come to Ganeshpuri immediately. Raghunath Shenoy came to know on the morning of the 8th and left for Ganeshpuri right away.

Wamnarao Khalkar, a devotee from Nasik, was on a special assignment given him by Bhagawan Nityananda. Several months prior to Bhagawan Nityananda's Mahasamadhi, Wamnarao was told to construct an octagonal dome on the top of the cave hill at the Kanhangad Ashram. This dome is still seen at Kanhangad and the area is used as a hall to sing bhajans.

In the center is placed a large picture of Bade Baba with a small statue of Lord Krishna. Just next to this hall is a shrine to Bade Baba and Akeri Keri Keri Bateri Baba's tomb. Wamnarao completed the construction of the dome and went to Janananda Swami to take his blessings to return to Ganeshpuri. He wanted to tell Bade Baba that he had completed the dome.

The Dome At Kanhangad Ashram

The Shrine to Bhagawan Nityananda With
Akeri Keri Keri Bateri Baba's Tomb
In Front of the Murthi of Bhagawan

Wamnarao Khalkar returned to Ganeshpuri sometime in June or July and said "Baba, as instructed by you, I have placed the crown on the hill." What we did not know then is that Bhagawan Nityananda had told Devrai Pai, "The day a crown is placed over the hill at Kanhangad, it will be time for this One to give up his body." With this last task completed, it was time for Bhagawan Nityananda to take Mahasamadhi.

On August 8, 1961 Bhagawan Nityananda of Ganeshpuri dropped his body for the last time at His Ashram in the village of Ganeshpuri. His body is buried in then great Ganeshpuri Mahasamadhi shrine that is visited by thousands of people each and every month.

Om Bhagawan Nityananda Bhagawan
Shri Bhagawan Sharanam Prapadye
Om

Chapter 5
His Wisdom and Instruction

THE CHIDAKASHA GITA OF
BHAGAWAN NITYANANDA OF GANESHPURI
With Commentary by Sadguru Kedarji

Introduction

I began reading and studying the Chidakasha Gita in 1982. During this period, Bhagawan Nityananda appeared to me often in Meditation and while Chanting. My unfolding understanding of the verses has explained many of the experiences I have had during the course of my Sadhana. These teachings ring true on every level.

I have read the entire Chidakasha Gita many times through, and I continue to read it, even now. Each time I read it I have a new realization and another breakthrough in the experience of the Abode of the True Heart. ALL of the teachings of Vedanta and ALL the teachings of Shaivism are contained in the Chidakasha Gita.

Although the Chidakasha Gita is ripe with many wonderful spiritual teachings, there are 12 main principles that, in my experience, Bhagawan Nityananda emphasizes over and over again. These 12 principles form the very essence of the work and the very foundation of His teachings.

1. Bhagawan Nityananda tells us that God is in humankind and humankind is in God. There is no difference between the two. Sentient and insentient are one in the same. All are reflected in the same "mirror" that is the Sky of Consciousness referred to as Chidakasha, the Heart space

or Triadic Heart of Shiva.

Bade Baba tells us that the Heart is not the physical Heart, nor the heart chakra located in the area of the physical heart. He tells us that the Heart is the one, indivisible Sky of Consciousness that is the Absolute. This Heart is beyond the body and the senses and can be accessed through the Crown Chakra in the head.

This Chidakasha, He states, is triangular with three points (Shiva, Shakti, Nara) and becomes a constant experience upon the dawning of Liberation. Chidakasha is the seat of Lord Shiva and the abode of His Shakti. It is comprised of Light, Vibration and Sound. From that sound manifests Omkar.

2. Bhagawan Nityananda wants us to know and realize where God is. He tells us that God is not in the Murti or statue or idol in the temple, but that God exists inside each of us and that each of us is the temple wherein God resides.

3. Sri Bade Baba tells us that Omkar, and the mantra Aum that it produces, is what gives power and form to the Universe of all sentient and insentient beings. It is also the very vibration of Chidakasha that is known in Shaivism as Spanda or Visarga.

4. Bhagawan Nityananda is not big on philosophy. He is very practical. In the Chidakasha Gita, He uses simple experiences from the interaction with objects of everyday life to help us understand the deepest most profound connection between God and humankind. He emphasizes a very practical means of attaining Mukti or Moksha by means of the Sushumna Nadi.

He declares over and over again that this central channel or central nerve (subtle body) that is contained in every living creature, is the only true spiritual path. He emphasizes that

Moksha (deliverance or liberation) cannot be attained until Kundalini Shakti is fully awakened by a Shakta Adept who is a Siddha Guru. Once this Kundalini is awakened, He states, Prana Shakti must be directed into the Sushumna Nadi and then constantly made to rise upward into the Crown Chakra in the head.

Bhagawan instructs that the breath must be directed in this way without taking any air in from the outside (this correlates to the Shaivite practice of "Sushumna breathing"). He refers to this as Prana Vayu and emphatically states that this is the only means to directing your awareness to become absorbed in Bindu Nada (point of sound emanating from the Sahasrar that is experienced in the crown chakra in the head). Once your awareness merges in this Bindu Nada, Mukti is attained.

The goal of meditation, he tells us, is to keep our awareness in this Bindu Nada, even while going about our daily, mundane activities. This, he states is true Dhyan and Dharana. This alone is Samadhi. It is the means to live in the world without being of the world and it can only be taught by a Sadguru.

5. Bade Baba describes this Bindu Nada in two ways; first as the sound similar to the dull roar of the ocean or the vibration of a large bell just after having been struck; and second as ajapa-japa, the sound made of the two syllables So' and Ham (the two feet of Lord Shiva) as one breathes in and out. Of these two, he emphasizes the first, telling us that even the mantra So' Ham (Hamsa) that sounds on its own (Anahata, the unstruck sound) dissolves in the vibration of Bindu Nada.

How will we know when we have attained Liberation? Bhagawan Nityananda tells us we will know when our entire conscious awareness is absorbed in this Bindu Nada constantly. He tells us that this Bindu Nada is the primary

quality and experience of Chidakasha. It is the very
Vibration of Ananda (Bliss) that is attained when Sat
(being) and Chit (pure perceiving awareness) unite. This
unification, He states, is brought about by causing Prana
(breath) to rise inside the Sushumna Nadi without taking
any air in from the outside. (Warning: Do not attempt this
practice without the direct instruction of one who has
mastered it.)

In this state, one experiences the Sky of Consciousness or
Chidakasha for one's self. This, He tells us, is the seat of
all Yoga. This is the true place of pilgrimage and, once you
have arrived here, no other pilgrimage to any other place is
necessary and no ritual is necessary either. In fact, Bade
Baba tells us to make this form of Pranayam our only
ritual; that, while in this state, the awareness of the Mantras
Om and Hamsa is the ritual bath.

6. Bhagawan Nityananda declares over and over again that
the goal of a human birth, the goal of all life is to merge in
the Absolute, to attain Mukti while still in the body. He
tells us don't wait, do it now. And then he emphasizes,
throughout the Chidakasha Gita, that the Guru is the means.
He is very clear about this. One must receive Kundalini
awakening and the leadership for Sadhana from a "Siddha,"
"Guru" or "Acharya" as he puts it, who has become a Jnani
(knower of the Truth).

At several points in the work, Bade Baba reiterates that,
"There is no place in the world for one who does not have a
Guru. Such a person is lost....You cannot realize the Truth
without a Guru." And he emphasizes that one needs to
follow the instruction of the Guru, until one is freed to
Liberation by that Guru's Grace.

7. Bade Baba does not leave us in the dark about who can
be a Guru or Preceptor. In this regard he is very specific.
He tells us that a Swami, Sanyasin, Brahmin, Jnani,

Brahmachari is not simply one who holds such a title and wears ochre robes carrying a copy of the Bhagavad Gita in his hands.

Likewise, one who is well-versed in the Vedas, Puranas and other sacred texts is not such a person either. Bhagawan Nityananda emphasizes that a Sadguru (true Guru), who may also be referred to as a Swami, Sanyasin, Jnani and so on, is only a person who is desireless and whose mind has merged with the Absolute One Paramatma or Paramshiva. He goes on to describe the qualities of such a Guru by stating that such a being sees all as the same one God and behaves in alignment with this state.

A Jnani, Sanyasin, Swami or Guru is one whose mind constantly rests in Buddhi, the Divine Will and Intelligence of the Atman. Such a being is one who sees only God in everything and everyone, everywhere and such a being does not distinguish between "mine" and "thine", "good" and "bad," "honor" and "dishonor," nor classes of people and races.

Such a being has a constant, uninterrupted experience of Bindu Nada and knows that there is no such thing as duality or diversity. Such a being experiences that the entire Universe is contained inside himself and that he himself pervades all objects (people, places and things). Bhagawan Nityananda tells us that only such a being can be known as a Sadguru, Siddha Guru, Jnani, Swami or Sanyasin and that one should only take such a being as one's Guru.

8. Bhagawan Nityananda tells us that, for the relationship between Guru and Disciple or Devotee to work, the seeker must have and continue to cultivate Faith in God and the Guru. This Faith is expressed by way of vigilance in daily spiritual practice as instructed by the Guru.

9. Sri Bade Baba tells us, over and over again, that the basis for Sadhana is the willingness to turn away from worldliness and the willingness to destroy our attachment to sense pleasures and worldly pleasures. He tells us that this happens through the destruction of the body-idea, also known as the ego (along with the senses). "Atma is not perceptible to the senses," He tells us. By this statement we understand that God can only be realized by going beyond the mind and beyond the senses. If our attachment to worldliness is not destroyed in this way, he tells us we will fail in the end.

10. Bhagawan Nityananda emphasizes the importance of Equality Consciousness and He explains what that is. Equality Consciousness is the experience of "sameness," the direct experience that there are not many individual experients (souls), but that there is only one Universal Experient, only one being who experiences through all of the forms. This one being comes and goes on the breath. Because all are this One God, all are equal. This, He tells us, is the real Equality Consciousness. Without it, we cannot know God.

11. He tells us that, "Without Bhakti there can be no Mukti." Here he emphasizes the absolute necessity for Devotion and Surrender to the Guru and the path. It is the intensity of your feeling for God and the Guru that causes Jnana (wisdom) to rise within you. Once your have Jnana, your Bhakti increases automatically. And with intense Bhakti, Jnana manifests of its own accord. The two work hand in hand. Through the cultivation of Bhakti and Jnana, limiting desire and craving for objects (people, places and things) is destroyed and perfect Peace is attained.

12. Bhagawan Nityananda tells us that Viveka (the ability to perceive the subtle in the gross) and Vairagya (dispassion or detachment) are vital to realizing the Truth. Without Viveka, he tells us, you cannot learn to choose

God over limiting desire because you are not able to discriminate between what takes you toward God and what takes you away from God.

And you cannot remain absorbed in your Natural, Free state of being without Vairagya. This elated dispassion is what allows you to keep your mind focused on Buddhi, long enough for you to realize that there is no outer world. All takes place inside the body of Supreme Consciousness, that Shiva-Shakti power or the Self that is also contained inside you.

These twelve paragraphs summarize my experience of the teachings and principles Bhagawan Nityananda offers us in His Chidakasha Gita. For these reasons, it is worth reading and contemplating over and over again.

With Supreme Love and Devotion, I offer this at the Lotus Feet of that Supreme Being, Sri Bhagawan Nityananda of Ganeshpuri.

The Chidakasha Gita

1. Jnanis are mindless. To Jnanis, all are the same. They have no slumber, no dreams, nor sleep. They are always in sleep. The sun and the moon are the same to them. To them, it is always sunrise. The glass of a chimney lamp, when covered with carbon, is not transparent. Similarly, the carbon of the mind should be removed.

Commentary: A being who is immersed in the state of Supreme Shiva, the state of Supreme Intelligence, is a knower of the Truth. One who sees and experiences God in everything and everyone, everywhere is called a Jnani. To such a person, only God exists. For such a being, this world-appearance is neither real or unreal. It is a reflection of the Bliss of the inner Self. A Jnani is immersed in

Equality Consciousness and is the Revealer of that Equality Consciousness. Equality Consciousness is the vision that all sentient and insentient manifestations are the same because the Self exists in them equally.

For one whose experience of Equality Consciousness is uninterrupted, the "Sun" of Pure Perceiving Awareness never sets. Such a being is always aware that the Revealer exists in that which is revealed. The physical covering is transparent for such a being. A Jnani is one who has destroyed the restless mind so that this Truth becomes a constant revelation.

2. There are three nerves in the body: the sun or the Sushumna; the moon or the Ida; the star or the Pingala. The first is red in color, the second, blue, and the third, green.

Commentary: Inside the covering known as your physical body, there are many channels or paths through which spiritual energy flows. These paths are subtle. Of these, there are three channels or paths of spiritual energy that are of primary importance to a spiritual seeker. Of these three channels, one is the most important. The subtle path that moves up inside your physical form through the right nostril is known as Pingala. The subtle path that moves up inside your physical form through the left nostril is known as Ida. The third subtle path is the most important because it is the path of the spiritually-perfected Love beings. It is through this path that the awakened Mula or Kundalini Shakti, once fully awakened, makes her journey through all the subtle spiritual energy centers of your being (Chakras) to union with Shiva in the Sahasrar.

This is why it is called the path of the spiritually-perfected Love beings. This is the subtle energy channel called Sushumna. This covering is also called the subtle body. This path begins at Muladhara chakra that is the entrance to

the Sushumna. This "gateway" to Sushumna, known as
Muladhara chakra, is red in color. This Muladhara is also
the "gateway" to the subtle paths of Pingala and Ida.
Depending on how a yogi directs his/her Prana (breath)
through these three channels, one can experience various
colors such as Green, Red and Blue.

**3. Where these three nerves meet is the heart space. As
we go on practicing yoga, the Bindu-sound is heard in
the head. This sound is one, indivisible.**

Commentary: The Ida, Pingala and Sushumna paths within
your being all merge in the Crown chakra at the top of your
head. When your witnessing awareness expands to the
point where you are able to direct your entire witnessing
awareness to become absorbed in this Crown chakra, there
is a sound that is heard on a constant basis. This sound is
called Bindu Nada or point of vibration. Some sages refer
to it as the ten different kinds of sound emanating from the
Sahasrar.

This sound is the Vibration of Divine Consciousness
known as Spanda or Chiti. It is called "one" or
"indivisible" because it is the very frequency of the inner
Self from which this entire cosmos is manifested. On
becoming absorbed in this sound, one sees the Light of
Divine Consciousness that falls downward from the
Sahasrar. This is Prakasha, Lord Shiva's Pratibha (light).
It is most excellent.

**4. Just as camphor is consumed by the flames of fire, so
also, mind must be consumed by soul-fire.**

Commentary: When camphor is consumed by flames it
burns completely and not even the seed of camphor
remains. In the same way, for a spiritual seeker who wants
to merge with his/her natural, free state of being, the
restless mind must be burned in the fire of the Shiva-Shakti

power. When the mind is silent, the impressions left behind on the mind still remain in subtle form. These impressions rise over and over again to make the mind restless. In the fire of a devotee's daily spiritual practice, by the Grace of a Sadguru, these impressions left behind on the mind are destroyed completely and the mind also dissolves in the fire of the inner Self.

5. The copra, detached from the shell, makes a dull sound when shaken; so also the body and soul must be thought of as separate. The first is light; by that light, all vices are consumed.

Commentary: When we remove the coconut kernel (copra) from the coconut shell, we do not mistake the shell for the kernel. We know that the copra is not its shell. In the same way, a person seeking to know the Truth should cultivate the understanding that the physical body and the internal soul are separate. One is a reflection of the other.
The internal soul is actually the light of Divine Consciousness. The body is merely a shell that this internal soul parades around in. When a devotee has this realization on a constant basis, all the ego attachments created by the false sense of individuality are destroyed.

6. Just as we draw water from a well, we should draw breath. When we breathe out, it should be like letting down the bucket into the well. When we breathe out, it is the carbon (the impurities of the body); when we breathe in, it is the breath of Omkar. Breath of Omkar is the manas (mind).

Commentary: In our approach, the breath is called Prana Shakti. The internal soul comes and goes on the movement of this Prana Shakti within your being. When you breathe in, the mind is born and creation manifests. When you exhale, the mind begins to calm down as the impurities of the body and the attachments of the mind are expelled from your being. The primordial sound, the mantra OM, is the cause of the manifestation of this Universe. When you breathe in, this act of manifestation occurs within your being, through ideation, due to the vibration of this same Omkar. The coming and going of Prana Shakti inside your being is the manifestation, sustenance and withdrawal of this world-appearance.

7. Manas is Jiva; but their positions are different. Jivatman is Paramatman.

Commentary: In our approach, Manas is a word for the Mind. The mind is considered to be the Jiva, the individual bound soul. When, by the Grace of a Sadguru and your own daily spiritual practice, you are able to turn the mind within to make it merge with the Supreme Principle, the mind becomes Jivatman, the reflection of the formless Absolute in the body. One who has fully realized the inner Self by merging his/her mind into That is said to be Paramatman or Jivanmukti, Self-realized while still in the body.

8. A man or woman should be educated. What is education? Jiva should know the secret that He is the Paramatman.

Commentary: Education in mundane life is limited knowledge. True education is complete knowledge and experience of That by whose light all things shine. This is the only real knowledge since it is by this knowledge that all other things are understood. Every individual should embark upon the path that will uncover the secret that he/she is really God himself.

9. Paramatman is in Jivatman. The real Mukti is to know the subtle in the gross.

Commentary: The one Universal Experient, the Self that is worshipped by so many different names, is actually the same one who takes the form of the individual bound soul. There are spiritual paths that espouse that Mukti or Liberation occurs when you achieve complete silence of mind while sitting for meditation. This is not Liberation. It is not Mukti. Mukti is the constant awareness that the subtle, the Supreme Principle, is contained in all the gross objects of this world. Mukti is the constant awareness of that fact.

10. We should leave off the gross sleep and sleep the subtle sleep. We should enjoy the sleep obtained from the practice of Pranayam.

Commentary: My Gurudev used to say that sleep is death. In the gross sleep, you experience the state of deep sleep where you are not aware of anything at all. The subtle sleep is one in which, while in the state of deep sleep, you are able to maintain the awareness that you are God and that your deep sleep is merely one of God's coverings.

The way to enjoy this subtle sleep in which you are actually fully aware (and therefore fully awake) is by means of Pranayam. One of the approaches to practicing Pranayam is the practice of controlling and directing your breath so that it enters the Sushumna Nadi and moves about there, rising and falling, without the necessity to take any air in from the outside. This is what Bhagawan Nityananda is referring to.

11. The upgoing breath is like the wheels inside a clock. Its movement is inside. When the movement of the breath is internal, one will see the world in himself.

Commentary: Prana Shakti is your breath. The upgoing breath is the Prana when it moves inside the Sushumna Nadi, rising through the chakras. This is what causes

Kundalini Shakti to rise after Kundalini has been fully awakened by a Shaktipat Guru. Just as the wheels inside a clock control the movement of a clock, the upgoing breath controls the manifestation, sustenance and withdrawal of the entire Universe. When a devotee, by the instruction and Grace of his/her Guru, is able to direct and maintain the Prana inside this Sushumna Nadi, without taking any breath in through the nose or mouth, the devotee experiences all 36 Tattvas (stages of manifestation and withdrawal of the Universe) inside his/her own being.

12. Just as we see the sky reflected in the water in an earthen pot, so also, to the internal vision, the sky of consciousness becomes visible.

Commentary: The water inside a pot has the ability to reflect the sky above. But when doing so, the water, which is the reflecting surface, does not become the sky. It remains as water and the sky remains the sky. This is due to the reflective nature of the Supreme Subject (the formless Absolute) who becomes the internal soul of all sentient and insentient objects (people, places and things). One who knows this from the personal experience gained by Guru's Grace, is able to attain the internal vision by which Chidakasha, the great inner expanse of Divine Consciousness, becomes completely visible.

13. If food is prepared in a gold vessel, the dog eats it. If it is prepared in an earthen vessel, then also the dog eats it.

Commentary: A dog's only interest is food. Regardless of what the food is cooked in, the dog will eat it because it has become absorbed in food. A person who is attached to sex, only wants sex, regardless of the context. One whose only desire is for money, will eventually pursue money, regardless of the means. You get what you meditate on. One who desires only God becomes God.

14. The sunlight is reflected in the salt water of the sea. It is also reflected in the clear water of a tank at the top of a hill. It is not enough if we see with the eye but we should experience it.

Commentary: Even though sunlight is reflected in water and other surfaces, to experience the sun directly, we need to sit in the sunlight. We can't get a tan by starring at the reflection of the sun. In the same way, it is not enough to have the intellectual understanding that the Self exists. We have to have a direct and ongoing experience of the inner Self, by going beyond the mind and beyond the senses.

15. On a tree grow numberless flowers. The flowers all perish but the tree does not perish for a long time. The visible is like the flowers, the invisible is like the tree.

Commentary: This world-appearance is like the flowers growing on a tree. Just as the flowers wither and die and then take birth again in an endless cycle of birth and death, but the tree remains as the source of birth and death of the flowers; so too, this world-appearance and all the objects in it perishes and is born again by the Shiva-Shakti power that remains changeless. Objects (people, places and things) are visible like the flowers. The power of Divine Consciousness that causes those flowers to manifest is subtle and not readily visible to those who do not have the subtle discrimination.

16. There are matches in a matchbox. Fire is produced only when the match is rubbed against the side of the box. So also, the Manas is the match; intelligence (Buddhi) is the side of the box. We should rub the Manas against Buddhi and then we get the kingdom of Self that is the same as the liberation from the cycle of birth and death.

Commentary: Buddhi (will) has two aspects;
transcendental and immanent. The transcendental aspect is
Lord Shiva's Svatantrya or God's sweet Will. When we
align ourselves with God's Will, we attain the kingdom of
the Lord and are able to bask in God's Grace all the time.
We become God's responsibility. This is a state that dawns
on a person when the mind is merged in one's natural, free
state of being. When the mind is "rubbed" against the
higher intelligence of the Shiva-Shakti power, it becomes
God. For this to happen one needs a Guru and a spiritual
path.

**17. A person should be quite indifferent to honor and
dishonor. He should not have the least love for his
body. Such a person will see the Supreme Being in
everything and everywhere.**

Commentary: To experience the state of Bliss, Joy,
complete Inner Peace and total Freedom, you have to rise
above praise and blame. You have to become immune to
the perceptions created by words and the energy of egoism
must be prevented from forming so that you no longer
respond to virtue or vice. This is Vairagya, dispassion. By
cultivating Vairagya, you are able to destroy the notion that
you are the body. In this way, once you have discarded the
false notion that you are just a person, you merge with the
Supreme Principle and see only That in everything and
everyone, everywhere.

**18. The Supreme Light and the Universal Light are
identical.**

Commentary: Shiva and His Shakti are identical. God's
transcendental and immanent aspects are two parts of the
very same Consciousness. There is no Shakti without
Shiva and there is no Shiva without Shakti. This world of
forms is identical to the Supreme I-Consciousness that
created it. Only God exists.

19. From a plank, are manufactured tables, chairs, etc. So also, Brahman is the primordial substance from which numberless worlds are formed.

Commentary: Planks of wood are used to manufacture wooden chairs and tables. Yet the chairs and tables remain essentially wood, even though they seem to have taken on a different form. Without the wood, there would be no chairs and tables. In the same way, this universe is not separate from Brahman (Divine Consciousness) because Brahman is the substance from which this universe is created. Therefore, this universe of forms is essentially that same Shiva-Shakti power fashioned into what we perceive as this universe.

20. Manas and the Atman are the same to all people. At the final stage of the universe, all is one. At the present stage, there is difference in their mode of breathing, thinking, and their mental tendencies.

Commentary: There are four ages known as Yugas (Satya Yuga, Treta Yuga, Dvarpara Yuga and Kali Yuga). These four form one world cycle. We are now in the fourth age known as Kali Yuga. At the end of this age, the entire Universe will be dissolved and reabsorbed back into the formless Absolute. When this happens all activity ceases, as all objects (people, places and things) are withdrawn into one formless Absolute. Prior to this cosmic dissolution, the Universe would seem to be full of duality and diversity, full of many different forms, seemingly independent of each other. In Truth, they are not. Only the One who creates, sustains and withdraws actually exists.

21. Fire, air, water, and earth are common to all. These may be used by all people alike. Similarly, well-water may be used by a brahmin, a pariah, and children alike.

Commentary: Just as all beings use fire, air, water and the earth and claim these as their own, regardless of race, creed, color, caste or past deeds; God belongs to everyone, regardless of race, creed, color, caste or past deeds. Also, anyone seeking the means to experience God in order to become a Liberated being, may do so. The water from the well of knowledge of Divine Consciousness may be drunk by all. On the spiritual path, no sincere seeker should be discriminated against. God wishes to redeem ALL His children.

22. Manas is the gingilly; Buddhi is the oil mill; Amrita (ambrosia) is the oil.

Commentary: To extract oil from a seed, you have to grind the seed in a mill. Then you get oil. In the same way, to extract the ambrosia of the Supreme Intelligence, you have to "grind" the mind in the mill of that inner Self. The restless mind must be made silent. This happens when the mind is fed to the Buddhi and devoured by this Supreme Intelligence.

23. Buddhi is the king. Manas is the minister. Manas should be subordinated to Buddhi.

Commentary: When the contracted intellect (Buddhi) of the individual expands and merges with Iccha (Shiva's Will), Buddhi then becomes the channel for real Intelligence. When this occurs, the mind should be subordinated to Buddhi so that the yogi always has access to That which is real knowledge, to That which is worth knowing. A yogi must learn to follow God's Will. This is what being a yogi means.

24. When a road is crowded with five or six thousand people, it is almost impossible to drive a horse carriage along the road. The driver must be careful in driving

the carriage. A cyclist's attention is not directed towards himself but towards the passerby.

Commentary: Being a yogi, being a devotee on a spiritual path does not mean you become a "space cadet." One who follows a Guru and engages in daily spiritual practice must also take responsibility for his/her worldly life. A yogi should become very focused and make his/her mind very sharp through Meditation. Such a person should perform his/her daily mundane activities masterfully, and in a way that is the heritage of sages.

25. When a person is entirely sunk in cold water, he/she no longer feels the cold of the cold water. A perfect person is not subject to anger.

Commentary: If you stay in cold water long enough, your body becomes indifferent to the cold and you are able to remain in the cold water without being affected by it. In the same way, a yogi should remain in the world without being of the world. A perfect yogi is one who is not swayed by anger or the other emotions that are common to this world. A perfected being does not lose his/her equipoise even for a moment, even though he is still immersed in worldly activity. He moves through this world as a spectator, remaining indifferent and unattached to that which is experienced by the body.

26. When a seed is fried, it cannot sprout. When a lamp contains no oil, we do not call it a "lamp." When the sun is shining, a gaslight becomes dim. It is the sun that gives light to the whole world. If Manas is regarded as the king, Buddhi may be regarded as the prime minister. When a tree does not bear fruits, it has no beauty. There is no effect without cause. In darkness light persists. Darkness is ignorance. Light is Jnana (knowledge). One must see the inner Self. One must return to the place from whence one started. One

must follow a path and Master that will allow him to realize this completely. Only then can one go home.

Commentary: This entire Universe manifests, is sustained and withdrawn due to the existence of the Supreme Subject, the One Shiva-Shakti power. Without this light of God nothing shines and nothing can exist either. Can you see yourself if there is nothing to reflect your form? No. In the same way, all objects in this Universe are reflections of that Supreme Subject.

Without the Supreme Subject, the object cannot exist and, in fact, objects (people, places and things) do not simply reside here in this world. They exist inside the body of Supreme Consciousness. Even darkness needs Divine light to be recognized as darkness. The form we are in is on loan from the Supreme Principle. We must follow a path and Master that will allow us to realize this fact completely. Only then can we go home.

27. A Guru (spiritual teacher) will lead any sort of man from a thorny path to the royal road. Such preceptors are of two kinds. One is the primary preceptor and the other, the secondary preceptor. Mind is the primary preceptor and the other, the secondary preceptor. One is not the preceptor of the other. He is only the secondary preceptor. The secondary preceptor is one who shows the water in the well. The guru who exists in the heart of all beings is the Jagad-Guru (universal preceptor).

Commentary: On the spiritual path, the living Master is the means. A Shakta Adept who has the power to bestow Shaktipat can lead any person from the ignorance of his/her own delusion to the royal road to Self-realization. The Shiva-Shakti power is the primary Guru. This Supreme Principle exists in the heart of all living beings. The living Master is not the Guru to the Shiva-Shakti power.

The cosmic mind, Shiva-Shakti, is the primary preceptor. The preceptor in the physical form of the Shakta Adept is the secondary preceptor. The secondary preceptor is spiritually-perfected Love being who has become the perfect reflection of the inner Self, and gives you Shaktipat and leads you in spiritual practice, until you are set on your own path. The secondary preceptor is that living Master who shows you the Self. The One Absolute Supreme Being takes the form of that Shakta Adept to bring you to Him.

28. People generally think that a teacher's body is guru. A man does not become a guru by simply wearing sandals and counting beads on a rosary. One who talks "Brahma Jnana" and gives stones to his disciples is not a guru. Whatever a Guru speaks in words, he must show it in action. First one must practice and after realization, he must begin to teach others.

Commentary: The Sadguru (true living Guru) is not the physical body, but rather the Grace-bestowing power of God at work through the Master. Someone who has been ordained a monk and wears the clothes of a Sanyasi should not automatically be considered a Sadguru. Someone who teaches from the scriptures and tells you that he/she is all knowing, but cannot give you a direct experience of God and the leadership necessary for complete Liberation, must not be considered a Guru.

Know the true living Master by the fact that his/her own actions are in alignment with his Liberated state and the instruction he espouses to you. The spiritual companion in the Self-Realized Love being is one who has attained the final state through his own spiritual practice, having followed the instruction of a Siddha Guru. Once Liberated, this person has an obligation to teach others and offer the leadership that will help people attain the same state of union with the inner Self.

29. One who has thoroughly wiped off the idea "I am the body" is fit to be called a Guru. There is none higher than such a one. There is no God above such a Guru. Such a Guru is God, and God is such a Guru.

Commentary: The true living Master is one who has risen above body-consciousness and remains in a state of total ecstasy, in a state of complete intoxication with the Self. Such a being is one who has merged his identity in the Absolute. For a Sadguru, only God exists and this world does not exist, separate from that Supreme Principle. A Sadguru has risen above the limitation of the ego by the destruction of the false notion of individuality.

Such a being knows from direct experience, that the body is merely a covering, a vehicle by which God comes and goes in this world-appearance. A Sadguru is not attached to his/her body, nor the senses. A spiritually-perfected being such as this is God. God expresses herself through such a being to bring His children back to Him.

30. If you keep sugar apart from us, we cannot have experience of its sweetness. If we eat it, then only we know its taste. A man cannot get Mukti if he simply repeats "Rama, Krishna, or Govinda" for a thousand years. He must repeat it heartily (knowing the secret).

Commentary: Sugar, apart from its sweetness, has no taste. We can only experience sugar and know what it is by tasting, and not by repeating "sugar, sugar" over and over again. Likewise, it is not possible to experience Mukti (Liberation) by simply repeating "Rama, Krishna, or Govinda" for even a thousand years (if this were so, Liberation could be had from simply reading a book, something we already know is not so).

No matter how hard we try, we will not attain Liberation unless we are able to realize the potency of these mantras and the secret to their power. The potency of the Mantra is understood through Shaktipat and the instruction of a Siddha Guru in the use of Mantra. And the secret to the power of Mantra is Devotion to the deity of the mantra and complete identification with the deity of the Mantra when repeating it. These are easily understood through the instruction of a Sadguru.

31. Cow milk can never be bitter. The stone fixed in the earth cannot speak. By visiting places of pilgrimage like Benares and Rameshvaram, a man cannot attain Mukti. What is essential is keeping the mind steady for a moment by introversion. Seeing earthen and stone images is not seeing God. It is mind's hallucination when you regard images as God. Without true Jnana, Mukti cannot be attained. Our taking the human birth is the effect. Giving it back is the cause. We must know the cause and effect. Likewise, we must know the good and the evil; the right and the wrong. Knowing all, peace must be attained.

Commentary: Everything is ordained by God. God's law dictates how things work. The Will of the Supreme Being is evident in the manifestation of this world-appearance. Cow's milk has its own taste that is recognized by the fact that it is not bitter. Stones can't talk. In the same way that God has ordained that cow's milk is not bitter and stones don't talk, God has also laid down the means and approach for attaining Him. God cannot be known by worshipping an object without the knowledge of the Self, the higher power contained in the reflection we call 'object.' Likewise, pilgrimage to holy places is useless without direct knowledge of the inner Self.

The true pilgrimage, the real Dhyan and worship is the act of fixing the mind steadily on the Supreme Being inside yourself. This practice causes the mind to become quiet, and eventually to dissolve. Once this occurs on a constant basis, one merges with his/her natural, free to state of being inside and such a person becomes the place of all pilgrimages, the holiest of places.

Taking a human birth is the effect of our past Karmas. The purpose of a human birth is to retrace our steps back to God. When we do this, we return to the Cause, the source of all that is. The purpose of life is to realize our oneness with That Shiva-Shakti power. Through this understanding you begin to cherish righteousness and Dharmic behavior. This is the way that peace is attained.

32. If a building has no doors, we cannot call it a "house." Without fire, we cannot heat water. Without air, fire cannot burn. Without food and sleep, a man can live for a few days but without air (breathing), a man cannot live even for a few seconds.

Commentary: Just as a building without doors cannot be called a house, just as water cannot be heated without fire, and just as a fire cannot burn without air, a person cannot live without Prana (breath). This Prana is the means by which the Supreme Being comes and goes in the body. It is spiritual energy. Awareness of this Prana Shakti is the basis for the spiritual path.

It cannot be said that you treading a path that will cause you to return to your primordial home, until Prana Shakti is awakened within you by the receipt of Shaktipat. This Shaktipat is given by a Shaktipat Guru. Having received this essential spiritual awakening, a yogi, by the Grace of that living Master, learns the true Pranayam. Only such a person can be said to be truly alive.

33. Destruction of the world means transforming it into Vayu (air with its blue color). Raja Yoga is the place of

indivisible monism. If you enter the ONE, you lose sight of the many.

Commentary: When you dissolve your mind in Pranayam by directing Prana into the Sushumna Nadi and upwards to the Sahasrar, the world dissolves. This is what is meant by transforming the world into Vayu. True Pranayam is Raja Yoga. To have this experience and make it consistent, you have to receive and master instruction in Pranayam so that your mind becomes steadily absorbed in the true heart, the Self. When your mind merges with the Absolute in this way, you lose all distinctions of "mine" and "yours." You see only the One Universal Experient in everything and everyone, everywhere. And then you realize that the Self alone exists.

34. In the infinite, there is no finite. To a Jnani, there is no Ajnani. To an Ajnani, there is no Jnani. If all the children beat a mother, she does not throw them away.

Commentary: In Truth, God alone exists. All objects (people, places and things) in this world are mere reflections of the Supreme Subject, the One, Universal Experient. Because God alone exists, there is no limitation, nothing finite in this Universe. How can that which has no beginning and no end be finite? One who has become absorbed in this Reality is a Jnani. Such a being sees only God in everything and everyone, everywhere. This is what is known as Equality Consciousness.

To one who is ignorant of the Truth (Ajnani), only ignorant people exist. One who is impure sees only impure people everywhere. The Ajnani does not know that God exists inside himself and he does not believe the spiritually-perfected Love beings (Sadgurus) to be real. Still, like a mother who shows compassion for all her children, even those children who abuse her, God accepts and embraces both the Jnani and the Ajnani as the same, and loves them both equally, as does the living Master. This provides the Ajnani with an open door, an open invitation to address his/her ignorance by embracing God.

35. You must not leave the feet of a Guru. Your mind should not flicker like the reflection of the sun in the shaking water.

Commentary: Once you have chosen your spiritual Mentor, the living Guru, keep both your feet in his world. Once you have made the commitment to become Liberated from the bondage of ignorance, do not allow your mind to sway from the path and practices as instructed by the Guru. Vigilance is an absolute necessity on the path to Self-realization.

36. The seawater is boundless. The tank water has a boundary. Our mind must be like the tank water. Mind is the cause of good and evil. A man may be good and bad according to his good or bad thoughts. God does not do good or evil to any man. The reason is, intelligence and knowledge are the divine faculties in man. A man protected by good thoughts, cannot be harmed even by a cannon shot. Without yoga, Liberation from karma is impossible.

Commentary: Don't take refuge in your mind. Take refuge in that One God, that ocean of Divine Consciousness that is beyond the mind. This is the only way to purify your mind. It is the only way to bring the restless mind under your control (like water in a tank) so that you can begin to master all the energies of your life. The mind is the cause of all good and bad actions and, therefore is the cause of all Karmas. These Karmas bind you to the cycle of birth and death.

Within your being there is a Supreme Intelligence that is superior to your individual intelligence. It is superior to your mind because it is the witness to your mind. When your mind comes into contact with that Intelligence, it desires to become pure (Sattva Guna) and then merges into the Absolute. Such a pure mind will protect you from all harm. This is Yoga. Without Yoga, Liberation from the cycle of birth and death is not possible.

37. Without knowing the secret (truth), if we simply decorate the exterior skin, our karma will not leave us. One cannot be a Sanyasi by external signs if he is internally a hypocrite. What you think, you must speak. What you speak, you must show by your acts. Do what you say. Say what you do. Such a man is a Jnani. He is a Paramahansa. He is a Yogi. He is a Sanyasi. One who has conquered desire is a true Sanyasi. Only a desireless man is fit to be a spiritual teacher.

Commentary: One should understand what Sanyas truly means. The world is full of monks who have taken vows and where orange or red robes (not to negate their worth, some who have taken the vows of monkhood are very great beings). This alone does not make them Sanyasins. True Sanyas occurs when one becomes a Liberated yogi. When you attain the state of Shiva Vyapti, the state in which you experience Bliss, Joy, Peace and total Freedom on a constant, uninterrupted basis that is Sanyas.

Only then are you a Sanyasi. That is the secret. Such a being sees only God in everything and everyone, everywhere. Only a being like this can be called a Jnani, a Yogi a Paramahamsa. Whether wearing a loincloth, ochre robes, a business suit, a dress or moving about with no clothes on, a Sanyasi can be recognized by these qualities alone. Such a person is free from attachment to people, places and things. This freedom from attachment and worldliness is the way in which you can recognize a Sanyasi. Only a person like this can be a spiritual leader, a Guru.

38. What is served for others should not be eaten by us. We must place a separate leaf for us and eat our food.

Commentary: Keep good company inside and out. This is the law for yogis. The beliefs, values and concepts perpetuated by those who are ignorant of the Truth should not be embraced by those who seek permanent spiritual transformation. For those on the spiritual path, you should "eat" the "food" that will take you to the opposite shore. You should embrace the values, beliefs and practices (and the lifestyle) that will take you to the inner Self.

39. There is nothing like "this one" has more and another has less. The power of thought, the ears, the nose, the hand, the eye, etc. are the same to all.

Commentary: No one is higher and no one is lower. That Shiva-Shakti power exists equally in everyone, everywhere. Shiva's Chiti or Shakti expresses herself through a body that is the same for all.

40. The nose is not the place where the eye is. Walking should be done by the legs only. Work done by the hands cannot be done by the head.

Commentary: Everything has its time and place. In one stage of life, habits and desires for things from previous stages of life are naturally surrendered. This is the understanding of those who take complete refuge in God. In complete surrender to Shiva-Shakti, your own Divinity, this understanding comes easily and the mind becomes a serene place of peace.

41. The head is the ocean of Ananda (Bliss). In it is situated the Prana Linga, the seat of Liberation. This cannot be learned from books. It is inherent in the brain. The book consists of parts, but Jnana is the indivisible one. A book consists of chapters, but Jnana

is single chaptered. For those who have not realized, a book is necessary. But to a man of realization, there is only one undivided being. When a man takes birth, he is not born with a book in his hand but he is born with the Supreme intelligence of the inner Self. While coming (to this world) and going away (from this world), a man has no book in his hand. Only in the middle period he takes a book.

Commentary: Books are born of the fluctuations in the mind. Some books, like scriptures and sacred texts, can be useful in directing the attention of the unenlightened to God. This is the purpose those books serve, to create understandings that, in turn, cultivate the desire for permanent spiritual transformation. In truth, all that is required for you to become liberated from ignorance of the inner Self is already contained within you.

The seed of Liberation and the destination of all spiritual practice is something you bring with you into this life and take with you when you die. The Prana Linga, the Lingam that is the form of the Shiva-Shakti power, is situated in the Sahasrar, the highest spiritual center. In this Chakra is a vibration that takes the form of a sound known as Bindu Nada. That sound also reverberates inside your brain.

When Shakti merges into this spiritual center and takes up residence there, the uninterrupted state of rapture that is the nature of pure Bliss is attained. Purnaham Vimarsha, the state of Liberation, then dawns. This state cannot be taught in books and is beyond the reach of any language used in an attempt to describe it.

42. When a man is born, he is perfect. When he goes away then also, he is perfect. In the middle, he is subject to Maya. That which pervades in all directions is ONE, indivisible. That which is limited is divisible.

Commentary: Maya is the illusion that a world actually exists. Maya is the plane of limitation that is subject to cause and effect, time and space and the limitations created by the false notion of individuality that give rise to the energy of egoism, attachment, attraction, aversion and the bondage created by the senses. A human being is only subject to these limitations while in the body. Karma is played out only after you have taken a form. Maya is limitation and, therefore, divisible. The Supreme Principle or inner Self, that which creates sustains and withdraws this entire Universe, is the One indivisible principle that pervades everything in all directions.

Chiti or Spanda Shakti is the cause of Shiva's Maya. When you are born, you are perfect. At birth, you enter this field of Maya, ignorant of your Natural, Free state of Being. Due to this ignorance, your thinking and actions become tainted and you become imperfect. When you die, the thinking that produces this ignorance also dies, temporarily. You enter into that which is perfect, temporarily, and then your soul transmigrates to different realms, based on your Karmas, before returning here to take another form.

When, through the Grace of a Sadguru, you develop the constant awareness that you yourself pervade the entire Universe, that you are That Shiva-Shakti power, you become perfect while still in the body. You leave this world Liberated, never again to return to the cycle of birth and death.

43. At the place where there is running water, there can be no mud. The place is quite clean. Ignorance (Ajnana) is mud. The current of water is Bhakti and Jñana.

Commentary: Where there is complete knowledge and direct experience of the Supreme Principle, ignorance cannot exist. The ocean of Bliss that is Divine

Consciousness is like running water that washes away mud.
Mud is ignorance of the Truth (Ajñana). Bhakti, complete
Devotion for God, and Jñana, the knowledge that rises from
within after Shaktipat as one practices the teachings of the
living Master, these two are like the current of water that
washes the mud away.

**44. It is not Bhakti to give a man some money or to give
him a meal as charity. Bhakti is universal love. Seeing
God, in all beings, without the least idea of duality, is
Bhakti.**

Commentary: Seeing and experiencing this world, this
Universe, as nothing other than a Play of Divine
Consciousness where all people, places and things are that
one Shiva-Shakti, seeing the entire Universe in this way is
true Bhakti, true Love. This is a Love without distinctions.

If you give someone a meal or money in an attempt to
dissolve your own guilt or to make yourself feel good about
the fact that you have given, if your ego is engaged in this
way, it cannot be called Love. If, on the other hand, you
give someone a meal or money with the understanding that
it is God giving to God, then there is no duality in it and
only Love is experienced. Ultimately, the greatest thing
anyone can give to another is the example of seeing God in
everything and everyone.

**45. Without the control of breath (Pranayama), a man
cannot be a yogi (a perfect man); nor is he a Sanyasi
(saint). Without a rudder, it is impossible to steer a
boat or ship.**

Commentary: Pranayama, the process of directing the
breath inside the Sushumna, is like the rudder that propels a
boat. Without a rudder, the boat cannot move. Without
Pranayam, as instructed by a Sadguru, one cannot practice
Yoga properly nor become Self-realized. Awareness of the

breath, along with the Mantra it sounds, is essential for guiding Kundalini Shakti to union with Shiva in the Sahasrar. One who has not perfected Pranayam cannot be a yogi and is not a Sanyasi either.

46. To a good man, every man is good; everything is good. A man can be good by his own exertion.

Commentary: For one who has experienced God everywhere, in everything and everyone, all people are good and all belong to God. To have this kind of Equality Consciousness, one must engage in spiritual practice (exertion) with discipline, under the direct leadership of a living Master.

47. We drink the juice of the sugar cane and throw away the refuse. Similarly, this body is a house for the Atman. When it is spoiled, we build a new one.

Commentary: To get sugar, we take what's inside the shell of the sugar cane and we throw the shell, the empty cane stalk, away. We value what's inside the shell and not the shell itself. In the same way, the body is merely a shell to house the Self, the All-Pervasive Consciousness. It is Shiva who comes and goes in this body. Therefore, the body is the temple of God. When the body withers and dies, we take another body and return to this plane of existence. The yogi should inquire into the nature of this process. Who has the power to come and go in this way?

48. It is the nest that perishes, not the bird. The nest is built of earth. The blood vessels and nerves are earth. In the blood vessels are the blood and semen. This body made of flesh is subject to death. If it is not washed for a single day, it stinks. We cannot trust the human body.

Commentary: This earth does not exist separate from the Self. It is really just a plane of existence. Like a bird's

nest, after a while, the body is abandoned by that Supreme
Principle, but that Shiva-Shakti power, the one occupying
it, remains. The body, too, is like the bird's nest. It is
subject to decay and dies, but the Supreme Principle that
occupies the body remains untouched and is imperishable.

Because the human body is a mere illusion, a shell that is
fashioned into form and then destroyed over and over
again, it cannot be trusted. One who is smart will place
his/her trust in that which is Omniscient, Omnipotent and
Omnipresent. God alone exists.

**49. Mind is the creator of ideas. When the gross ideas
are suppressed and the man lives in the subtle, this state
is called "Nirvikalpa Samadhi" or Samadhi without
ideas. Just as we teach a bird how to talk, keeping it in
a cage with its feet bound, we must keep our mind in
our Buddhi. A man must learn for himself.**

Commentary: The mind weaves a countless number of
fantasies and thoughts. By Meditation, you can remove all
thoughts and notions from your mind. This thought-free
state is called Nirvikalpa Samadhi. Just as one trains a bird
to do what one wants and keeps the bird under control in a
cage, one must also tame the restless mind and bring it
under one's control by immersing it in the Self. One
should experience this for oneself.

**50. Holding the nose with the hand, with eyes turned
upwards and holding the breath in tight as if winding a
clock spring with a key are similar to circus feats or a
cinema show. These are not what is called "Samadhi."**

Commentary: A seeker of the Truth should exercise
caution in how he/she goes about spiritual practice. There
are many techniques that promise samadhi. In actuality,
they are not only empty practices but some can be quite
harmful. The state known as samadhi is a state of complete

rapture and uninterrupted Bliss. It is a state in which the yogi's identity with Shiva-Shakti is constant.

It is a state in which there are no thoughts, no cravings, no desires and no expectations of sense pleasures or worldly pleasures. It is a state in which you experience the Bliss of the Absolute in all the objects of this world-appearance. It is Meditation in action, while going about all the mundane activities of your life. This state is attained through the Grace of a living Siddha Guru, and the vigilant spiritual practice of the devotee, after receiving Shaktipat. One should choose such a Guru carefully.

51. The sense of equality is the greatest thing in this world. People go mad after shadows. Very few are mad after the invisible (the subtle). True madness is very rare, it being found only in one among a lakh or two. Other people run mad after sixteen things in a ghatika (twenty-four minutes). "I want this," "I want that," "This is different," "That is different." Such is their mad talk. Entertaining various motives is madness. Fickleness of mind is madness. Greatness is madness. Practicing and seeing the reality is the opposite kind of madness. Liberation from birth and death is Divine madness. Those who have not realized the truth are mad after the gross. Everyone has one sort of madness or another. Thousands of people possess houses, diamond-jewels, gold and property. They did not bring these with them at birth nor will they take these with them at death.

Commentary: The sense of equality is seeing God in everything and everyone, everywhere. It is the understanding and experience that all objects (people, places and things) are equal because all are the ONE indivisible Shiva. This sense of equality is the greatest thing in the world to have. People chase after the pleasure and pain of worldliness. This is madness. Entertaining an endless stream of desires, notions and fancies, these people cannot keep their minds quiet. People drive themselves crazy chasing after the illusion of this world-appearance and the objects in it.

Now there is another kind of madness. It is the madness that liberates you from the bondage of worldliness. It is mad love for God. This is Bhakti. Armed with this Bhakti, you are able to free yourself from the cycle of birth and death. With Bhakti you stop chasing after happiness, love, peace, joy and freedom where they are not and you find these right where they are -- inside yourself.

Everything that belongs to you already exists inside you. Possessions and people, places and things do not belong to you. You did not bring these with you at birth and you cannot take these with you when you die. You can be mad for the Truth or you can be mad after illusion. Being mad for the Truth leads to Equality Consciousness. To chase after that which you did not bring with you and cannot take with you is pure delusion.

52. It is not the body that exists nor disappears. He is the ONE who is the supreme doer. It is the breath that man brings here at birth and it is the breath that man takes with him when he leaves this world. Property and fame are here only. There, everything is one. Duality exists here only. On the other side, there is no duality. A perfect man (Avadhoota) is the greatest of men. Yogis and Sanyasis want some Siddhi, i.e., power acquired through yoga or tapas. An Avadhoota does not want anything.

Commentary: There is only one Universal Experient. It is this same ONE God who comes and goes in the body and on the breath of every living creature. He alone is the one who experiences. This world-appearance is His play. There is no duality in this Supreme Doer. Property and

fame do not exist in this Supreme Being who is the body of
Supreme Consciousness on which the play of worldliness is
superimposed.

Duality and distinctions are manifestations of the limitation
of the Ego. They are imaginary and, in fact, do not exist.
Supernatural powers, the money, fame and power to
dominate others, these are desires of one who is still tainted
with the impurity of individuality. A perfected being has
merged with the Truth and wants nothing else.

**53. When SAT unites with CHIT, Ananda (bliss) is the
result. This Ananda is Paramananda, Sri
Satchitananda. Paramananda is experienced in the
head. In the head is in the Brahma-nadi.
Brahmananda is Paramananda. Jiva enjoys this bliss
when he is one with Paramatman. This bliss is also
called Shivananda. Paramananda is experienced in the
head. This state is eternal joy. This state is Jivanmukti.**

Commentary: Sat-Chit-Ananda means Being-Awareness
and Bliss. When your witnessing awareness unites with
Chiti, the independent Shakti of Shiva, Bliss is the result.
This Bliss is the ever-present Joy of the Self. When you
allow your mind to turn in on itself in Meditation and there
are no thoughts, this is the experience of your own sweet
Bliss. When you continually direct that awareness to the
Sahasrar, to Shiva Dvadashanta, the spiritual center that is
reflected in the head, you become one with this Bliss.

This is the Bliss of Shiva known as Shivananda. This is the
Joy of the Absolute known as Paramananda. It is
experienced in the Brahma-nadi, the heart center that is
reflected in the head. A Jivanmukta, one who is Liberated,
experiences this state of Jivanmukti all the time. It can be
reached by the instruction of a Siddha.

54. He is a Jnani who has given up worldly pleasures and, by practicing yoga, seen God. Ananda (bliss) is not in what you hear. Bliss is a matter of experience. Such a man is called a Mahatma. Those who have seen earthen and stone images do not become Mahatmas. He is a Mahatma who knows himself.

Commentary: A Jnani is a knower of the Self. One can only know the Self, one can only know God, by giving up all *expectations* of sense pleasures and worldly pleasures and by ending the mad search for these. Then, with steady spiritual practice, one sees God. The Bliss of Shiva cannot be experienced by listening to what others say they have experienced. It can only be experienced for oneself by going inside. It cannot be had from the worship of statues either. To know God, you have to experience *That* inside your own being. The one who does so continually is a Mahatma, a King of kings.

55. An Avadhoota has conquered death and birth. He has no consciousness of the body. An Avadhoota has gone beyond all Gunas (qualities). He is the knower of the "Omniscient Light." He has no consciousness of the "i." Such is a Raja Yogi, not a Hatha Yogi. When he comes to a village, he feels glad, whomsoever he may see. He has no consciousness of duality though he moves here and there. He has no hunger. He eats plentifully if he gets plenty of eatables. If he does not get, he will not ask anybody.

Those who give to him poison and those who give to him milk are the same to him. Those who beat him and those who love him are the same to him. To an Avadhoota, the universe is the father, the mother, and the relation. He becomes the universe and the universe becomes he. The universe is merged in him. Note: At times, in his spontaneous talks, Bhagawan Nityananda would describe some of the qualities of a spiritually-perfected Love being so that people could understand how to recognize a such a Self-realized being. This is one of those moments.

Commentary: An Avadhoota is a Self-realized being, a perfected master of yoga. When we say Yoga, we are not talking about Hatha Yoga (the yoga of postures and stretching). Yoga is only that practice that causes you to be Liberated, Self-realized. Such a person is not attached to the body. And, although a Self-realized being may appear to be ordinary, he/she is only the Consciousness of Shiva and recognizes his body as the expression of that Shiva-Shakti power, not mere flesh.

An Avadhoota is one who is no longer bound by the three Gunas (Sattva, Rajas, Tamas), having risen above virtue and vice, pleasure and pain. The activity of the Gunas does not affect such a being because she has given up the craving for sense pleasures. Such a person accepts what comes to him unsought. His equilibrium is not affected by changes in his circumstances from good to bad or bad to good. An Avadhoota considers all people to be God, whether they are friend or foe. Such a being does not differentiate between those who beat her and those who love her.

To such a Siddha, only God exists everywhere and God is the father, mother and all the relations. To an Avadhoota, the relationship between husband and wife does not exist. It is a relationship between Shiva and Shiva. To a Siddha, the relationship between father and son does not exist. It is a relationship between God and God.

An Avadhoota is a Liberated being who has realized that the entire universe is contained inside himself and is reflected on his own inner screen. This state is the result of Raja Yoga practiced under the direct leadership of a living Master, and is not attainable by Hatha Yoga alone. Such a being is merged in God, regardless of his outward appearance and manner.

56. In Pranayama, Pooraka is drawing up the breath. Kumbhaka is retaining the breath. Rechaka is exhaling the breath. These three kinds of breath are from within. Nothing is taken from outside. While thus the practice is going on, the Prana will move only in one nerve. We then feel the internal joy. Who can describe this Brahmananda? The outside world will then be forgotten. We will then be in the world beyond.

Commentary: Pranayama is a specific meditation technique that involves instruction in how to direct the breath into the central nerve, also known as the subtle body or Sushumna Nadi. This central channel is one of three, primary channels in the body. Pranayama is a technique that involves Pooraka, the inward/downward breath and, Rechaka, the upward/outward breath (also called Prana), and the retention of breath while focusing on the pause or space between the breaths.

When instructed properly, this movement of breath is directed inside the Sushumna and, while continuing to move, remains in the Sushumna Nadi. While the breath moves in the central nerve, no breath is taken from outside. In this way, Kundalini Shakti moves upward through all the Chakras in the subtle body and enters the heart space (Chidakasha) reflected in the head. When this occurs, the yogi experiences a profound sense of peace and joy and remains focused inside himself, with no awareness of the outside world as such. This is the world beyond, the world of the Supreme Principle.

57. "This world" means Jivatman. The "next world" means the union of Jivatman and Paramatman.

Commentary: The Jiva or Jivatman is the individual bound soul who creates endless karmas out of ignorance of the Truth. This world-appearance is the realm or plane of the Jiva. It exists for the sport of Shiva that is a Play of Divine Consciousness in which these karmas are being worked out as part of the free evolution of beings. The "next world" is the world in which the Jiva becomes Shiva by merging her individual, limited identity with the Divine Consciousness of Shiva-Shakti, with the Absolute that is Paramatman or Paramashiva. This union is the "next world."

58. Just as small rivers enter the sea, our attention must be fixed on the internal breath.

Commentary: Every river eventually merges with the ocean. In the same way, every person will, eventually have to retrace his/her steps back to God. The internal breath is the means. The internal breath is the movement of Prana inside the Sushumna Nadi. Through internal breathing or "Sushumna breathing," Kundalini Shakti is channeled into the Sahasrar. When our attention is focused on internal breathing, the individual identity is united with God and, just as the small rivers enter the sea, our limited identity is merged in the ocean of Divine Consciousness.

59. What is visible is transient. It is perishable. When the mind is merged in "Bindu" and "Nada," Nirvikalpa Samadhi is attained. Our attention is then entirely towards Ananda (eternal joy). Fixing the attention between the eyebrows, the Prana should enter the holy Brahmarandhra. Here the light of lights becomes visible to the divine eye. This is Mukti. This is eternally supreme joy. This is the place where the Manas ought to dwell. This is the eternal being whence the Vedas have sprung. This is seeing Paramatman in all. This is the real place of Jivatman.

Commentary: This world-appearance is transient and temporary. It is perishable because it is an illusion of Maya. When the mind is merged in Bindu-Nada, the firm point of sound that is the Vibration of Divine Consciousness in the Crown Chakra, all thoughts cease, the notion of a world is erased and Nirvikalpa Samadhi is the result. Our attention is then turned entirely within and we experience our own Bliss, our own eternal Joy.

By fixing one's attention on the command center of the third eye, known as Ajna Chakra, with the proper instruction from a Sadguru, one can direct the exhalation of the breath (Prana) upward into the Crown Chakra in the head. Here there is the light of a thousand suns that is visible inside one's own being. This is Liberation. This is where endless Supreme Joy can be tasted. A yogi should keep his mind one-pointed on this inner Light and sound.

It is from this perfect state that the Vedas and all sacred texts have been realized. This is the state where one sees God in everything and everyone, everywhere. This is where the Jiva should travel and roam.

60. The real place of Jiva is formless, indivisible. God pervades all things movable and immovable. He is the ONE without a second. God is the origin of Vedas. He is the Lord of the body. He is the Lord of Jivanmukti. Man, to be man, must meditate upon God.

Commentary: In truth, the Jiva does not exist. Jiva is an illusion since it is Shiva, the formless God himself, who takes the form of the Jiva. Nothing exists anywhere that is not Shiva. God pervades all things sentient and insentient. Shiva is the ONE without a second. He is the origin of the Vedas and all other scriptures and sacred texts. All forms belong to Him, including the body that is on loan from that Supreme Being. Shiva is the Lord of Liberation, the place of deliverance. Human Beings, to be human, must meditate on the ONE God, Shiva.

61. He who meditates on the Reality is a sanyasi. He is a yogi. The distinction of "Pariah" exists in the external. Internally, all is one without distinction. What is "Pariah" is not after death. A "Pariah" is he who has envy and pride, who holds vain discussion about religion, who talks ill of others behind their backs. Sewing is not stitching thread and cloth, but stitching Manas and Buddhi, i.e., merging Manas in Buddhi. Now the distinction of male and female: A true female is one who is merged in the external. A true male is one who is merged in the internal. One whose Buddhi is firm is male. One whose Buddhi is fickle is a female. This distinction of male and female is external only. Internally such a distinction does not exist at all. When the Manas and Buddhi are merged in the Atman, one who is physically a woman becomes spiritually a "man."

Commentary: A Sanyasi is not defined by orange robes and lectures on God. To be a Sanyasin, you have to be a Yogi. A Yogi is one who meditates on the Reality, on God. Many believe that certain people are of an inferior caste or class or have inferior genes. This is a political distinction that has nothing to do with the Truth. Those who are bound to the false notion of being just a person, out of which manifests the imaginary ego idea, are contracted. They are the ones who suffer.

To remove this and all other useless conditions, one must merge Manas (the mind) in the Supreme Consciousness (Buddhi) of God. This is what should be sewn, and not crops of worldliness. When the Manas and Buddhi are merged in the Atman, one who is attached to the world of forms becomes spiritually "virile."

62. The body is the cave. In this cave dwells the Atman. Atman, dwelling in the body, must attain "Moksha" (liberation). The outward bodily parts are various. In the invisible (subtle) all is one, indivisible. OM is Pranava. Pranava pervades the form (body). OM is bodylessness and formlessness.

Commentary: The physical body is a mere shell. Inside this shell is the indweller, the Witness known as Atman or the Self. Shiva becomes the Jiva in order to realize Shiva. This is the Play of Divine Consciousness here – that God plays at becoming the individual bound soul and then plays at developing amnesia, looking for God, until He realizes Himself by attaining Liberation. The body has many manifestations but the Self has only one indivisible quality. This quality is made up of Light and Sound and is embodied in the sacred Mantra, Om. Om is known as the Pranava Mantra. It is the very nature of Shiva. It is formless without any body.

63. Bhakti in the beginning, is selfish. Afterwards, there is no selfishness in it. When a man attains perfection, the whole universe becomes to him, his guru.

Commentary: Love/Devotion (Bhakti) in the beginning, is selfish. Before we have the experience of the inner Self on a consistent basis, we give love with selfish aims and are engaged in the process of "buying and selling" where we barter attachment, attraction, words, affections and sensations for individual limiting desires and cravings, seeing each other as objects of the senses, as objects of desire and craving.

Through the leadership of the living Master, and in keeping the company of such a Siddha, our Love/Devotion becomes pure and we come to understand that Bhakti is Love for the Self and Compassion for ourselves and others. We come to understand that Love has no distinctions, that it is unconditional. When a person attains this knowledge, he/she becomes perfect and the entire universe becomes his Teacher.

64. What is called "Hatha Yoga" is selfishness. In Hatha yoga, a man seeks his own goodness. He seeks fame. He can stop the sunrise of tomorrow. He can create a mountain of gold. To say "I am Brahma" is not just. "Thou (O God!) art ALL; ALL art thou," we must say. A yogi is one who thinks the whole universe to be a yogi. He should regard all as himself.

Commentary: Yoga is not a spa. In Hatha Yoga, one studies techniques for strengthening the body for a good meditation posture, stress relief and wellness. This is very useful. Some branches of Hatha Yoga also teach certain Siddhis or psychic/supernatural powers that can be used in conjunction with certain postures and mantras. Some use these powers to create wealth and fame for themselves. Other branches of Hatha Yoga place the entire focus on physical health/well-being and sexual vitality, missing the point of spiritual transformation altogether. The problem with these approaches is that they feed the ego idea of the aspirant and cultivate the senses, rather than helping the aspirant to rise above the senses and the false notion of individuality.

To say "I am greater, I am better than others because I have this strong body and these great powers" is unjust and deluded. A yogi should follow a path that will bring her to the realization and experience that she is not the body or the senses nor sense pleasures, and that God alone exists. The yogi's practice should be one that leads to the realization that this world does not exist but is really a Play of Divine Consciousness that unfolds on his/her inner screen. That is the only true Yoga.

65. If a man goes to a forest and there lives in a cave, it is just like a beast in a cave. Even the milestones are better than such a man because by the milestones, we can count the distance in miles. Such people are of no use whatsoever. A thoughtful man should gradually go on renouncing the world. When a man eats food, it is for his own benefit. Others are not benefited by it. It is not enough if we leave darkness. We must always live in the light. If we have a light on a dark path, we have no fear. There is fear in walking in darkness.

Commentary: There are many who believe and teach that the world must be renounced in order to realize God. These people give away all their belongings, dress in a worn out sac, and flee to forests and caves. What they don't realize is that they take all their karmas, all their limiting/binding notions, all their useless attitudes, all their useless beliefs and psychological problems and all their limiting cravings and desires with them.

These limitations cannot be removed by a change of clothes or location, nor by a change in outer behavior. Such a person is just like a beast in a cave who is a victim of the fickleness and fluctuations of nature, having no control over itself. A person who makes gradual, recognizable progress on the spiritual path that is sustainable, that is permanent, is much better than a one who specializes in this kind of outward renunciation.

When you drive a road that has mile-makers (milestones), at least you know you are making progress because, with the mile-markers, you are able to measure the distance you are travelling to know how far you have travelled, and when you have arrived at your destination. Following the instruction of a Sadguru is just like this. You are able to make lasting progress that is measurable. Bad habits, useless attachments and poor thinking can be given up gradually as one becomes stronger in Sadhana.

Don't try to change the world. What you practice and do is like the food you eat. That food only benefits you, not others. So, if you want to see change in the world, become the change you wish to see in the world by changing yourself and transforming your own vision.

Changing your environment because it appears to be 'negative' is not enough. You create the world you live in. Merge your identity and awareness in the Self. Then, even if you live in the most difficult of circumstances, you will have no fear and no worries. Fear is a state of mind created by the notion of separation from God and the notion that you are imperfect and different/separate from others. When you change by the inner experience of the Self, your outer circumstances and environment will naturally change without struggle.

66. If you perform tapas for thousands of years with the desire for results, it is of no avail. But if you perform tapas for one ghatika (twenty-four minutes) without any desire for "fruits," you will see ALL in God and God in ALL.

Commentary: Tapas is intense penance. And, in Yoga, penance is ardent and vigilant spiritual practice and worship done regularly. Once a man asked Gurudev, "When will I attain Siddhahood and what practice can I do to acquire it quickly," to which Gurudev replied, "There is no such thing as Siddhahood."

Intention is everything. Motive is everything. Gurudev used to say, "Spirituality is not a field to grow crops in." On the spiritual path, the best intention is the simple longing for the Supreme Principle, the Self. If you do your practices with a burning Love and Devotion for your own Self and the living Master, this is enough to secure the goal.

In fact, after understanding that the goal of Yoga is Liberation or Self-realization, it is best to forget about Liberation and simply focus on the joy of daily practice. God responds to pure Love, not the tainted qualities of limiting desire that are the trademark of the false notion of individuality. Armed with this Love without distinctions, God comes looking for you and you see ALL in God and God in ALL.

67. Hatha yoga is duality. The most excellent is Raja Yoga. No man should think he is the doer. Everything is ordained by the great Self. Salt is obtained from sea water. When it is mixed with water, it becomes one with it. Similarly, Maya springs from Paramatman and finally merges in him.

Commentary: Due to its focus on the body, Hatha Yoga can promote the notion that you are the doer, that you are your body and its attributes. This becomes an obstacle on the path to Liberation. The most excellent is Raja Yoga that is the path or approach that embodies Shaktipat, the spiritual leadership of the living Siddha Guru, and spiritual practices focused on merging one's individual identity in God. In such an approach, the focus is on realizing that you are not the body or the senses and that God alone acts through you.

Through the focus of rooting out the Gunas and the Malas, and the practices taught to attain that goal, one comes to acknowledge that the body is on loan from God and that it is the Shiva-Shakti principle or God-principle that ordains and does everything. Just as salt comes from the sea and dissolves in seawater, this illusion of Maya that we call world is a manifestation of the Absolute and finally merges back into the Absolute.

68. Vedanta means Prana (breath). To be entirely merged in Prana, is Vedanta. Vedanta is one,

indivisible. It is unbreakable. What is called Veda recitation is not from the tongue. Veda recitation should be from the throat. Those who know this secret are Brahmins. Veda is the one letter OM. It is the fire of inspiration. Vedanta is formless and changeless; indivisible. Light is caused by Veda. What is called Dharana in yoga is the real recitation of Veda.

Commentary: True Vedanta is not the recitation of the Vedas, but the firm realization and awareness of That which the Vedas point to. Practice of Vedanta is attained through the awareness of the space between the breaths. It is the awareness of ajapa japa, the Hamsa mantra that sounds on its own with each inhalation and exhalation. To merge with that Consciousness experienced between So' and Ham is true Vedanta and nothing else. Dharana is the act of remembering God at all times. That is true yoga and the real recitation of the Vedas.

69. Just as a tire of a bicycle is filled with air by a pump, the Nadis (nerves) should be filled with "Vedanta discrimination." Prana should be raised to Brahmarandhra, the highest point in the brain. The nerves should be purified and such purification should be done step by step. Buddhi and Manas should become one with Paramatman. You should play with him. You should sit in the upper story and look around downwards. Buddhi's place is above. Buddhi must become one with Jnana.

You should always drink the water of eternal joy. You must be one with the nectar of Ananda. You must know those who are always merged in this eternal joy. You should know the very secret of this Ananda. Truly, the Kundalini must be awakened. Just as we rock a child in a cradle, we should fix our attention in the head and examine what takes place there. Paramananda (supreme bliss), Sadananda (eternal bliss) are there in

the head. Shiva Linga is also in the head which should be one.

Commentary: A bicycle needs firm tires to move and those tires are filled with air. In the same way, the true understanding of Vedanta is experienced when the yogi directs Prana (the breath) into the Sushumna and raises the breath to the Crown Chakra at the top of the head. Then the outlook of the sages that is expressed in the Vedas can be experienced for oneself. Pranayama purifies all the nerves of the body step-by-step.

In order to experience the Absolute, the individual intellect (Buddhi) and the Manas or mind (along with the ego) must be merged in Shiva Consciousness through Meditation. You should play with the Lord in this way by identifying with Him. Have the outlook of Shiva by experiencing this world from the upper story, the highest point of existence. Buddhi's place is being absorbed in Shiva-Shakti, in the Divine Will. In this way, Buddhi becomes the storehouse of true knowledge. Drinking the nectar of Self-awareness in this way is eternal joy. Become one with this nectar, with this eternal Bliss.

Keep the company of those who have attained Liberation. The secret to the constant rapture of this Bliss is Shaktipat, the awakening of Kundalini Shakti that is imparted by a Shaktipat Guru. This is the secret to attaining uninterrupted Ananda. After receiving Shaktipat from such a Siddha, practice, practice, practice. Just as we rock a child steadily and gently in its cradle so that it can experience peace, we must meditate on the Crown Chakra in the head and examine what takes place there (Bindu-Nada). The Bliss of the Self, the Bliss of Shiva Consciousness is experienced in the head, in that spiritual center. Shiva dwells there in his fullness where Buddhi becomes one with the Shiva-Shakti power.

70. When you rub a match to the side of a box, you obtain fire. You should cook everyday. You should avoid all distinctions. When the recipient is fit, he should be initiated. That person who has the power of discrimination should be initiated.

Commentary: When you rub a match to the side of a box, you obtain fire. Likewise, when you receive Shaktipat initiation from a Shaktipat Guru, the inner fire is ignited and the intellect, ego, mind and the senses are cooked in the knowledge and experience of the Self. Therefore, you should cook everyday. Avoid all distinctions of high and low. This is the way to prepare yourself for the descent of God's Grace. When you are ready, the Master appears and you should receive Shaktipat. You should take it by your stubborn desire to experience God. This is the kind of discrimination that makes you worthy of initiation.

71. If food is given to a man who has no hunger, it will cause indigestion in him. Those whose belly is full have no hunger. Those who are well dressed feel the cold, the greater.

Commentary: For God to be experienced, desire to know God must be present. To become Liberated from the bondage of ignorance, you have to want to know the Truth. Yoga cannot be taught to those who have no longing for it, just as feeding someone who is not hungry is a waste. Also, to receive what a Sadguru has to offer, you have to empty yourself so that the Master can fill you with God's Grace. People who only want sense pleasures cannot be taught Yoga. Just as putting on the wrong clothing in winter makes you feel the cold even more, engaging in sense pleasures only increases the desire for them. For this reason, a seeker has to be willing to set aside worldliness and sense objects in favor of learning the path to God.

72. One must go to Kashi by train. One must reach the town of "Shivanandapuri." One must go to the country of "peace." One must stop his journey at "Brahmanandapuri."

Commentary: Just as you have to take a train to get to Kashi, you have to practice the Yoga of Meditation to get to the inner Self. The purpose of Meditation is to reach the other shore of Shivanandapuri, the abode of the Supreme Principle. This is the place of peace. Have no other goal but the journey to Sahasrar (the highest spiritual center), the union of Shiva-Shakti. This journey begins with the receipt of Shaktipat from a living Master and ends in complete absorption in the Self.

73. A man must know himself. He who has conquered the mind is the man. He is the ascetic. He is the yogi. He sees the one Atman in all. Suppose you come into a dark room after wandering in the sun. What do you see? Look at the sun for five minutes and come into a dark room. You see nothing. This is as it ought to be. One must see with the inner (spiritual) eye.

Commentary: On the spiritual path, to know yourself means to know the Self, to know your Natural, Free State of Being that is the inner Witness. The person who conquers his mind by removing all thoughts and notions is a true being. One who accomplishes this is an Ascetic. She is a yogi and sees God in all. Experiencing God inside is like coming into a dark room after staring at the Sun. Your senses are blinded, your mind stops and all your habits are turned away. You are forced to see with the inner eye of true knowledge. This is as it ought to be.

74. A ripe fruit is very sweet to the taste. The same fruit when it is unripe is astringent. Both are produced by the same tree. The difference between the two is caused by time. As soon as a coconut is planted in the

ground, it does not grow into a plant. First, it sprouts, then it becomes a plant and finally it becomes a tree. A tender coconut tree can be easily plucked from the ground. But a fully-grown coconut tree cannot be easily plucked. So also, our mind must be unaffected, whatever people say to us or whatever they say about us. The mind must always be under our control.

This is what a man must accomplish in life. This must be "the one object" in life. This a man must accomplish even if his head is to be struck off. We should give a blow with the mind itself, not with a cane or a hand or something. We should learn to tie a man without a rope. This is what a man should accomplish in life.

Commentary: Progress on the spiritual path takes time and requires tending to, just as one cares for a garden and does not harvest the vegetables or fruits before they are ripe. Make the mind your friend gradually, and with daily spiritual practice. The goal is *Equality Consciousness*. The goal is making your mind so pure that you experience every circumstance as a gift from God, whether the circumstance is favorable or unfavorable.

Make your mind immune to praise and blame. This must be your goal. Just as a clever man can outwit a person twice his size in a fight by being smarter (not necessarily stronger), don't beat your mind up. Don't try to take it by force. Woo the mind by cultivating Shakti through Meditation and the other spiritual practices. Witness your thoughts and allow them to pass like watching clouds pass in the sky, while remaining unmoved, unaffected by its ramblings. Tell your mind, "You are God. I love you because you are Chiti, that one who creates the entire Universe. You are my friend because you are going to reveal God to me." Accomplish this in your life.

75. The 'mind' is the seat of "sin." It is the cause of action, good and bad. Mind is the cause of all these. 'Mind' is, itself, a condition superimposed on to the Self. If there is no mind there is no speech. Without the expression called 'mind,' nothing can come and nothing can go. But for the mind, nothing can be accomplished. Suppose one knows how to speak English but he does not know how to write it. Then we cannot say, he knows English fully. When he knows both, then only he can secure a passing grade in English.

Commentary: The 'mind' is the seat of all restlessness and the notions and ideas it weaves are responsible for the bondage of ignorance that we experience in our lives. The 'mind' is the obstacle to realizing God. However, nothing happens without the help of the mind. You need your mind to realize God also. So, purify the mind through the instruction of a Sadguru. Purification of the 'mind' means the direct experience that 'mind' does not exist separate from the Shiva-Shakti power.

What we call mind is an energy that manifests when an object needs to be recognized in Consciousness. It is actually the Self that does the recognizing. Complete your study and "secure a passing grade" by steady spiritual practice that expands your awareness so that, once again, it becomes one with the witness to your mind and senses, that *Pure Perceiving Awareness*. In this way, you will come to understand that the mind is God and not a mind at all.

76. Even a child of five years old knows that there is God. But the child does not know where God is. The sun sees all. But very few, one in a lakh or two, look at the sun. In this world, three-fourths of the people are fond of sexual pleasures like beasts. Even those who have reached the middle state are less than one fourth of the people. Good deeds are very few in this world. Evil deeds are many.

Commentary: In this Kali Yuga age, God has been abandoned and ignorance is worshipped by the majority of the world population. A young child knows that God exists but does not know where to find God. God exists in everyone and everything, yet very few seek him out. This is the disease of the modern age. Most people behave like beasts, worshipping sexual pleasure and feeding their cravings for sense pleasures and worldly pleasures as if they are starving animals. Those who have reached the middle state where even a little balance and virtue are practiced are very few in number. Virtue has been lost to vice and evil deeds are commonplace. Only the act of taking total refuge in God can reverse this tide.

77. Swami is he who has united the Chit with Sat. Upadhi means the tree of peace. We must take shelter under this "tree of peace."

Commentary: Sat is Being. Chit is pure perceiving awareness. When these two unite permanently, the Bliss of Nirvikalpa Samadhi is experienced. The awareness "Shivo'ham. I am Shiva. All things are in me and I am in all things," becomes the permanent state of the yogi. Only when this occurs can one be called a Swami, regardless of whether or not he wears orange clothes or she has shaved her head. When Sat merges with Chit, the Bliss that is experienced culminates in a state of sublime peace. Seekers of the Truth should take refuge there.

78. Those who are always one with Brahman are the Brahmacharies. Such a man may even belong to a pariah caste. One does not become a Swami by simply holding an ascetic's wand in hand or by holding a copy of the Bhagavad Gita. Nor by putting on red clothes, nor by discussing God with whomsoever he meets.

Commentary: Those Yogis whose minds are immersed in the Self (the Supreme Principle) all the time, and whose experience of the Self is uninterrupted, are the true Brahmacharies, the pure ones. Such a person may even belong to a lower caste or class or be uneducated and an outcast. Such a person may even work a full-time job and be a householder. One does not become a swami simply by taking vows, wearing orange or red clothes and memorizing the Bhagavad Gita or other scriptures. A swami is not one who can give a well-prepared intellectual discourse on God. One who can be called Swami is one who lives in the Purnaham Vimarsha state of the nectar of Self-awareness at all times.

79. If gold is melted in fire, it shines with lustre. So also, one should purify oneself, killing desire and anger internally. By introspection, he should move internally. A man's mind never remains stationary.

Commentary: By its very nature, the mind is restless and wanders in many directions at the same time. This is due to its desire for this and that and the anger it experiences when these desires are not fulfilled. Through Meditation, one should experience the inner Self, God within. Then, in the inner fire of Meditation, the mind melts, becomes pure and shines like gold.

80. However wicked a man may be, within five minutes his wickedness may be changed into goodness. So long as there are clouds, the sun's rays are not visible. As soon as the clouds scatter in all directions, the sun becomes visible. OM "the tower of peace!" OM "the form of peace!" OM! Salutations to OMKAR!

Commentary: However evil a person may be, however bad his/her karmas may be, within a short period his limited, binding tendencies may be purified. With the leadership of the Guru, a person can root out the Gunas and the Malas (the impurities). If a person is willing to set aside his desires and cravings for five minutes and experience the power of the Mantra, God will become visible. The Pranava Mantra *Om* is such a mantra. It is the tower of peace! Om is the form of peace! Salutations to Omkar!

81. There is not a fixed rule about the taking of food. It has not been said that one should not take his meals. Moderation! Moderation is the rule. Half stomach, food; one-fourth water. Do not love sleep too much.

Commentary: On the spiritual path, there is no fixed rule about diet and no one particular diet that a yogi should follow. Eat food that is well-balanced, nutritious and right for your body. Nowhere is it ordained that fasting is better than eating. Take food in moderation. That's the rule. When you eat, don't eat to fill your stomach. When you finish eating your stomach should be half filled with food, one quarter filled with liquid and the other quarter Prana. Always leave room for Prana and don't sleep too much.

82. Fire consumes anything and everything. It does not distinguish between good and bad. Likewise those who are doing "karma" may eat anything. Those who do not know what "karma" is are not aware of what they should do. Such a one suffers from indigestion. One whose digestion is alright may eat anything he likes. It will be digested. Sleep is necessary. Moderate sleep. Do not eat when the stomach is full. Be always regular in your meals.

Commentary: Inside every living being is a Yagna or sacred fire. This fire is Shakti and is also responsible for your digestion. It does not distinguish between which food should be digested and which shouldn't. If you are engaged in selfless service (karma yoga) and you offer your food to God before eating it, you may eat anything, as long as you do so with the understanding that it is God feeding God.

Those who do not offer food in this way, do not practice proper diet and suffer indigestion. Sleep is necessary but don't sleep too much as this will make you dull. Take sleep in moderation. If you're full, don't eat more food, but be regular in your meals and take them at approximately the same time each day.

83. Gold chains around the neck, gold jewels on the ears, gold rings on fingers. These are the causes of the fear of being robbed when they are on the body. Money is a cause of fear.

Commentary: Those who chase after possessions, seeking to increase their lot day-by-day; those who believe they are their possessions and are attached to objects (people places and things); such people live in constant fear of losing what they wrongly believe they possess. Attachment to objects is a taint that leads to fear. When you live with the understanding that all objects belong to God and are on "loan" from God, you stop living in fear.

84. What is called "fear" is the creation of the mind. For the internal sight, there is no fear. Fear exists for the man who has no internal eye (Jnana). It is impossible for a blind man to describe what the cart is like. Similarly to a man who has no Guru, there is no place in the world.

Commentary: The notion of fear is a thought-construct, a vikalpa, created by the presence of the Malas in your Consciousness. The Self, Shiva-Shakti, that God inside you, fears nothing. In fact, it is only by the light of the Self that there can even be a notion called "fear." For a person afflicted with Anava Mala, believing himself to be imperfect and separate from God, there is no true knowledge. This condition gives rise to fear, automatically.

Just as a blind person cannot describe what a cart looks like because he can't see it, a person without a Guru, without a spiritual leader, cannot realize God and is truly homeless. There is no place that such a person can go where he/she will not experience fear and duality.

85. Food full means Prana full. Food means Prana. If we store our money in a box without much thought about it, it remains in a great store. If we spend from it, it becomes less and less. Money (wealth) is life. The box is intellect (Buddhi). The box requires nothing. Similarly, if a man knows himself, he does not want anything. If by the internal exercise of the Sadhana (practice) that is with us, we lead the Prana to the Brahmarandhra (the top end of the Sushumna canal), and there if Prana and Shiva are united, then we do not require anything. Restraining the Manas from going down and showing it the royal road of the "middle path" is what is called food.

Commentary: A yogi is one who attributes everything to the Shiva-Shakti power, to God. For such a being the experience of Jivanmukti is his food. Humankind mistakenly believes that it is "meat and potatoes" that creates and sustains life. But one who is Liberated knows that life is sustained by the movement of the life force known as Prana Shakti. It is this Prana Shakti, the treasury of Shiva's powers that creates, sustains and withdraws this entire Universe.

Prana Shakti takes the form of your breath. Life comes into being through Prana. It is Prana that keeps the heart pumping. Without Prana, there would be no physical form. Prana, the life force, should be regarded as money. It should not be wasted by exhausting the body in the pursuit of sense pleasures and worldly pleasures. A yogi should live a temperate life of moderation. Buddhi, the intellect, is the "box" that houses the Self in the body. When Prana is caused to rise and remains centered in Buddhi, all one's desires dissolve.

If you know this, you know all there is to know about yourself. Shiva, the Primordial Being, makes his home in the thousand-petal lotus in the Sahasrar, the Chakra above the top of the head. When Prana is made to rise on the royal road or "middle path" known as the Sushumna Nadi, and merges into Sahasrar, into Shiva, all limiting desire is removed. Then, just as you are content after filling your belly with your favorite food and drink, similarly, when limiting desire is destroyed, you become completely content within yourself.

86. The repetition of Rama is true delight. It is the eternal Atma delight, eternal true delight, internal Atma delight, Kundalini grandeur delight. The lord of mind is Rama. Rama means Atman. That which governs the ten Indriyas (five Karmendriyas and five Jnyanendriyas) is Rama. Ravana means all the wicked qualities in us. Sita means Chitta. Lakshmana means attention (thought control). Krishna means introspection. This introspection is the eternal Atma delight.

Commentary: The deities we read about and experience in the epics and scriptures of our tradition are all representations of God and His many aspects. For example, Lord Rama was an incarnation of Vishnu. He is also another expression of the formless Atman, the inner Self. As such, he became a great Saint. Even now, repeating his name brings pure delight in the Self. Rama became one with Shiva, one with Divine Consciousness. Therefore, he is that one who governs the powers or energies behind the senses that are the seat of the senses (the Karmendriyas and jnanendriyas).

The demon Ravana, who was slain by Lord Rama, represents all the wicked qualities and limiting/binding tendencies in each of us. Ravana represents that which each of us needs to rise above. Sita, the wife of Lord Rama who was kidnapped by Ravana, represents Chitta, the mind. The kidnapping of Sita by the demon Ravana is symbolic of how the mind is kidnapped by poor and evil thinking.

Lakshmana symbolizes awareness and the ability to focus the mind to cause it to remember God. He represents that power. And Lord Krishna represents Meditation on God. Each of these saints whose lives are documented in great epics like the Ramayana and Mahabharata, is an aspect of Divine Consciousness. These saints can also be meditated on to experience the Self.

87. All are men. There is no incarnation higher than man. Man is the greatest of animals. But those are the best of men who ponder over the subtle.

Commentary: There is no incarnation greater than that of a human being. Only through a human body can one become Liberated. This makes human beings the greatest of the manes, the greatest of animals. The best of human beings are those whose aim is to realize God.

88. "Ekadashi" means the worship of the "ONE." To such a man, everyday is Ekadashi. Those are called "men" who have such an Ekadashi. A man should think very little about the gross. He should spend much of his time in meditation of the subtle.

Commentary: Ekadashi means first or the number one. But for a yogi it means worship of the One God by remaining absorbed in God within. To one who experiences the constant, uninterrupted rapture of the Self, worship of God happens every moment of every day. A person should spend little time involved in the mundane activities of this world (just enough to earn a decent living) and spend much of her time in Meditation and spiritual practice.

89. A man becomes "desireless" when he sees a dead body burning. This desirelessness is temporary. This is the secret of the body. Desirelessness imparted by a Guru should not be abandoned. From desirelessness a man obtains liberation from bondage. This desirelessness is the best. Guru is secondary. The desire that a man be initiated is of the third class. Getting a Guru is of the second class. By practice; getting experience for oneself is the real desirelessness which is the goal of human life. When one practices and imparts his knowledge to another, it is "Yogananda Desirelessness."

It is the imperishable and the indivisible state. It is the tree of peace. The climbing of the tree of peace which is in the head and being one with that "peace tree" is the real imperishable desirelessness. The cutting of the primary root of passion and anger is the imperishable desirelessness. Being in Samsara, enjoying a little of its pleasures and then renouncing it is the second desirelessness. Desirelessness is liberation from bondage in this very life.

Commentary: When you see a dead body burning (being cremated) or buried, you realize how transient life is and how limited the body is. You are reminded that you too will pass one day. But this realization is temporary because, out of fear of your own death, you begin clinging to life again by pursuing your attachment to desire and craving for people, places and things.

True desirelessness is not the fear of whether or not you will go to heaven when you die. True desirelessness is freedom from the limiting desire for people, places and things. You can only gain this true desirelessness from following the instruction of a true Guru. This desirelessness should never be abandoned. Through spiritual practice, as instructed by the living Master, one is freed from attachment to the body, the ego idea, the senses. In this way, one is freed of desire for anything other than union with God.

This state of desirelessness (the absence of limited desire known as Karma) is the supreme state of Liberation. Liberation from limited desire is the goal of all Sadhana, the goal of retracing one's steps back to God. It is the best state and is the primary goal of all spiritual practice. The physical relationship with the Sadguru is designed to foster this state and, therefore, that relationship is not the final attainment. The final attainment is union with that which is desireless. This is primary.

The experience of eternal peace is had through union of Shakti with Shiva in the Sahasrar. When, through the Grace of a living Master, and daily spiritual practice, the yogi experiences this union, this is the state known as desirelessness. The nectar of peace flows from this state and is like a tree with its roots in God, *imperishable.* To experience this peace tree, one must cut away the root of ignorance that is anger and passion. To experience the samsara that is this world while remaining detached from it, to renounce the ego idea while leading ones' life, is the stage that leads one to the ultimate realization of God and Liberation from bondage.

90. Those who have no "faith" have no desirelessness. Similarly, those who have annihilated the Manas, have no Vasanas. So also, those who have no faith, do not reap any fruit. We buy a diamond for five or six thousand rupees. This is all rental delusion. If we have no mind to buy a diamond, its value is nothing more than that of a lump of earth.

Commentary: Faith in God, faith in the Shiva-Shakti power, this God-principle within, is the most important ingredient for a seeker. Without faith, you can't reach the desireless state. And if you can't reach the desireless state, your karmas will keep you bound to the play of the Gunas and the Malas. Those who have merged the mind in the Self through Meditation have no more latent tendencies or impressions. Their samskaras are burned in the fire of Yoga. This is the "fruit" that must be reaped. But it cannot be harvested without Faith.

In this world-appearance, objects only have the value that we give them by naming them. The fact that a diamond has a value of five or six thousand rupees is really an illusion created by buyers and sellers. These things only have the power and value that we give them. We project that power on to them. The real power and value exists inside our own being in the form of that Supreme Consciousness that is reflected in the diamond and all other objects around us. The purpose of engaging an approach that takes you beyond the mind and beyond the senses is to learn to go to that sacred place inside, all the time, rather than getting caught up in the reflections of that source.

91. Elements are not five but four. Earth, Water, Fire and Air. Space is no element. It is one indivisible. The earth is extended. Air is above water. Space is above air. The sea is the boundary. The earth is the bed. Space is the house. The air is above. The earth is below. The earth is red. The air is white. The earth, made of four elements is not round. It is triangular. Between the lunar nerve and the solar nerve is Sushumna (the star nerve). The earth is like our face.

Commentary: Everything in this world is contained inside the body of Supreme Consciousness and that body of Supreme Consciousness is also contained inside a human being. The elements of Earth, Water and Fire are also contained in our being in the form of Nadis or subtle energy channels. Earth itself appears inside as Shiva-Shakti Trikona and is comprised of the three main channels (nerves) or Nadis known as Ida, Pingala and Sushumna (the central or star nerve).

These three nerves also form the three points of a triangle known as the triadic heart of Shiva (Shiva-Shakti Trikona) or the abode of the true Heart. This earth is like our face. Air or space is contained in the Sahasrar, representing the formless Absolute.

92. Vayu (air) is imperishable. It is one, indivisible. It exists in everything. When the glass chimney of a lamp is shut, there is no light. When it is not shut, the lamp shines brightly. If we take "earth" and imagine it to be sugar, it is sugar only in thought. The nature of earth is not changed. So also, even if a man becomes a yogi or a jnani, the nature of the body does not leave him. Manas becomes one with the Brahman, not the body. Jnanis are subject to the limitations of the body. Since their Manas is annihilated, they are not aware of their bodily condition. A man in sleep, if bitten by a cobra, is not aware of the cobra bite and he is not affected by it.

Similarly, Jnanis are not aware of their body and hence, the bodily conditions do not affect them. When a letter, written in English or in any tongue, is given to a child of five or six months old, the child throws away that letter and it cannot know what is contained in it. A child of six months old does not at all know the difference between a diamond and a lump of earth. Such children have no idea of the body. They are always in the thought of Atma. Children have no idea of duality. When their brains develop, they become aware of differences. When the brain is not developed, Prana in such a child is in the Sushumna.

Commentary: Vayu, the air we breathe, is imperishable. It is that which sustains the Earth and it is one with Brahman. Air exists in everything. Even a flame cannot burn without Vayu. The essence of this earth is Vayu. Just as imagining this world to be sugar does not change the fact that it is the earth, imagining the Earth to be something other than the life-breath of God, does not change its essence as God. The perception that this world is something other than God only exists in our thought, not in reality.

This earth is a limitation in Shiva's Maya, a divine expression of the inner Self. Its nature remains the same. In the same way, a Jnani (knower of the Truth), who is a spiritually-perfected being, is still bound by the body and the laws of nature (the three Gunas). However, such a being's mind has merged in Brahman, in the absolute, Shiva. For this reason, a Self-realized being no longer identifies with the body and his/her exalted state is no longer affected by what the body undergoes.

Just as a person in deep sleep can be bitten by a cobra and not be aware of it, the Jnani's awareness is firmly established in Shiva and that awareness is never changed or diminished by the fluctuations of the body nor the passing of time. Just as a young child cannot read a letter and sees no value in doing so, a child of 5 or 6 months old is not concerned with this mundane world or its activities. At this age, the child's awareness is still rooted in God. Children of 5 or 6 months old have made no distinction between objects and have no awareness of their own bodies. They are completely absorbed in the Self and have no notion of duality.

Until children are engaged in developing their brains with the mundane knowledge of this world-appearance, they have no sense of separateness, no sense of difference and no idea of duality. Before the learning of empirical knowledge, Prana in such a child is still centered in the Sushumna. A Jnani's state is like that of such a child, except that the Jnani has direct, uninterrupted knowledge that he/she is the Supreme Principle.

93. As the child is growing month by month, it gets knowledge of various things. Earlier knowledge is of no use. When a man is in the know of all, he must be like a child. A true Jnani is just like a child of six months. Such a child is not conscious of its own calls of nature. It does not distinguish between the two calls of nature.

Jnanis are similar. They do not like one thing and dislike the other. They have no idea of poison. The administrator of poison should think about it. The eater never cares for it. Likewise, a Jnani does not say, "I want dinner," "I want that." They are always well established in the internal Atman.

Commentary: As a child grows up his/her Witnessing Awareness becomes clouded with empirical knowledge of mundane things. As a child matures into adulthood, she comes to believe that her earlier experience of the Absolute is of no use in the pursuit of worldly pleasures and she begins to abandon her true nature. A smart person, that person who knows all that is worth knowing, is the one who becomes like a child again by embracing the fact that God exists in everything and everyone, everywhere. A true Jnani is like a child of six months who is not conscious of differences and duality. These great beings are like young children.

They see all as the same ONE God and accept whatever comes to them unsought. Being well-established in the Self, Jnanis do not chase after sense pleasures and worldly pleasures. They have no craving for these, having eliminated all craving in the fire of their spiritual practice. Because this is the case, they are able to transmute the "poison" of difficulty, the "poison" of pain and pleasure, into Divine Consciousness itself. They have risen above the influence of the three Gunas and the three Malas no longer exist in their Consciousness. Such is their perfect equipoise. The person seeking to harm or embarrass such a Jnani should think about this first.

94. Our head is like a coconut fruit. In the coconut there is water and kernel. Likewise, there is water and kernel in our head. In the head is Chidakasha. It is the well of Hridayakash. We should draw water from this well and drink it. It is no use digging a well in the earth and drinking water from it.

Commentary: The head is like a coconut fruit. There is a delicious center of nectar located in the crown chakra in the head. Chidakasha, the inner expanse of Divine Consciousness, is accessed through this chakra. Chidakasha is the very heart of the Lord, Shiva. It is the well of one's being. Drinking the "water" from the "well" of ignorance that is the mundane knowledge and experience of this world-appearance is useless. Draw water from the well of God inside yourself and drink that water. It is the only Reality.

95. You have a certain thing in your hand. If you look for it somewhere else, you will not find it. If you sit in an upper story, light a lamp there, and close the doors, those who are below cannot see the light. See the biscope! See the drama! All these are seen in the head. Everything should be seen from the same place. You need not go to several places to see several things. The city of Madras can be seen from there as well as from here. It is better to see it from one place. We must "idealize" it in our brain.

What we call the heart is not below. It is above (the neck). When we are cooking, the flames go upwards. So is the heart upwards. There is light in the heart. There is no darkness in it. If a man's head be struck off, we cannot say who the man is by simply looking at

his trunk. It is the heart that sees through the eye. A man must have the internal eye. What is called the "heart space" is the face that is triangular. We can know a certain man by looking at his face. A man must know his own secret. A man must know himself.

Commentary: Whatever you hold in your hand, will be found in your hand. If you hold an object in your hand, everyone understands the foolishness of then looking for it somewhere else, because it's right there in your hand. The drama of life and the contradiction of our existence is that we go looking outside for what we already have within ourselves. All of the Joy and Happiness we seek through the body and the senses is really already contained in the highest spiritual center that can be accessed through the crown chakra in the head. Yet we close the doors on this "upper story" of our existence and conceal it from even ourselves. This is the paradox of life.

Instead, we should merge with our true nature inside and have the outlook of Shiva. Everything should be seen from the perspective of the Divine. All that there is to be experienced in this world can be experienced by going inside. You need not go elsewhere. Even a city like Madras can be seen with the inner eye of knowledge, without physically traveling there. It is best to see all things from God's perspective inside our own being. This Equality Consciousness must be our only ideal.

What is known as the heart is really the Shiva-Shakti power emanating from the highest spiritual center. There is a great light in this spiritual center. It is the place where the Supreme Principle dwells. There is no darkness there. If you decapitate a person, without the head, that person is unrecognizable. In the same way, without the Supreme Subject, this world does not exist and cannot be known or experienced. It is God who sees through the eyes and experiences through the body and the senses. This is the secret that everyone must realize. In that highest abode of the true Heart, there is a triangle. It is Shiva-Shakti-Nara. This is the face of God, our face. A person must come to know this. A person must know the Self.

96. Mukti is according to the nature of our Bhakti. If you try hard, you get good salary. If you try a little, you get a small salary.

Commentary: Just as earning a good salary requires effort and expertise, Liberation from the bondage of ignorance requires Bhakti (longing/devotion to the living Master and discipline in practice). If your Devotion for the Master and God is weak, if your Devotion and love for the practices instructed by your Guru is weak, you cannot attain Liberation and your experience of God will be unsteady. Complete Bhakti, perfect Surrender, is the key to Liberation.

97. When we are little children, we do not know who is our father and who is our mother. When we grow up, we come to know our parentage. When a rooster eats, it scratches everything towards it with its feet. Similarly, when a person's intellect is developed, he becomes selfish. Everyday people die. Everyday people are born. But rarely do they burn their selfishness. Selfishness completely disappears when the divisible becomes one with the indivisible. From rice various kinds of eatables such as ambada and halva are prepared. These preparations are not called rice.

Commentary: As young children, when we are only five or six months old, we have no sense of difference. We experience all as the same and we have not yet learned the distinction represented by the labels "mother" and "father." At this age we are in awe of everything and everyone. It is a state of pure wonder that is our Natural, Free state of Being. Then, as we grow older, we become like the rooster that grabs for everything, scratching after objects as if mad. As we develop in the ways of the world, we become selfish. This is due to the limitation of an intellect that believes it must concern itself with comfort and security in order to possess objects.

People are born and die everyday. By observing this, we know that what can be possessed in this world cannot be taken with us. Nor are we born bringing objects into this world with us. Yet we remain obstinate, refusing to surrender our selfishness. This selfishness disappears when we merge our individual consciousness into Divine Consciousness. When the intellect is purified in this way, we realize that God alone is. Just as rice that is fashioned into halva and ambada or other dishes remains, essentially, rice, we have to recognize that, although we call a person by a name and we differentiate a building from its owner, all these are still That ONE, indivisible Lord.

98. A vessel without water is of no use. Bhakti is water. Intelligence (Buddhi) is the vessel. He who has no subtle Bhakti is no man. It is not the work of Shakti when a person dances an oracular dance. This dance is a trick. Trickery's course is downwards. Shakti follows a middle course. Trickery belongs to the body. Shakti is Atmaic. Trickery is powerless before the fire of Shakti.

Commentary: To be a water pot, the vessel has to be useful in collecting and holding water. In the same way, the individual intelligence or Buddhi is of no use unless it is absorbed in Love and Devotion for God (Bhakti), since a person only acquires real intelligence by merging her Buddhi into the Supreme. Attachment to sense pleasures and pain is not the work of Shakti. This attachment is due to the free will of the individual.

It is illusion, a trick born of wrong understanding. This illusion, known as Maya, has one purpose; to keep a person bound to ignorance. This is known as the downward path. Shakti follows the middle course, known as the central nerve or Sushumna. Trickery belongs to the body. Shakti is the power of the Absolute. It is Divine Consciousness. The illusion of this world-appearance is powerless when deposited in the fire of Shakti, inside. The purpose of Meditation and all other spiritual practice is to burn this illusion in the fire of Kundalini Shakti.

99. Almost all fruits have their seed inside. But cashew apple has its seed outside. Our mind, like the seed of cashew apple, must be outside Samsara. One must not reserve sugar for himself and distribute sand to others. One following the royal road should not lead others to the path covered with forests. Upon realizing the Self, it is one's bound duty to lead others by the royal road. This must be done at once. We are not sure about the future.

Commentary: The seed of most fruits is contained inside the fruit itself. But cashew apple has its seed outside. Like the seed of the cashew apple, we must bring our minds to rest outside the ocean of worldliness (samsara). For the yogi, it is important to learn how to be in this world without being of this world. This is the purpose of taking a Sadguru and performing spiritual practice.

Once Liberated, a yogi must not keep her knowledge secret from others. Once perfected in Yoga and established in the state of Purnaham Vimarsha, one must teach others and should not lead others astray. It is the duty of the enlightened to lead others to God. This duty must be embraced and carried out at once since the future is uncertain at best.

100. When a train leaves a station, the next station is alerted that a train is approaching, by the sound of bells

ringing. What is called Bindu-Nada is the bell. Just as we hear a sound when we throw a stone into a well, we hear Bindu-Nada inside the head.

Commentary: The Primordial Being that is the Shiva-Shakti power makes a sound. Just as you know a train is approaching by its sound and the alert you get from bells ringing in the station, as you direct Prana to rise inside the Sushumna Nadi, you are alerted to the approach to Sahasrar by Bindu-Nada, a multiple vibration that can be heard inside the head. Just as you know that a stone has fallen into a well by the sound it makes, you know that your awareness is becoming absorbed in the Self when you hear this Bindu-Nada vibrating inside the head. This sound emanates from Shiva's Light and, therefore, can be called Bindu-Nada or point of sound emanating from Light. It is the signal that Prana Shakti is entering the Sahasrar.

101. When a boy has passed the first standard and he goes to the second standard, books of the first standard are no longer required by him. When a man is in sound sleep, he sees neither the stars nor the sun nor the moon. He is aware of nothing. Then the mind is nill. Sleep is a subtle condition. It is not gross. In sound sleep we are not conscious of the body. Then we are conscious of Atma alone. We will have sleep when Prana is in a fixed plane in the body. When the ego is completely destroyed, everything seems to be like "reflection." The mind's delusion is not permanent. It is not Shiva.

Commentary: When a student graduates from a class and moves on to another, he is no longer concerned with the books he used in the class he just graduated from. In the same way, when you pass into *sound* sleep, you no longer experience the objects from your waking state and you are no longer concerned with them. You are not aware of anything in deep sleep because the mind has stopped completely and merged into a void.

For this reason, deep sleep is a subtle condition. It is a different plane than the waking state and is very close to God. In deep sleep you lose all body consciousness and enter into Divine Consciousness. It is the Self in which you are floating in deep sleep. But you need an awakened awareness to fully understand and experience this for what it is, rather than projecting false notions on to it. Otherwise, you miss making use of that experience.

The ultimate sleep occurs when Prana Shakti has pierced all the other three states of being (waking state, dream state, deep sleep) and become centered in the Sahasrar. When this occurs, the ego is completely destroyed and all objects are recognized as being mere reflections of God, Shiva or the Self. The delusion of the mind is not permanent. Only That which always has been, always is and always will be, only That which is both the cause and the effect, only *That* is permanent.

102. When a man has become a graduate in law, he receives a university gown. This gown covers the body from head to foot. It has four hands (two hands and two legs). When SAT and CHIT become united, we have Ananda, Brahmananda, Paramananda, Sri Satchidananda, Sri Yogananda. When we discard worldly pleasures, we enjoy divine pleasures. When we realize the truth about Jiva, we enjoy Ananda.

Commentary: When a person graduates from a university, he/she is covered from head to foot in a cap and gown. This covering is quite regal but also illusory, since it has nothing to do with what the graduate will retain and use. In the same way, the body, no matter how fit and how perfect looking, is a facade, an illusion that has little to do with the Reality.

When Sat (being) and Chit (awareness) become united, you experience the Bliss of the Absolute and the Omniscience, Omnipresence and Omnipotence of the Shiva-Shakti power dawn on you. When you turn away from (by way of breaking your attachment to) worldly pleasures, you enjoy these Divine pleasures. When you realize the Truth about the limitation of the body and the senses, you enjoy Supreme Bliss.

103. Those who have no guru, have not realized the truth. In this world there is no effect without cause. When the darkness in this world has appeared as light, that is called Jnana. Darkness is ignorance. Light is knowledge. Do not be a hypocrite and earn fame.

Commentary: It is not possible to realize your true nature, in order to resolve the identity crisis, without first Surrendering to and following the instruction of a Sadguru. *Only the person who obeys can command.* In this world there is no effect without cause. What is learned well is first taught by a Master. The Guru is such a person. Only a Liberated Sage, a perfected Master of permanent spiritual transformation and ultimate Liberation can awaken Kundalini Shakti in you and guide you from the darkness of your own ignorance into the Light of Divine Consciousness known as *Jnana.*

Ignorance of the Self and *attachment* to sense pleasures and worldly pleasures (not contact with but attachment to) is what we call darkness. The experience of God within and the act of *merging* your individual identity in the Self is what we call Light or Jnana. Once you are led to *That* by your Guru, in Sadhana, and experience your full worth inside, do not be a hypocrite by trying to earn fame. Remain humble and share your experience with others.

104. Say what you do and do what you say.

Commentary: For a yogi seeking Liberation, it is extremely important to align one's actions with the Supreme Intelligence. As you progress on the spiritual path, become aware of the vibration you are creating with your speech and make the effort to align your speech and actions with the Divine Will of God. This is very necessary in the quest for Truth and Wisdom.

105. Before you die, leave the forest path and follow the royal road. When you are on your deathbed, you may suffer the agonies of hell, your Prana being obstructed by the three humors (Vatha, Pitha, and Kapha).

Commentary: You can only become Liberated from ignorance, moment-to-moment, you can only realize God completely *while alive in the body*. Many people believe that they should eat, drink and party for as long as they are physically able, putting off the pursuit of permanent spiritual transformation until old age. Many do not even consider God until they are on their deathbed. At this point, it is too late.

The future is uncertain at best. Before you die, stop wandering in the forest of illusion that is this world and take up the royal road of spiritual attainment. Spiritual instruction and practice cannot be taken up when you are suffering the agony of a body that is near death. If the subtle body, the Sushumna, has not been purified of all latent impressions at the time of death, it is not possible to go to God. So, you should take up spiritual practice under the leadership of a Sadguru now. The saints tell us, do it now. Don't waste any more time.

106. There are many people in this world to take care of those who have passed the I.C.S., but there is none to inquire about the path to Divinity. No one can describe what the Bliss of Mukti means and what it is. That religion which was taught by Shiva from the beginning of creation is one and one only.

Commentary: So many teachers, so little wisdom! There are many who teach and encourage people to pursue comfort, security and reward. There are spiritual teachers and then there are Sadgurus. The world is full of "experts" on this and that, waiting to advise you at every turn. But few are those who can lead you to God.

The Bliss of Liberation cannot be described. It must be experienced. To experience it, you need agency. **That agency is Grace and Grace comes from a Master.** Nityananda Shaktipat Yoga is that path that has been taught by Lord Shiva since the beginning of time. It is the path Kundalini Shakti travels on in the Sushumna Nadi to union with Shiva in the Sahasrar. It is the easy path imparted and guided by a Sadguru. Such a path is the only path to Self-realization.

107. Adversity given by Shiva is no adversity. Sorrow given by Shiva is no sorrow. It is your mental delusion. At the time of our birth on this earth, there is some difficulty. So also at the end. When a person comes out of the mother's womb, tears trickle down the child's eyes.

Commentary: We are all subject to the law of Karma. Past actions will be suffered in the present life. Karma involves the ego's perception of both suffering and delight, both pleasure and pain. Therefore, it is the ego idea that must go. Then everything is experienced as Joy, even in the midst of facing your karmas.

What you experience in this life is a direct result of your past actions. Therefore, *you* are responsible. The purpose of the spiritual path is to lead you to the understanding that will get you to stop creating new Karma for yourself, whether it be perceived as 'good' or 'bad.' It is due to Karma that you have taken birth. Your present lifetime exists for you to work out the karmas you created in past lives. That's why you are here.

This is why the newborn's first action upon birth is to cry. It knows that it has suddenly entered the realm of limitation where all consequences of actions must be suffered. On the spiritual path, God creates obstacles to test you, to obliterate your ego and to remove anything that is an obstacle to your realizing the Self. This type of adversity is really no adversity at all. It is God's Grace, God's blessing for your existence here.

Once you are Liberated, no new karmas are created and, upon your death, you are not reborn. This is the goal of Sadhana, to prevent future births by removing your ignorance of the Truth. You may not always perceive Grace as being pleasant. But that's due to your ego-idea as well, that is born of your false notion of individuality and your own resistance. When you Surrender completely to God's Grace, your mind becomes so positive that you experience all circumstances, whether good or bad, as a gift from God. In this way you become invincible while still in the body.

108. All is Shiva. Justice and its opposite both are Shiva. O Mind! Leave off injustice and be one with justice.

Commentary: This world-appearance is the result of Shiva's Maya (the illusory aspect of this world appearance). Due to Maya, we experience duality. However, this duality, this diversity, is a *perception* created by Shiva, by God. Therefore, justice and injustice both belong to Shiva. Both are created by *That*, the Self. A true yogi chooses justice over injustice by reaching for Sattva Guna -- meaning he/she chooses to face his/her Karmas, rather than trying to avoid them or make them someone else's responsibility.

Facing the karmas you have created is justice. A yogi realizes that his own power of existence is God's power. Understanding this, a yogi becomes very mindful of how he/she is vibrating and what he is putting out. Therefore, the yogi's responsibility is also to choose justice over injustice in order to spread God's virtues in this world. In this way, one becomes very pure.

109. OMKAR is one without a second. Omkar is the cause of both creation and dissolution. Omkar destroys Manas. Omkar is really the Atman in you. Omkar is indivisible. A divisible object can never be indivisible. From the beginning there is only one religion taught by Shiva. If you sit in a room closing the doors, you do not see anything outside. When the doors are closed, Jiva communes with Shiva. When the doors are not closed, Jiva is separated from Shiva.

Commentary: The mantra *Om* is the sound of the Shiva-Shakti power, the Ultimate Reality or Cause. It is also known as the Supreme I-Principle. It creates and destroys. Om is the primordial vibration from which the Universe is created and also dissolved. Om is the Self that is you. Becoming absorbed in its vibration stills the mind. Om is indivisible. Objects (people, places and things) are only a reflection of this vibration of OM. Therefore, they are divisible.

From the beginning, the only path to Liberation is the approach taught by Shiva. The full, uninterrupted awareness of That Shiva-Shakti power, that Supreme Intelligence, is the goal. When you close the "doors" of your wandering mind and withdraw your entire attention inside yourself, the world disappears and you commune with That Supreme Principle. When you open the doors of your mind and focus your attention outside yourself, the world is created again and you are separated from Shiva because, in that moment, he is concealed from you. This predicament is resolved upon the full realization of *That.*

110. OMKAR is indivisible. Omkar is creation. Omkar is Maya, action, manas, Consciousness, Light of Consciousness. Chitta is the cause of desire.

Commentary: Omkar, the primordial vibration of OM, is indivisible. It is also known as Aham, the Supreme I-Consciousness that vibrates forever. It is the descent of Chiti that is responsible for the Manifestation, Sustenance and Withdrawal of this entire Universe. Om becomes Maya and The City of Eight (the false notion of individuality, the mind, the ego-idea and the five senses). It contracts to become all the objects of this world.

It is the Shakti that assumes all the forms of this world-appearance. Chitta is the individual, small 'i,' the contracted notion of being just a person that gives rise to the ego-idea. It is the Jiva, the individual, bound soul. This chitta is the cause of limiting, binding desire and craving.

111. SAT is the one, indivisible. It is the one "subtle" which is everlasting. CHIT is always changing.

Commentary: Divine Consciousness has two aspects; the transcendental and the immanent. Sat is also known as the transcendental aspect or the passive, observing aspect of Consciousness or the Self, which is both the Cause and the Effect. Chit (awareness) expresses itself as the active or immanent aspect of That Supreme Principle or Self. The immanent aspect of this world-appearance is always changing, like a play that is constantly being rewritten.

In truth, Sat, the Self or Supreme Principle, and its' active aspect or Shakti are one in the same. One is the expression of the other. Indeed, that Sat which is indivisible, threads through all that appears to change. What appears to change is the Shakti of the Supreme, Sat.

112. When the "SAT" unites with "CHIT," the result is Ananda. This Ananda is the Satchitananda, Sri Nityananda, Sri Paramananda. Union of Jiva and Paramatma is Ananda, Yogananda, Paramananda, Satchitananda and Brahmananda.

Commentary: Sat is also a reference to Existence, without beginning or end. Chit is *awareness* of *That* which exists without beginning or end. When these two unite, the result is the experience of the indescribable Joy of the Self. This Joy is Love. It is God, the ONE without a second. When you merge your individual identity in *That*, there is union of the individual with Paramatma, the formless Absolute. This is the experience of Oneness with everything.

113. You must see that God who is in the heartspace. Yes, you must see Him. You must see that Krishna who is eternal bliss (Nityananda). It is delusion to regard stone as God. Pain of death given by Shiva is no pain. All sorrow is mental delusion. Praise God within yourself. Praise Him in your head! You must know the secret of Parabrahma who is eternal joy. Yes, you must know that secret. Look for Him in the heart. See Him with your inner eye, not with the outer. See the royal road with the internal eye. Leave the downward path and come to the central path. The downward path is that path followed by those people who decorate the external body without knowing the secret of God.

Commentary: For seekers of the Truth, for those sincerely wanting Liberation, the desire to see God, to experience the Self in it's most exalted state, must be cultivated. You must find God, not in the stone statue, but inside yourself. Through spiritual practice, offering all your desires to that Supreme Intelligence, God, the death of attachment to the senses, the death of the ego-idea, the death of your limited identification with the body comes easily.

In this state, to the yogi, even the Universe dies and only God is seen. There is no pain in this death. It is actually Nityananda, the incomparable, eternal Bliss. The secret to praising God, the secret of all Puja (offerings of worship), the secret of performing oblations, the secret of service to God, this secret is the practice of merging your awareness in the space between the breaths. It is the secret of Hamsa that carries the Prana to the head, through which it enters into the Sahasrar, the highest spiritual center known also as the Abode of the Heart. Looking inside in this way, you find God.

Turn away from the pursuit of sense pleasures and worldly pleasures and become absorbed in your own Self. The downward path is that path that takes you away from God through the false notion that you are the body, just a person, just the mind and the senses, and that this body mechanism is all there is.

114. No one is mad in this world.

Commentary: No person is more or less intelligent than another. No person is greater than another. All people are God. At one time, everyone was wise, everyone knew his/her true, primordial nature. Eventually, everyone will tread the spiritual path back to God. Sooner or later, you will have to retrace your steps back to your true identity as the Self. For this reason, all are the same.

115. Leave the gross pleasures and enjoy the subtle pleasures. Leave off the physical sleep and enjoy the subtle sleep. Enjoy that sleep which is eternal. This sleep is enjoyed only in our subtle state. Burn to ashes the delusion of the mind.

Commentary: If, by Shaktipat and your own spiritual
practice, you turn away from worldly pleasures, you can
enjoy the eternal, subtle pleasure of your own Divine state.
The Bliss of this state is incomparable. It is the subtle sleep
that is more satisfying than even physical sleep. Leave off
the sense pleasures of the body and become one with your
own eternal Bliss! This Supreme state can only be
experienced when the mind dissolves, moment-to-moment,
as all thoughts, notions and ideas of this and that dissolve.
These are burned to ashes in the fire of true Meditation.

**116. He is a Brahmin who has performed the
Upanayana ceremony. Establish what is called
"Upadhi" in you. Being desireless, look inwards in your
heart. See with the eye of desirelessness. Discard
distinctions. Burn to ashes the idea of "you" and "I."
Yes, you burn it to ashes.**

Commentary: One who performs the sacred ceremony and
is invested with the sacred thread is known as a Brahmin.
During the caste system in India (this was also during
Bhagawan Nityananda's existence here), the Brahmin caste
was the only group of people in India who could engage in
the kind of spiritual approach or path we have the privilege
of freely engaging in here. In this way, Brahmins were
automatically revered as spiritual authorities. People of
this caste were considered to be the only ones who could
know God.

Bhagawan Nityananda refuted this false notion. Here he
states that the real consecration does not take place in such
a ceremony or caste. The real consecration and initiation is
to become established in the power and silence of the Self,
inside your own being, which anyone, regardless of caste or
class, can do. Establish Upadhi (silence) in yourself by
removing your *expectations* of sense pleasures and worldly
pleasures.

Become desireless by Meditation on God that is your very nature. In this way, over time, you will burn all notions of duality to ashes and see the ONE God, the ONE, Shiva-Shakti power vibrating inside your own being and in everything and everyone, everywhere. This state is what is called desirelessness, and when you have attained this state, that is the real Upanayana ceremony. Then no other ritual is necessary.

117. In the beginning, there was only one religion propagated by Shiva. In the beginning, there was no difference like "man" and "woman" among human beings. This distinction was only in the gross nature. In the subtle nature, all was one. The subtle has no qualities. The subtle receives only the eternal Ananda everywhere. Having and seeing is all mental delusion. The visible world is transient.

Commentary: In Satya Yuga, the first of the four ages that comprise one world cycle, there was only one religion on the planet taught by Lord Shiva himself, who existed here in a physical form. In Satya Yuga, *Equality Consciousness* reigned supreme. People saw each other as absolutely equal in God, regardless of gender or ethnic background. This is why Satya Yuga is known as the Golden Age. In its highest form, Divine Consciousness, the Supreme Subject or Supreme I-Consciousness, has no qualities and no divisions. It experiences its true nature as Bliss everywhere. This world is an illusion because it and everything in it is transient. Only that ONE God is everlasting.

118. Hari is no Lord. Shiva is the Lord. What is called Hari is delusion. We must not be fooled by the shadow (reflection). What is called Maya is delusion. To distinguish between the subtle and the gross is delusion. The delusion caused by the subtle and the gross are the same. The delusion caused by the gross is multitudinous.

Commentary: He who sustains the Universe as we know it, he is called "Hari." In truth, Lord Hari is a manifestation of Shiva, the Absolute. Hari is Maya Shakti, that aspect of Shiva that brings creation into being for Shiva's sport. Maya Shakti is concealment of Shiva. It is the *illusion* that there is a Universe separate from him, the illusion that a Universe actually exists. The sustenance of this illusion is said to be Hari, also known as Vishnu. (These are all just names for aspects or expressions of the One God.)

With the limitless understanding brought about through the complete realization of God, Hari is seen as a play, a creation of Shiva. To say that Shiva and this Maya are different, that they are separate, to view the cosmos in this way is itself delusion. The experience of objects (people, places and things) as separate and apart from Shiva is delusion.

To say that God is separate from this world, having nothing to do with it, to worship God in this way is the same delusion experienced as if one believes God does not exist. Nothing that is not Shiva can exist anywhere, since That Supreme Principle (Shiva) threads through everything, everywhere. To say that there is anything other than Shiva, any one other than God is delusion.

119. Realize your Self. When you see another and yourself as different, it is delusion. Identify yourself with another. Realize the secret that is in yourself. It is not enough if you talk of this identity but you must act according to it. What you see with the external eye is of no use. The feeling of distinction will be the cause of trouble at the time of death.

Commentary: Realize God. Seeing differences and duality in this world is delusion. You are one with everything and everyone because all are God. Identify yourself as being the same as others in this way. Realize the secret of your own true nature. God dwells within you as you. Worship God by becoming God. It is not enough to have intellectual knowledge of the Self. You must become *That*, and act accordingly. Investing yourself in the objects of this world is of no use. Seeing duality and difference, making distinctions between objects, between yourself and others is the death that causes rebirth.

120. Same-sightedness is the "Oordhva Shwasa" (gasping upwards) at the time of death.
Samesightedness is the indivisible one. This is supreme Bliss. This is the subtle. This is the eternal. In the upward breath, there is no cawing sound. O Shiva! B y your grace, permit us to breathe in and breathe out harmoniously. One must meditate in the head. One must meditate upon the ocean of eternal bliss. Meditate in the Ida, in the Pingala and in the Sushumna. Ananda-Kundalini! Rise! T he match is in the matchbox. Light is in the match. Rub the match and kindle the fire.

Ajnana is darkness. Jnana is the light. Kundalini is the eternal Bliss. Yes, it is so. Eternal Bliss is in the heart. Infinite light is Kundalini! Kundalini is the Light of Brahma. The sunlight is the subtle light. The solar nerve is the Sushumna. The lunar nerve is the Ida and the stellar nerve is the Pingala. The nerve of the third eye is the seat of Jnana. In this nerve is Jnana.

In this nerve is sleep, Sushupti. In sleep, there is no wakefulness. Enjoy this sleep. Harmonizing both Prana and Apana, enjoy the subtle sleep. Harmonizing the Prana and Apana, enjoy the eternal Bliss. The seat of breath is the truth. It is the internal space (Chidakasha). In the eternal space is the tower of eternal bliss. This tower is the seat of eternal peace. In the "unconscious sleep" enjoy the "conscious sleep" of Bliss. This is not the sleep of beasts or the "sleep of man." Enjoy that sleep which must be the aim and end

of humankind. Sleep the sleep of the "spiritual eye" (Upanayana).

When talking, when sitting, without any desires, without any thoughts, sleep this spiritual sleep. Fixing your attention on breath, sleep. Perform the natural Japa of the inward and the outward breath. Have mental (subtle) Bhakti. Yes, have it. Attain Liberation from bondage. Have constant Bhakti. Never interrupted. Breathe up and down without any restraint. Drawing the breath upwards is Pooraka. Stopping the breath is Kumbhaka. Kumbhaka is your real seat. Breathing out is Rechaka.

While breathing in, it should be like drawing water from a well. Draw the breath up to the Brahmarandhra in the brain. By such breathing, kindle the fire of Jnana. Purify the nerves. Burn the three humors (Vatha, Pitha and Kapha) in this fire. What is called discrimination is such a fire. It is the yoga fire. It is the food-digesting fire in the stomach. The discrimination is the solar light. God pervades the universe in the form of subtle energy. Creation is caused by the doubts of the mind. Creation is purely a mental affection. When you have attained the same-sightedness, there will be no creation.

Commentary: Samesightedness is the state of Purnaham Vimarsha. It is the exalted state of Liberation, the state of a Siddha who sees God in everything and everyone, everywhere. At the time of death this samesightedness is the Urdhve Kundalini that rises into the Sahasrar for the last time and remains there, rather than leaving the body. This is called *Mahasamadhi* and is the final resting place of one who is God-realized.

Upon exhalation (Prana), the breath moves upward. When Prana is centered in the Sushumna, it is very subtle and

powerful. It purifies everything, including all the Chakras
and the 72,000 nadis or energy points throughout the
physical and subtle bodies. This is the state of eternal Bliss
that is our very nature. O Shiva! Permit us to breathe
steadily in an unobstructed fashion, paying close attention
to the space between the breaths as we inhale and exhale.
Permit us to realize you in this way!

A yogi's duty is to learn this secret from the Master, to
learn how to direct the Prana into the three main channels;
Ida, Pingala and Sushumna and, ultimately, to direct the
Prana solely into the Sushumna Nadi, causing it to rise into
the head to remain there. By doing so, one comes to
Meditate on the ocean of eternal Bliss that is Shiva.

Rise! O Kundalini, awake! The match is in the box. The
fire is in the match. By drawing the Guru's power to you
through Shaktipat, awaken the dormant Kundalini and
begin your journey back to God! The sleep of ignorance
(Ajnana) is darkness. Knowledge and experience of God
within (Jnana) is Light. The inner energy that is awakened
through Shaktipat is known as Kundalini Shakti. This
Kundalini is eternal Bliss because, when it merges with
Shiva in the Sahasrar, it liberates the yogi from the bondage
of ignorance.

This eternal Bliss is experienced in the heart of Shiva.
When Kundalini is transformed back into its transcendental
aspect, *Chiti*, it is experienced as the infinite light of God.
It is the Light of Divine Consciousness. This Light is
subtler than the light of the sun and much more powerful.
It exists in the central channels, Ida, Pingala and Sushumna.
The third eye is called Ajna Chakra or the sixth Chakra. It
is the subtle spiritual center in the middle of the forehead,
just above the eyebrows. This is the command center.
Once Kundalini pierces this center completely, the yogi is
set on his/her own path and Liberation is very near.

It is from this Chakra that Kundalini is dispatched into the Sahasrar, uniting with Shiva. That is why it is called the seat of wisdom, the seat of Jnana. In this Chakra is the sleep of eternal Bliss. When Prana and Apana (exhalation and inhalation) are harmonized and centered in the Sushumna Nadi, you enjoy the subtle sleep of Divine Consciousness that is eternal Bliss, eternal Happiness, eternal Joy.

The seat of the breath is Shiva. It is the seat of Truth. It is the inner expanse of Divine Consciousness known as *Chidakasha*. This is the place of eternal peace. When you withdraw your entire awareness to this place, you enjoy the "conscious sleep" of Bliss. This is not deep sleep or the sleep of the unenlightened. This is not the physical sleep that everyone sleeps. This is the Supreme Awareness of Shiva-Shakti. It is the Turyatita state of the spiritually-perfected beings.

This state must be the aim of all people. When you attain the outlook of Shiva, you have the spiritual eye of knowledge. Remain absorbed in Shiva-Shakti, remain absorbed in God within, even while you are talking, sitting, and active. Remain in this thought-free state and sleep the spiritual sleep. Perform ajapa japa, the natural mantra repetition that happens on its own when you maintain the awareness of your breath and the space between the breaths. This is Hamsa. By Hamsa, have mental Bhakti.

Yes, praise God in this way by becoming God! Through this kind of steady Devotion attain Liberation from the bondage of ignorance. Attain the uninterrupted state of Purnaham Vimarsha. Breathe up and down without any restraint and retain the breath in the central nerve (Sushumna). This is your real seat. Breathing out is Rechaka or Prana. Breathing in is Pooraka or Apana. When you breath in it should be like drawing water from a well. Draw the breath up into the Heart space in the head. By centering the breath in the Sushumna Nadi as instructed by a Sadguru, kindle the fire of Wisdom. Breathing in this way is a powerful technique that purifies all the nerves and functions of your body.

This Sushumna breathing is the inner Yajna, the inner fire of Yoga. It is the fire of discrimination. It digests your food and cleanses your being. God pervades the universe in the form of subtle energy called Chiti or Chit Shakti. The world that we have come to know is a gross manifestation of this subtle energy brought about by the fluctuations and doubts of the mind. What we call this world is really a Superimposition in Maya, created by our own mental representations. When you merge your individual identity into Shiva, this creation will disappear and God alone will remain.

121. The subtle state is common to both mobile and immobile beings. The difference is in the casual (Prakriti). Difference is delusion. Difference is in the body. Bodies are transient. Prakriti is evanescent. When you realize the subtle in the gross, that state is called Moksha. Mukti is the indivisible. Mukti is in the heart space. In the heart space is Shiva Linga. It is self-existence. This is also called the "Prince-Prana." This is the upward breath. This is known in yoga as Prana. Prana is the ONE. Prana is the ONE in all. Prana is the existence.

This is known only to those who have practiced yoga. Those who have not practiced yoga are not aware of this fact, they being bound by desires. So, cut asunder the bondage of desires and hence attain salvation. Realize the one Tatwa; Paramatman. Realize him by the "internal eye." He is a man who has realized God by the "internal eye." Such a man feels that the universe is in him and he is in the universe. Mind, engrossed in the world, is not steady. Shiva who dwells in the heart space is the ONE, everlasting. Shiva is OMKAR.

OMKAR is Pranava. When united with forms, it is Pranava. Omkar is the "unawareness" of bodily existence.

Commentary: God and the Shiva-Shakti power exists in all sentient and insentient beings. The difference between these two is in Prakriti. Prakriti is The City of Eight or Visesha Spanda. Prakriti is the contraction of Chiti that becomes the individual will, ego, mind and the senses. In truth, this is not a real difference, since Prakriti only enables a human being to engage in Shiva's Maya, which itself is illusion.

Prakriti exists so that Shiva can take a physical body. This is the only difference between an individual and a rock. The physical body is transient but the underlying principle of Prakriti, which is Shakti, is eternal. When you fully realize that the Supreme Subject exists in all objects of sense, your state is one of pure Bliss and God-realization. You become Liberated and this Liberation is indivisible. It is the heart space where the Shiva Lingam, the symbol of the Absolute, resides.

This state is called the "Prince Prana" because it is attained by the constant practice of directing Prana into the Sushumna Nadi and retaining the breath inside in this way. This type of exhalation is called Prana. Prana is existence and nonexistence. It is the abode of Shiva and can only be experienced by one who has practiced Yoga under the guidance of a Sadguru. This is the only way to cut through the bondage of desire and craving for pleasure and pain.

Realize the Shiva-Shakti principle, the realm of Paramatman, by directing your attention inside. This is the internal eye of Jnana. Regardless of physical gender, one is a knower of the Truth who has realized God by this internal eye. Such a person then feels that the Universe is contained inside herself and that she is contained in and one with the entire Universe. If you allow your mind to be absorbed in the mundane world of objects, it will not become steady. The way to steady the mind permanently is to Meditate with the conviction that you are God. Doing this over and over again brings Liberation, in time.

Shiva is everlasting. Shiva is the Pranava mantra Om. Shiva is both the cause and the effect. This God-principle, the Self, is the cause of everything created and uncreated in this universe. When the Self takes all the forms of this world, it is Pranava still. The nature of the Absolute is not altered in the least by the fact that it appears to become bound by form. When properly practiced, Omkar is this realization.

122. OMKAR is the elite of all. Omkar is like the dawn of the sun. Omkar is the witness of all. Omkar is the most frightful of all forms. Omkar is fire. There is not a greater thing in this universe than fire. Fire is pervading both internally and externally. In the middle is the earth. The earth is below. Air is above. Air pervades the universe. The universe is in air. The first is air. The second is fire. The first is discrimination. The second is sound.

Soundlessness is in the form of air. Soundlessness is eternal Bliss. It is existence, knowledge, Bliss. The Self should be merged in soundlessness. The visible world is in the Self. When SAT unites with CHIT, Ananda is realized. This Ananda is Vivekananda, Chaitanyananda, Sri Brahmananda, Paramananda, Sri Nityananda, and Satchitananda. What is manliness is the realization of this Ananda. This is Brahma Jnana, Yoga Jnana, Kala Jnana. This Trikala Jnana is in the heart. In the heart is Mukti. Nityananda Mukti is in the heart.

Commentary: The constant state of rapture in which Om is heard and experienced without interruption, is the elite state of all. It is like the dawning of the sun. This is Witness Consciousness. This inner witness is the one who witnesses all. It is the most fruitful of forms. This inner witness is Shiva. Shiva is fire, the Light of Consciousness. There is no greater thing in this world. This Light pervades all the internal and external realms.

In the middle of this Light is the earth. Just as air pervades this universe, this Prakasha of Shiva pervades all of existence and nonexistence. Just as there is air before fire and fire needs air to stay lit, first there is Prakasha, Shiva's Light, and then there is Vimarsha, that manifests first as sound. Shiva's Light is like a pulsation with no sound, just as air does not make a sound when there is no wind. This Prakasha is eternal Joy.

Shiva is of the qualities of existence without beginning and without end, pure knowledge and complete Joy. This is also called Being-Awareness and Bliss (Sat-Chit-Ananda). Your individual consciousness should be merged in the silence of Satchidananda. The visible world is actually contained in Shiva. When Sat unites with Chit, Bliss is the experience. This Bliss, this indescribable Joy is the state that all the deities are named after in different ways. What is called "manliness" is the realization of God. This realization is wisdom, knowledge, yoga and pure consciousness. This knowledge of Trika, Shiva-Shakti-Nara, is contained in the heart. In the heart is Liberation. The eternal Bliss of the Self is in the heart center that is accessed in the head.

123. Bhakti is prema (love). Giving to eat or eating is not Bhakti. It is the delusion of the mind. It is pertaining to the body. There should be "subtle" eating and drinking. One should drink the water of discrimination. Peace is water. Yogananda is sitting on

the water of peace. O Mind! Leave off worldly
pleasures and enjoy eternal Bliss! O Mind! Leave off
worldly joy and enjoy eternal Joy!

Enter into the eternal, O Mind! Run into the heart.
The real enjoyment is in the heart. Enjoy that pleasure
which is called Mukti. Live in it. Enter into the
internal, leaving off the external. O Mind! Open the
third (divine) eye. Do not be thinking of anything else.
See the world with the same-sightedness.

Commentary: Bhakti is Love and Devotion for God.
Eating and drinking and exchanging needs out of emotional
craving is not love but merely a delusion of the mind.
Sense pleasures pertain to the body only. There should be
subtle eating and drinking that is the taking of the food we
call Jnana, the wisdom and knowledge arising from contact
with the Self. Drink the water of this kind of
discrimination. Peace is this water. The bliss of Yoga is
what is experienced by sitting in this "water" of peace.

O Mind! Leave off worldly pleasures and enjoy eternal
Bliss! O Mind! Leave off worldly joy and enjoy eternal
Joy! Enter into the eternal, O Mind! Run into the Heart.
The real enjoyment is in the Heart space that is Chidakasha,
located in the head. Enjoy that pleasure which is called
Liberation from bondage. Live in it. Enter into Shiva,
leaving off the Jiva. O Mind! Lose yourself in the divine
eye of wisdom. Stay focused on Shiva, inside, and do not
think of anything else. See the entire world as an unfolding
of Shiva Consciousness. See God in everything and
everyone.

**124. Japa cannot be performed by the finger tips. Japa
cannot be performed by the tongue. Shiva cannot be
attained by Manas. Karma cannot be done with the
hand. Karma cannot be done with legs. O Mind!**

Perform karma without attachment. Being desireless, see the world.

Commentary: Mantra repetition (japa) is not accomplished by touching the japa mala beads. Japa is not even performed by repeating the mantra aloud. Although these are helpful, true japa is the awareness of the mantra Hamsa (ajapa japa) that is being repeated inside your being by God himself. This is true japa.

Shiva cannot be attained by engaging the mind (manas). *Shiva can only be attained by stilling the mind.* Karma Yoga is selfless service (Seva) or the act of performing your work while remembering only God, without concern for what you will gain yourself.

Karma Yoga is not the act of doing work. It is not engaging yourself in hard work. It is the act of working *without becoming attached to your work, without involving your ego in your work,* without becoming deluded into thinking that you are your work. It is the act of working while maintaining the understanding that all actions and their fruits are His - that it is God who acts and God who receives as a result of action. This experience is that of desirelessness. See the world by it.

125. Mean dispositions of the mind are senselessness. This senselessness is the pariah (outcast). Joking and mocking at others, hypocrisy, pride and envy, etc. are the pariah characteristics. He whose skin is black, he whose clothes are black, is not a pariah. A man who has a turban on his head, a wristwatch on his wrist, is pariah if he does not recognize the equality in all. One who is a pauper is not a pariah, but he who is selfish and is full of differences is a pariah. He is not a man who has not realized the truth of Vedanta. Liberation in one's lifetime is that Vedanta which is like a trained horse. But the Vedanta which is like a wild elephant is not Mukti, but delusion.

Commentary: Having a mean disposition is senseless.
Having prejudice is senseless. This kind of disposition is
the pariah. Joking and mocking at others, hypocrisy, pride
and envy, are the characteristics of the ignorant individual.
He whose skin is black, he whose clothes are black, is not
ignorant. A person who has a lot of wealth, great clothes, a
fine house, an expensive car, a gorgeous woman or man,
real estate; such a person is still ignorant if he does not
recognize the Equality in all.

One who is a pauper is not a pariah, but one who is selfish
and is full of differences is a pariah. Only one who realizes
Equality Consciousness practices true Vedanta. Only such
a person is a true human being. Discipline in the practice
of Yoga for attaining Liberation in one's lifetime is that
Vedanta that is like a trained horse. All other paths are
delusion itself.

**126. A selfish mind is not steady (firm). A subtle
discrimination is steady. What is creation is peace.
What is creation is "witnesshood." What is creation is
subtle discrimination. Subtle discrimination gives us
health-giving contentment. Subtle discrimination is the
seed of Mukti. Trickery (Yukti) is not superior to
Shakti. Trickery is subject to Shakti. Trickery is the
delusion of the mind. Shakti is from Atman. Subtle
discrimination is the real Buddhi. Shakti truly so called
is subtle discrimination.**

Commentary: A selfish mind is subject to a sea of cravings
and desires. Such a mind is completely under the influence
of compulsion, being easily swayed due to its own
fickleness. For this reason, the path of Yoga teaches us to
have discernment which is the kind of subtle discrimination
that allows you to operate from the outlook of Divine
Consciousness.

This requires a spiritual practice that includes Meditation so that the mind can be brought under the control of the Self. This Self is the inner Witness, the Shiva-Shakti principle that is both the cause and the effect. This God-principle is the power behind all manifestations of thought, including Trickery. When the mind is turned within, it loses its trickery and merges with the subtle discrimination of the Absolute. It becomes That.

127. What you see with the physical eye, is the gross intellect. What you see outside is the gross intellect. What you see inside is not Hari. What is visible is not Shiva. What you see inside is not the universe. In Shiva is Hari; in Hari is not Shiva.

Commentary: What is seen in the physical realm of existence that we call this world is a perception created by Hari, Lord Vishnu, an energy aspect of the Absolute. What you see with the physical eye is perceived by your Buddhi, your individual intellect. This is the gross intellect. What is seen in Chidakasha, what is seen in the inner expanse of Supreme Consciousness, in the Heart, is Shiva, not Hari. Hari, Lord Vishnu, is the sustainer of Maya, of what is perceived through the senses. This is our visible world. What is seen inside in Meditation is Chidakasha. This is not the physical Universe. It is the very Heart space of Shiva. Shiva is the cause of Hari, having created him. Hari is not the cause of Shiva.

128. The subtle intellect is Buddhi or Jnana. The internal concentration is one pointed. The gross intellect is like a horse that is not controlled by reins. The intelligence that is acquired from others is not permanent. It is not Hari. It is not Shiva. That which is imparted by the Guru is the subtle intelligence. It is never gross. The gross intelligence is bestial. He is not a man who does not return what he has received.

Commentary: The subtle intellect is God's Will. This is
Jnana or direct knowledge of the Self. When the individual
Buddhi is merged in Supreme Consciousness, it is purified
in the fire of Jnana, the direct experience of the Shiva-
Shakti power. This is the energy substratum of all things
perceived and unperceived. This Shiva-Shakti power then
becomes the subtle intellect. This transformation occurs
through one-pointed, internal concentration that is
Meditation on the inner Self. The gross intellect is the
impure Buddhi or individual will that is like a wild horse
that cannot be controlled.

The will of the individual bound soul is absorbed in
mundane knowledge learned from other bound souls. This
knowledge is not permanent and cannot yield Liberation
because it is born of the ignorance generated by lack of
awareness of one's true nature and the Unity of all people,
places and things. It is transient, worldly knowledge only,
spiritually bankrupt.

That intelligence that you acquire from keeping the
company of a Siddha Guru is the subtle intelligence of the
Self. It should not be confused with the gross intelligence
experienced in worldly affairs and sense pleasures. Gross
intelligence is bestial due to it being based on spiritual
defects. Once you have experienced this Truth to the
fullest, it is your responsibility to return God's gift of direct
knowledge and experience of the Self by sharing it with
others.

**129. He who is ignorant of the true goal of life is a
beast. This goal is desirelessness. He who is ignorant of
this fact is not a man. Man who is the crown and
culmination of God's creation, must not be like a frog
which sinks below water and rises above water
repeatedly. This human life is not a comparison to that
of the frog. This life cannot always be attained. When
we have acquired it, we should make efforts to reach the**

goal of life. Meals cannot be had before cooking. Discrimination is the fire. Intelligence is the vessel. Mukti is the goal of life.

Commentary: True Man is a human being and a human being is that person (male or female) who is completely absorbed in God, being Liberated by his/her own spiritual practice and the Grace of the Guru. The goal of a human birth is Liberation from the bondage of ignorance that keeps God concealed. This is the goal of life. People who are ignorant of this fact are like beasts cast about at random in the survival game of the fittest.

The human form is the greatest treasure in Shiva's Maya because it is only through the human form that one can know God and become Self-realized. This human form is the culmination of God's creation. It is the penultimate position in the cycle of karmas, the cycle of birth and death. It is not always possible to acquire a human body after death. Many times, your Karma at the moment of death dictates that you take a lower life form. For this reason, it is extremely important not to waste a lifetime in the human body immersed in worldly pleasures and sense pleasures. It's important not to become a bogi who uses spiritual contact with the Self only to become better or greater at the game of worldliness.

Make the effort to reach the goal of God-realization while you have a body, and long before your death approaches. Most food has to be cooked before you can eat it. Likewise, your mind, ego, intellect and senses have to be cooked in the fire of Jnana, in the fire of instructed spiritual practice, before you can truly acquire Mukti. Mukti, Liberation, is the purpose and goal of life.

130. One is the dwelling. One is the eternal dwelling (Mukti). That dwelling is OMKAR. That dwelling is formless, changeless, indivisible. Future is not happy.

Today is the happy day. Tomorrow is not, day after is not. Nine o'clock, ten o'clock is not the time. Now is the time. The indivisible time you realize by discrimination is "the time." The time that you spend forgetting the goal of life is beggarly.

Commentary: Purnaham Vimarsha, the state of constant rapture in the uninterrupted awareness of Shiva Consciousness is the dwelling place or home of all true human beings. This state is Mukti or Liberation. It is the constant, uninterrupted awareness of OM. This final state of Liberation is formless, changeless and indivisible. It is a state and experience of timelessness.

There is no happiness in living for the future. Your happiness is not in the future that does not exist. It is in the present moment. In the present moment, you can have an experience of your own Divinity. Right now, you can see God and become *That.*

So, perform the practices as instructed by a living Sadguru. Do so every day. Perform them now. Now is the time! Don't put it off until nine o'clock or ten o'clock or tomorrow. Put both feet in the Guru's house now. Remember God right now in this and every present moment! For, transformation can only occur in the present moment, that moment of choice in which you are fully present with your true nature.

Become that timelessness that is your own indweller! Forgetting this as the goal of your life makes you a beggar, exposing you to the elements of pain and pleasure, limiting desire and craving. In this way, you become limited and bound, confined to a prison of your own making. You should want what is greater than that.

131. The seat of Mukti is "Gokul Nandan." "Govardhana," "Gokul." The third eye is the "Gokul."

The internal eye is "Gokul." It is Mathura. It is Vrindavana.

Commentary: The real place of pilgrimage is inside a human being. Your church is there, inside. The seat of Liberation is that Gokul Nandan, that temple and place of worship that is in Chidakasha, the triadic Heart of Shiva. All places of pilgrimage begin and end there, inside. Becoming absorbed in Shiva Consciousness is the internal eye. It is the real worship of God. Doing so, no other pilgrimage is needed.

132. Look for the all pervading God in the head! Truly look at Him in the head! Hence enjoy the eternal bliss! See this creation in the heart.

Commentary: To experience God, the all-pervasive Lord, you first have to go inside your own being to that place where He dwells inside you. Look at Shiva-Shakti by becoming absorbed in the Heart Space, Chidakasha, in the head. This is the space where all of manifestation is reflected. This space is the threshold to the Sahasrar, that highest spiritual center. The direct knowledge and experience of this is revealed by a living Sadguru. Enjoy eternal Bliss by going to that place. Ride the train of Prana Shakti that takes you directly there! No lines, no waiting!

133. Realization of OMKAR is the annihilation of the world. Realization of OMKAR is the destruction of the Manas. When honor and dishonor have become one to a man, he attains Ananda, eternal joy, exhaustless joy, real joy. Then all that appears becomes nothing but joy.

Commentary: When you attain Mukti (Deliverance or Liberation), that is OMKAR. This realization occurs when the mind is destroyed, when it dissolves in the Heart space in the Sahasrar. When this occurs there is no desire for pleasure or pain, no desire or compulsion towards honor or dishonor. This is a place of pure, boundless and endless Joy. From this state, one sees everything and everyone, everywhere as nothing but a Paradise of Joy. This Joy is indescribable and all-pervasive.

134. "Shiva is from Kasi." The heart space is Kasi. Manas is Kasi. Everything is Kasi. The eternal Atman is Kasi. What is Kasi is in the head. The ten Nadas (sound) are eternal. The subtle Kasi is the Nirvikalpa Kasi. What is Haridwar is the nine gates in the body. It is the heart space. It is the place of peace. Yajna (sacrifice) is the immortal Jnana (wisdom).

Commentary: One does not have to make a pilgrimage to Kashi (city in India that is considered the abode of Lord Shiva) to experience Shiva. One does not have to go to any of the great Shiva temples or caves to experience Shiva. One does not have to travel to Haridwar to bath in the waters there in order to experience God.

All these holy places of pilgrimage are contained inside you. The Atman, the Self, Shiva-Shakti, is inside you. What is the true Kashi temple is the Shiva Lingam in the Sahasrar (highest spiritual center located at a distance of 12 fingers above the head). The true place of worship, the real temple is that place where the ten Nadas (sound vibrations out of which Mantras form) and the nine gates (subtle spiritual energy centers in the body) all merge in Chidakasha. Direct knowledge and experience of this Heart space of Shiva in the Sahasrar is the real Yajna, the true ritual sacrifice.

135. "Yukti" (skill) is like walking on foot. Shakti is that which enters the heart. Sanyasa is like going on a train. He who goes on foot is a wanderer. (Manas is fickle). The body is the train. The passenger in the train is Manas. If there are no passengers (Manas), the

train will not move. Tickets will not be issued. People will not gather. Then there is neither the first class nor the second nor the third. Manas is the class of peace. The master of the chariot is Buddhi. The engine is the head. The nerves and the blood vessels are the screws. That which moves in the nerves and blood vessels is Vayu.

Commentary: The effort and struggle to perfect various Hatha Yoga postures and the effort to become perfect in knowledge of the scriptures is like walking to a place on foot when you can get a train to the same location in far less time. The train is Prana Shakti that travels inside the Sushumna Nadi.

True Sanyasa is the act of getting on this train and being carried to the Sahasrar, the ultimate and final destination of all travel. The mind is a passenger on this train of Prana Shakti. When it dissolves in this Prana, all distinctions and differences are destroyed and one experiences the pure Buddhi, the highest intelligence that is God. Prana Shakti is that which causes the body and all the organs to function. It is Vayu, the breath or life force that, when directed into the Sushumna Nadi, reveals God on a permanent basis.

136. He that saves you at the time of death is Shiva. It is not Hari. Shakti is in Shiva. Maya (delusion) is in Hari. Bodies are earthly. The bodily senses are all looking outwards. Shiva is internal. He is the Brahma-Randhra. That which is taught by others is no real knowledge. That which has come to your experience is real knowledge.

Commentary: In order to become completely Liberated, in order to be free of the bondage that is the wheel of birth and death, you have to merge with the Guru-principle, that Shiva-Shakti power that is the energy substratum of all things. It is only Shiva, the Ultimate Reality, who saves you from the samsara of this world, not Hari (the sustainer of worldliness also named 'Vishnu').

Shiva and Shakti are one in the same. They are the cause of everything created and uncreated everywhere. What is known as Hari, or the sustainer is really Maya Shakti or Shiva's Maya that is responsible for the illusion of a Universe of all the worlds.

So, why become attached to the reflections (objects) of Shiva, the Supreme Subject, when you can turn your senses within and experience the Supreme Subject directly? Shiva is Chidakasha. Shiva is the Sahasrar, the triadic Heart (Shiva-Shakti-Nara). You cannot understand this simply from the speech of another. You have to experience it for yourself, in the laboratory of your own existence, by way of a Sadguru's instruction.

137. When you have attained perfect peace, there is no necessity of going anywhere. There is no necessity of seeing anything. There is no necessity of going to Kashi, Rameshvara, Gokarna and other holy places. All is seen in the mind. Going and coming are delusions of the mind. When peace is attained, ALL appears to be the ONE. Liberation from bondage is seeing the ONE in ALL and the ALL in ONE. This is desirelessness. The thing in the hand must be seen in the hand itself. You cannot find it anywhere else. So also, everything must be tested in one's own thought.

Commentary: The perfect peace of God-realization causes you to become the place of pilgrimage. God exists inside you as you. When you realize this completely, when you merge with the Self in the great inner expanse of Chidakasha, there is no need to go to Rameshvara or other holy temples to experience God. When Liberated, the mind becomes Chiti once again and all places of pilgrimage and worship are contained in this state.

One does not have to go anywhere else to experience the Supreme Self. Seeing God in everything and everyone, everywhere is Liberation. This is desirelessness. Just as you don't go searching elsewhere for something you already have in your hand, don't go looking for Joy, Happiness and Peace outside where they are not. Go where they are, inside yourself. This can be tested by directing your mind and your thoughts back to the source, the inner Self, inside your own being.

138. The real sunrise is to be seen in the sky of Consciousness. This is the most excellent sunrise. The whole universe is to be seen in the heart space in one's Self just as the sun is reflected in the water placed in a small mud vessel. When we travel by a cart, the whole world seems to be moving. Likewise, the whole universe can be known in yourself.

Commentary: The real sunrise is seen only in Chidakasha, the Sky of Divine Consciousness that is the Heart space in the head. Inside, thousands of great Suns (Adityas) can be seen. They are most excellent and much brighter than the sun in our solar system.

Just as you can see the reflection of the sun in water, what you experience as this world, this Universe, is really a reflection of what can be experienced in the Heart space inside your own being. When you get into a moving cart, it seems that the whole world is moving. But, really, you are the only one moving.

In the same way, activity in this world is a perception created by God's force inside you. The entire universe is contained inside you. Your own Spanda Shakti creates a perception of activity where there really is none. You experience this perception inside your own being, and nowhere else. By the Grace of the Sadguru and your effort at Sadhana, the whole universe can be known inside yourself.

139. He who is hungry knows what hunger is. Similarly, everything is known to the Atman. When a train leaves a station, a wire is sent to the next station. When you throw a stone into a well, a sound is heard. So also, when Vayu is moving in the nerves, "ten kinds of sounds" become audible.

Commentary: You know what hunger is because you have experienced it. Likewise, the Atman, the Self, is the one and only experient - the Universal Experient. Everything is known to God who is both the cause and the effect. When a train leaves the station, a wire is sent to the next station. When you throw a stone into a well, a sound is heard. So also, when Prana (Vayu) moves though the 72,000 Nadis in the body, a message resounds throughout the body – embodied in the ten kinds of sounds.

This message is like a reverberation that is heard when you throw a stone into a well. This reverberation creates a "ripple effect" that sends Shakti throughout the nerves and three channels, purifying everything. As Prana moves through the 72,000 Nadis, all the ten kinds of celestial sounds can be heard. They are heard in one point known as Bindu Nada.

140. Suppose water is boiled in a vessel whose mouth is closed. Then all the heat energy is concentrated in the vessel itself. When water comes out of a pump, we hear the sound of Omkar. We should abandon the forest path and tread the royal road. The energy moving downwards must be made to move upwards. The mind should know mind's place.

Commentary: Human beings should turn their entire focus inside and keep it there. Just as you concentrate heat energy inside a pot of boiling water when the pot is closed, in the same way, when you close off the outer focus and become absorbed in the Self, Shakti builds up in your being and purifies it.

God, Shiva, exists in all things. Nothing exists anywhere that is not Shiva. This is why even water makes a sound that can be traced back to the Primordial OM. The forest path is the path of worldliness and sense pleasures. We should abandon this path for the royal road, the Siddha Path of the Sushumna Nadi that takes us to God.

This can be accomplished by learning, from a Siddha, how to direct Prana Shakti upward inside the Sushumna Nadi to merge in the Sahasrar. This is also the mind's true place, to merge in Chidakasha.

141. A boat does not sail where there is no water. So also, if Vayu does not move, there is no blood circulation. When circulation is stopped, heat ceases to be generated. When the generation of heat ceases, there is no digestion of food. So also, a train cannot move without fire.

Commentary: A boat needs water to sail. A train cannot move without the energy generated from its engine. In the same way, the body cannot function without Vayu, which is Prana (the breath and the force inherent in the breath). It is Prana that causes the heart to pump and the blood to circulate. Without Prana, the body is a corpse. This Prana is also responsible for digesting food that is needed to sustain the body. Therefore, the body is not life. Prana is life. Prana is God.

142. Without a rope, water from a well cannot be drawn up. In the body, breath is the rope. Drawing the inward breath harmoniously is like drawing up the water from a well.

Commentary: In order to get water from a well, you have to lower a bucket into the well and pull it back up with a rope. In Sadhana (daily spiritual practice), the well is the Sushumna Nadi, the bucket is Kundalini Shakti and the rope is the breath (Prana). Drawing Kundalini Shakti upwards into the Sahasrar by directing Prana into the Sushumna is the key to experiencing the nectar of Self-Awareness. It is like drawing water from a well.

143. In order to make planks of a wooden beam, it should be sawed up and down. Similarly, breath should move upwards and downwards in the body. It should be led into Buddhi and made always to move in an upward direction. To take a stone uphill, requires great effort but to bring it down by the same route is not difficult. So also, going up is difficult but coming down is easy. It is difficult for the Prana to leave the body. To receive a thing is easy but to return it is difficult. Those men who do not return what they have received are not worthy of the name of "men." They are merely animals. They have no virtue.

Commentary: Wooden planks have to be sawed uniformly in order to fit properly when making a beam. In the same way, Prana has to be drawn in and out of the body uniformly, in an even fashion, in order for the Bliss of Supreme Consciousness to be experienced.

Buddhi is Shiva dwelling in the Sahasrar. During exhalation, the breath should be directed upward and into the Sushumna Nadi so that it can touch the thousand-petaled Lotus in the Sahasrar and advance to Vyapini or Turyatita in the spiritual center above the head. This requires effort, discipline and practice under the instruction of a Siddha Guru.

It is easy to be lazy and to destroy our equanimity by engaging in the bad habits of sense pleasures that make us forget God. Turning to God is more difficult because we are not in the habit of doing so. Nonetheless, God has given us life so that we can attain Him. We should return what we have received from God by fulfilling the goal of all Life, Liberation, so that, upon death, we can return to God by way of breaking the cycle of birth and death.

144. It is impossible to describe the pangs of death. Jnana is attained by subtle thinking. So breath should be controlled. The mind should be merged in the sound.

Commentary: Death is the sleep of ignorance. Going through life without full awareness of the Shiva-Shakti power, the Supreme Self, is ignorance. When you carry this ignorance with you at the final moment of death, you do, indeed, suffer the pangs of death.

This death is an indescribable horror. For, not only do you have to travel to other realms to work out karmas that cannot be experienced in the body, but then you have to return here in another form to relive your ignorance all over again.

Jnana is attained by the subtle thinking derived from Shiva Consciousness. Through Sadhana (daily spiritual practice) as instructed by the Guru, your mind becomes very subtle and, eventually, merges in Bindu-Nada, the constant reverberation of Chiti that is experienced in Chidakasha. When this occurs, and you remain in this state on a constant basis, you do not die. You cast off this body for the last time and merge with Infinite Consciousness. For such a person, death does not exist.

145. He who has a burden on his head, has his attention on the burden. Similarly, he who acts the part of a king in a field drama, has his attention fixed on the crown. Likewise, Jnanis have their attention fixed on Buddhi.

Commentary: You become what you think on the most. Whatever you invest your mind in, you become. You get what you meditate on. You become what you obey. Just as one who is sad or depressed feels this way because he/she has become absorbed in his burdens or suffering, just as an actor playing the part of a King merges his mind in the character of the King, Jnanis, the truly wise, have learned to keep their attention on the Self. In this way, they worship God by becoming God.

146. Manas (mind) is inferior to Buddhi. Buddhi is the king. Manas is the prime minister. The prime minister must go to the palace often to see the king. So also, Manas is the king of the body.

Commentary: The mind is a contracted form of Chiti, the subtle intellect also known as Buddhi. This Buddhi is the place of Omniscience. As such, it is superior to the mind. Just as the prime minister's job is to run the Kingdom in the way the King instructs, the mind's job is to run and operate the body and the senses in the way that Buddhi, God, instructs. To accomplish this, just as the prime minister needs to go to the palace often to consult with the King, so too the mind needs to travel to the palace of the inner Self to consult with God.

147. Gas light has no luster before the midday sunlight. Light is of use only when it is dark. When a man is hungry, he does not consider the difference of castes. Similarly, in sound sleep, there is no hunger. Then, Manas is absent. Just so, a man must sleep the sleep of yoga. Only such men are Jnanis.

Commentary: In the direct light of the sun all other light dissolves and only the sun is seen. Similarly, where there is no darkness, light is not even required. Just as when you are hungry and go to a restaurant, you will eat food without asking the race or background of the cook, in the same way, when your awareness is merged in God, differences dissolve and there is no longer any duality. Only God exists.

Just as there is no hunger when you are sleeping soundly because the mind is absent in deep sleep, in the same way, you must sleep the sleep of Yoga and allow your mind to dissolve in Shiva Consciousness. In the uninterrupted state of constant rapture that is Mukti, the mind dissolves, the world dissolves, the Universe dissolves, and only Shiva, God remains. Those in this perfected state of Equality Consciousness experience only God everywhere. Such people are Jnanis.

148. Take ten men; their Bhakti is not of an identical nature. When ten people are going on a journey, if one of them sits to take rest, the remaining nine will also do the same. Likewise, one man is inspired with Bhakti, other people, by seeing or hearing him become also Bhaktas.

Commentary: People love God and desire to know God in varying degrees, and some not at all. But, just as people on a hiking trip will stick together and stop for rest together when the leader designates, those whose love for God is weak or nonexistent can be encouraged to increase their Faith and Devotion, just by the example set by one person who loves God completely.

Therefore, keep good company. Keep the company of those saints who have realized God, who have become absorbed in the goal of the path. By doing so, you will be taken across by your Love and Devotion for such Siddhas. Just by keeping their company you can be transformed into a lover of God.

149. You do not feel the scent of a flower that is in your own hand. Flowers that are distant smell sweet. Babies

whose brains are not developed, see no difference in the
things of the world. When their brains are developed,
they see the difference in things. Until a baby is six
months old, it feels no differences. A first class yogi is
like a baby of this type. If you give a diamond to a
baby, it throws it way. To such babies, pebbles and
diamonds are the same.

Similarly, to true Jnanis, a lump of earth and money are
the same. They have no desires of any sort. They see
the one Atman everywhere. All is seen in the Atman
and the Atman in all. This vision is internal. What is
called internal vision is "subtle discrimination." Subtle
discrimination is Shiva-Shakti. Shiva-Shakti is the
indivisible Shakti of the Para-Brahma. What is Para-
Brahma-Shakti is the Atman. This is the ONE reality.

Commentary: As we grow older and become more and
more attached to the ramblings of our own mind in the
pursuit of worldly pleasures, we consider ourselves to be
mature and more intelligent. So intelligent that we start to
take many things for granted. Just as we smell the scent of
a flower at a distance, but cannot feel the scent of a flower
in the hand, with the passing years, we learn how to make
distinctions and differences that prevent us from seeing the
One in the many.

A baby of six months or less does not have a "developed"
brain that makes such distinctions. At this age, we see no
differences. A diamond is the same as a hand full of dirt to
us at this age. We have not yet learned distinctions like
"mine" and "yours" and we simply dwell in a state of
constant wonder where we see our own simple nature
reflected everywhere. This is the state of a child up to six
months old.

A first class yogi is like a baby of this age. Such a yogi
lives in a desireless state seeing everything and everyone as

that same Shiva-Shakti power, that same indivisible Parabrahman that is the Absolute. For such a person, only God exists and nothing else has value aside from that One God.

150. Reality is the Prana in man. He is a man who thinks (ruminates) rightly. This correct thinking (right discrimination) is the real goal of man. Everything is attainable by practice. By practice, everything becomes known.

Commentary: Shiva Consciousness is the Reality. This Reality takes the form of Prana in a human being. That person is God who constantly contemplates his/her own true nature by experiencing God within. This experience is correct thinking. It is right discrimination and is the real goal of life. Through Sadhana under the direct guidance of the living Sadguru, all this becomes known firsthand. By practice you become That – the Self that you already are.

151. If you keep a seed safe in a box, it will not yield plenty. If you sow it in the earth and cultivate it, one seed yields thousands. From one lamp, you can light a thousand lamps. One tree produces thousands of flowers. Flower is the downward state. The tree is the upward state.

Commentary: It does not take many seeds to create others. Even one seed sown in the earth will yield thousands more. From the flame in one lamp you can light thousands of lamps, just as even one tree will produce thousands of flowers.

In the same way, it does not take many people to change the awareness of the masses. Even one Siddha can affect transformation in the lives of thousands. We should all become like those saints, those perfected beings, by inquiring as to the true nature of their state inside. Rather than becoming attached to the objects and forms of this world, we should seek to know the upward state that is Supreme Consciousness dwelling inside a human being.

152. If we sow a gold coin in the earth, it will never sprout.

Commentary: A gold coin will not multiply into other gold coins if we put it in the earth. That would be the wrong way to invest it and a waste of time. To make a gold coin multiply, you have to invest it properly. In the same way, if we invest our entire being in sense pleasures and worldly pleasures, and if we only establish an intellectual understanding of God, these will never transform us. We will never know our true worth, our real value, our own Divinity. In order to experience our own worth, we have to go to the right place inside our own being and merge with the Absolute there. We should invest our time and our entire being in this way.

153. A lifeless thing is soundless. It is gross. A living thing has Shabda-Brahma. The universe is nothing but Consciousness. When you build a house, you must first lay a foundation and afterwards, raise the walls. So also, there is no effect without a cause.

Commentary: Just as something that is dead cannot produce a sound, an object (person, place or thing) has no life without God. In living beings and things, there is the existence of the primordial sound Om, Shabda-Brahma. The Universe is nothing but this Supreme I-Consciousness pulsating as Om.

Contracting to become the sound inherent in living things, Shakti takes all the forms of existence. It is this Spanda Shakti that is the cause. Objects are only reflections or effects of this unifying God-principle. Without Shakti, the energy substratum of everything, nothing can exist anywhere.

Therefore, God himself is inherent in all forms, sentient and insentient. As in the building of a house, society must be built on a solid foundation that is imbued with the recognition of the Supreme Self. Otherwise there can be no real intelligence.

154. Those who are physically blind have no knowledge of forms. To such, light is of no use. Those who have destroyed mental modifications, have destroyed all desires. Such people are not subject to dreams.

Commentary: To the blind, everything and everyone is absent of form. A blind person has no use for light. Similarly, a Siddha who has destroyed all mental modifications and notions of this and that, a spiritually-perfected being who has destroyed all expectations of sense pleasures and worldly pleasures, no longer has use for craving or desire. Such a person is not subject to the manifestations of the restless mind in the waking state or in dreams and is not subject to pleasure and pain.

155. Those who do not breathe through the nose, have no desires of any sort. Their breath is purely internal. They concentrate their breath in the Brahmarandhra where the Ida and the Pingala meet. They have realized the Great Self. They look upon all things as Self. This is Swarajya (Self government). What is Swarajya is Jiva's true place. The light of life is Prana Vayu. Prana Vayu is the capitol of Swarajya government. Atman is the lord of the Swarajya government. Swarajya is one's own energy. This energy must be kept under perfect control. What is Swarajya is not a hill; it is not gold. Keeping under control both desire and anger is Swarajya. A man must say what he does and do what he says.

Commentary: A realized being, is one who has mastered Sushumna breathing, also called internal breathing. For such a being, the breath moves upward in the Sushumna automatically. This breathing is not the external breathing through the nose or mouth. It is spontaneous Kumbhaka where Prana is concentrated in the Sahasrar where the Ida, Pingala and Sushumna meet.

One who has mastered this Prana Vayu is a God-realized being. Such a person sees all as her very own Self, as God. This state is the birthright of all souls. It is your place and the goal of all life. This state allows you to govern your mind and your senses so that you are able to maintain Equality Consciousness. This Equality Consciousness is self-governance (Swarajya) and it allows you to keep your ego and senses in check so that you vibrate at the highest level of Consciousness.

156. If you are afraid of water, you cannot cross a river in a boat. If you are afraid of fire, you cannot heat water. Fear must be banished. To accomplish anything worth doing, one must be thoroughly fearless. Mind is the cause of anything we do.

Commentary: Fear prevents transformation and, therefore, should be removed completely. In order to accomplish anything in life, you have to be fearless. In spiritual life also, in order to make progress in Sadhana, you have to destroy your fears. Action is filtered through the mind. For this reason, the mind has to become very focused. It cannot maintain focus when fear exists. So, one of the primary goals of spiritual practice is to remove fear. With the primary goal of the destruction of the ego-idea attained, you automatically become fearless.

157. On a mango tree, all fruits do not grow at the same time and ripen at the same time. First, we have the tender fruit. By and by, the fruit ripens. The ripe fruit

is eatable. So also, men must be like mangoes. In every respect, we must cultivate peace.

Commentary: In Sadhana (spiritual practice), people advance at different rates, depending on their personalities and their discipline in practice. The goal of Sadhana is peace. One's Sadhana has ripened when one experiences Supreme peace inside and begins to operate from that place of peace in every situation and circumstance. In every respect, we must cultivate peace.

158. The head is the mango. In it, is the sweet ambrosia. This ambrosia is the essence of the five senses. This ambrosia is the supreme energy in man.

Commentary: Like the inside of a ripe mango, the delicious "fruit" of Yoga is in the head, in the Crown Chakra. In this Chakra is the sweet ambrosia of Chit Shakti. This Chiti is the essence and cause of the five senses. It is nectar, the Supreme energy in all human beings.

159. A house in which there is no lamp at night has no beauty. Whatever the nature of a house, the house is perishable. What a lamp is to a house, is Jnana to the body. The light is the light of Kundalini. A thing hidden in mire, fetches no value. When it is recovered from mire, all make use of it. If you discover a diamond in mire, you do not throw it away.

Commentary: If you were to walk around your house at night without light, you would not be able to see the objects there. It's the light that allows you to see in the dark, not the house with its objects. In fact, without light, nothing would have any value since you wouldn't be able to see it to attach any value to it.

So, the house and its objects are perishable and really have no value. It's the Light that has worth. In the same way, the physical body has no value. It is perishable. It only has worth because there is the Light of Knowledge (wisdom) inside it. Without that Jnana, the body would not exist. That Light is Kundalini, the rising Shakti that leads one on the royal road back to God. Like discovering a diamond in the dirt, discover your very own Self inside your being. All can make use of that!

160. A man falls into a well. We should take him up, not allowing him to die. We must not think that a man will always be bad. We must try to correct him.

Commentary: Many sway off the spiritual path and many are completely ignorant of the fact that such a path even exists. We should not think badly of such people. We should have compassion for even the worst in character. Regardless of past deeds, anyone can be transformed by the hand of God. We must try to bring such people to the spiritual path, by way of the living Sadguru.

161. If any powder falls into the eye, our attention is turned on the eye. Similarly, if our outer attention is directed inwards, it is called introversion (internal sight). Ignorance is like a casket of powder. The possessor of a box only knows what is contained in it. Others do not know it. The real wealth is the energy of life. Intelligence is the box. The box is locked after the wealth is stored in it. Locking the box is giving the Manas its proper place in the head. That thing received is the soul in man. Turn your soul to God within yourself. Realize internally your own secret. The universe is in you and you are in the universe. The inner man is the ONE in All. He who is "there" and He who is "here" is the ONE and the SAME.

Commentary: What's inside is what is of value. A box containing powder owes its value to the powder inside. In the same way, what's inside a human body is of real value. By turning your entire attention within, through Meditation, you can come to experience your real value, your real worth, by going inside.

Ignorance is the state that most people are in. People walk around not knowing who they really are. The possessor of the powder box is the only one who knows what's inside it. Similarly, the Supreme Being who created and owns all bodies, all forms, is the only One who knows the real value and purpose of such forms. That Supreme Being dwells inside you and if you turn your mind within by Meditating, you gradually come to realize the secret; that you and that Supreme Being are One in the same.

The real wealth is the energy of life known as Shakti. This energy substratum of everything is locked inside your body also. To come to know it is a process of closing off or locking the doors to the outside world so that you can direct that energy inside and keep it focused there. Once your individual intelligence is merged in this Shakti, the mind is trained to focus on it, to see God everywhere at all times.

162. The supreme light is the universal light. O Mind! Abolish the idea of "otherness." Have the idea of "sameness."

Commentary: The Supreme Light is the Universal Light that is the cause and substance of every form in this universe. O Mind! Abolish the idea of difference. Abolish the idea of separateness and imperfection. Have the conviction that you and God are one in the same, and that you exist eternally, everywhere and in everyone.

163. When you were born, you were born with breath. When you leave this world, you leave with breath only. This body of earth, you never made it nor can you take it along with you. That which Shiva gave us is the same

in all beings, both mobile and immobile. All seeds have the same power in them. The subtle in seeds is one. There is difference in their behavior only. The delusion of the mind is not permanent but transient. What can be seen and heard is all transient.

Commentary: When you were born, you were born because the breath, Prana, entered your body. When you leave this world, you leave in the form of the breath that carries The City of Eight from your body to the next realm. You did not make Earth or anything in it and you cannot take any of it with you.

This earthly realm belongs to Shiva (God). Shiva has given all beings, sentient and insentient, the same Shakti, the same Divine Conscious Energy. This Spanda or Chiti is the subtle element common to all living things and inanimate objects.

The only difference is an insignificant one in that, owing to Shiva's Maya, we perceive that these things have different behaviors and different uses. These perceived differences are actually delusions brought about by thinking and our superimposing from past impressions left behind on the mind. The mind sees and hears and processes experience. It is transient and these experiences are also transient. They are of Maya and are not real.

164. When we call a man "pariah," it is nothing but mental delusion. A piece of cloth goes equally well into the mouth of a "pariah" or a "brahmin." A Brahmin does not use even the chunam touched by a pariah. He does not sit on the same mat with a pariah. Some one acts like this; another sees it or hears of it and he blindly imitates it.

Commentary: Seeing differences in others is not only delusion but it is stupidity. Considering yourself to be

better than others, to be of a superior race, to have a better set of genes, to be of a better quality of ethnicity; these are foolish notions that will keep you separate from God.
In many societies there have been caste systems that place one group or race of people below another. This notion is still prevalent today, even in countries like the USA where racial discrimination and Eugenics are outlawed.

The problem is ignorant people are copycats. They see the wealthy and most revered people of the society behaving in this foolish manner, and they blindly imitate it. Wake up! It is only God staring back at you through the eyes of that person you claim to be inferior. God alone walks among us.

165. Those who call another a "pariah" are themselves pariahs. Suppose there is a bunch of plantains. From the plantains of the same bunch, we prepare various sorts of eatables. The plantain is a fruit. If it is cut into slices and fried, it is no longer called a plantain. It is called "fried slices." So also, variously named preparations are made from plantains (of the same bunch). In the beginning, there was only one bunch. Preparations are manifold. The original form is one only. So also, in all creatures, the sound of Omkar is the one only.

Commentary: Those who discriminate against others are themselves the lowest of the low. One who knows God has *Equality Consciousness* and believes this to be the most important. Plantain is a fruit that, when cut up and cooked in different ways, is called by different names. But it is still plantain, no matter what people may call it when it is made into a particular dish.

In the same way, in this Universe there is only God whose existence is first known by the sound of *OM*. This reverberation of Om, this God, this Shiva is the only thing that truly exists. It is Shiva who becomes this manifold universe. However, although Shiva, the Supreme Self takes many forms, those forms are all Shiva, the Primordial Being whose sound is OM. So, in all creatures, OM is the only one, the ONE in all.

166. There is a station where four railroads meet. One train goes to Calcutta, another to Bombay, a third to Madras. They all start from one station and they reach one station only. Similarly is Maya. Maya is born of us and it disappears in us. It is like butter in milk. Butter emanates from milk and it merges in milk. The sayings of a great sage last long. Even if there is none to hear them, they continue to live long.

Commentary: Like trains that all leave from the same station and then return there at the end of their runs, so too, Shiva's Maya emanates from that one Chit Shakti and returns there. Maya, which is this world-appearance or the perception of activity, this Maya unfolds from inside each of us and dissolves there. It is like butter in milk. Butter emanates from milk and it merges in milk. This teaching is the Truth experienced by sages. This teaching survives all the four Yugas (ages of existence). Even when the Universe is dissolved in Shiva for a time, this teaching remains, even if none exist to hear it.

167. There was a bare plain. There a traveler's bungalow was erected. Scarcely two days had passed, a meeting was held there. Chunam was used to cement the stones. The walls were all white washed. On the very day of white washing, a meeting was held. A certain cooli was appointed to warn the people, attending the meeting, lest their feet and bodies be besmeared with the chunam.

The meeting was over and all the people dispersed. But the cooli stayed behind. Afterwards, many a meeting

**was held in the bungalow. There was no body in the
bungalow to tell the cooli, "You were engaged with a
certain salary a month. Now take your salary up today
and go away. From tomorrow, your services are not
required." Yet the cooli continues to do his duty.
So is a Jnani in the midst of worldly people. There are
many people in this world who behave like the people in
this bungalow. They are ignorant of the subtle. They
are ignorant of what karma is. Hence the comparison
of the world to this bungalow.**

Commentary: In this story, Sri Bhagawan is comparing the
bungalow to the human body and to this world. The cooli
is likened to the Siddha who warns people not to become
attached to worldliness. The chunam is likened to the dross
of worldliness, with attachment to the senses and to worldly
pleasures that cause people to believe they are the body and
that the goal of life is the pursuit of the pleasure and pain
they experience in this world.

The ignorant wander through life like the travelers visiting
that bungalow. They return, again and again, to the body to
live out their karmas, not realizing that those karmas, that
which causes them to return to the cycle of birth and death
over and over again, is due to their own ignorance of who
they really are. The Siddha, like the cooli in the story, even
without compensation of any kind, continues to live in God
and to share knowledge of the Truth with others. The duty
of those who are God-realized is to lead others.

**168. In a similar way, you must understand all matters.
One is standing still. Another is working. All are
imitating one another. They are ignorant of both justice
and injustice. After knowing justice, they will not stoop
to injustice. For a just man, it is very difficult to do
injustice. Such a man will never tell a lie, even though
his tongue were to be torn asunder. An unjust man
wants everything. A just man wants nothing. He is not**

afraid of anyone. The whole world is in him. The minds of the unjust people are in the world. It is the duty of every human being to know what is justice and what is injustice.

Commentary: It is important for you to understand the essence and workings of Shiva's Maya that is this world-appearance. In this world appearance, people who do not have the direct knowledge and experience of God resort to imitating each other. These people are ignorant of the fact that God's Will is justice. Because they don't understand this, they commit actions believing that they each are the doer of those actions.

This ignorance leads to a lack of discrimination that eventually leads to injustice. After becoming absorbed in God, a person will not stoop to injustice. Such a Jnani understands that her thoughts, speech and actions create a vibration that reverberates in this world-appearance and, therefore, she does not want to commit actions that will create a useless or harmful reverberation in Consciousness. Such a person is also virtuous and will not harm others by lying.

A Jnani has no desire for sense pleasures and worldly pleasures. He has no fear either. The entire world is in him. The minds of unjust people are absorbed in worldliness and the pursuit of pleasure and pain. Your life exists so that you can retrace your steps back to God. In this way, you will come to know for yourself what is justice and what is injustice. It is your duty to know these two.

169. Rivers and streamlets enter into the sea and there become one. Similarly, finite things become one in the infinite. Dualism loses itself in monism. Monism is oneness. This realization of the oneness is the most supreme.

Commentary: All forms and creatures in this universe are finite. Duality is transient also. All these are reflections of Supreme Consciousness. Just as rivers and streamlets enter into the sea, all sentient and insentient beings, and all perceived duality emanates from and is reabsorbed back into Shiva, the great ocean of Consciousness. This is Monism. Realization of God in this way is the most Supreme.

170. After a man has realized the oneness, he will no longer be born. Those who are immovably fixed in the idea of oneness die only when they desire to die. Such men are perfectly desireless. Realization of oneness is the most subtle one. What is the samesightedness (the indivisible sight) is realizing the Atman in all. This equality consists in realizing the one in the many. This is known as introspection. When the next world and this world are realized as one and the same, a man has attained same-sightedness. This is also called the union of Jivatma and the Paramatma. What is Jiva is mental modifications (vrittis). Paramatman is the Great Silence, who is above the three qualities. He knows not good and evil, cold and heat. He is qualityless, formless. He is No-Thing.

Commentary: Once Liberated, a yogi is not born again. Such a person leaves his body only when he decides it is time for him to pass. A Liberated being, a Siddha, is perfectly desireless and has complete samesightedness, seeing God in everything and everyone, everywhere. This is the subtle realization that such a Siddha has attained.

The Liberated yogi has complete Equality Consciousness. This Equality Consciousness consists of seeing God in all things. This is known as true introspection. When you realize that this world-appearance is a reflection of the next world, the inner realm of God, when you realize that all this is contained inside the body of Supreme Consciousness you attain samesightedness with the realization "As there, so here." This is the union of Shakti and Shiva, the union of the individual intellect with the divine Buddhi or will of God.

The Jiva, the individual bound soul, is a mass of mental modifications, an entity filled with notions and ideas that are limiting by their very nature. Paramatman, God, is the Great Silence who is above the three Gunas (sattva, rajas and tamas). Paramshiva (the formless absolute) does not experience good and evil nor cold or heat as such. The Absolute, Paramshiva has no qualities. That is formless. That is no thing. Shiva Consciousness is the Consciousness or outlook of this formless Absolute, God.

171. If you cover your body, then the more you will feel the cold. Those who decorate their bodies, feel the prouder. It is very difficult to banish the ego from us. Whitewashing is required for the inside of the wall more than the outside. The outer cleaning is to show to others but the inward cleanliness is for one's own benefit.

Commentary: The ego is very subtle and resists purification. For this reason it is difficult to banish. Attachment to the body, attachment to outer appearances and objects of desire, all these feed the ego and serve to further taint it with impurities. Just as the inside of a wall requires more attention and cleaning, our inner state requires much more attention than our outer appearance. Destroying the ego is for one's own benefit. This requires Sadhana. It begins with the desire to purge ourselves of ignorance of the Truth. This is an inner process and it is most important.

172. All is He, pervading everything. He is the One, pervading all creatures. Qualityless, the one Omkar, one, whose form is everlasting peace. Blesser of those

who have faith in Him. The same being punishes those
who ridicule His devotees. He makes the death of His
devotees easy. O Shiva! Do not lead me towards hell
but lead me towards You. The giver is Shiva.

Commentary: All is Shiva Consciousness (God). The
Absolute formless God known also as Paramshiva pervades
everything. He is the ONE pervading all creatures. Shiva
is the one without qualities. He is Omkar (the
reverberation of the Mantra Om). Shiva is everlasting
peace. He blesses those who cultivate Faith in him and
punishes those who ridicule and harm His disciples. He
makes the passing from the body of his disciples effortless.
O Shiva! Do not lead me towards hell but lead me towards
You. The giver is Shiva.

**173. A dead thing is without motion. It is soundless. A
living thing has the delusion of sound. It has
Consciousness. Conscious creatures have impressions
and movements. Creatures, conscious of sound, have
the delusion of sound. They have the light of Brahma in
them. Consciousness of creatures is light.**

**Men know the distinction between justice and injustice.
Lower animals have no distinction of such a sort. Man
stands at the head of all creation. There is nothing
impossible for man in this world. Man is in the
universe and the universe is in man. Man is the greatest
of animals.**

**Mind in man is fickle. In man, both this world and the
next, merge. Shivaloka is the third (divine) eye. The
Shiva nerve is the Sushumna nerve, also called the
Brahma nerve. The lord of Shivaloka is nothing but
Shiva-Shakti (Shiva's energy). What is Maya is in
Shiva. Shiva is not in Maya. Creation and destruction
are both Maya caused by Him. In the Great Self,
everything becomes latent-effect, soul, Manas, Brahma,**

**waking consciousness, Taraka, sleep, extreme
ignorance, and the whole of the external world.**

Commentary: A dead thing is motionless and soundless
because Chiti (the energy substratum of everything) has left
it. The perception of sound (the delusion of sound), the
ability to hear sound where it really does not exist, is
caused by Chiti. Creatures have movement and
impressions due to Chit Shakti. This energy is the Light of
Divine Consciousness inside them. The awareness of
forms is also the Light of God.

All human beings are endowed with a Conscience.
Therefore, they know the distinction between justice and
injustice and are able to embrace Conscience in the absence
of the ego. Those with restless minds who are attached to
egoism cannot make this distinction. Human Beings are
the greatest of all creatures. Nothing is impossible for them
because they have the ability to realize God and become
Liberated. The mind is fickle and must be made to dissolve
in the highest reality, Shiva. Shivaloka, the plane of
existence or abode of Shiva, is the realm entered when
one's Prana pierces the Ajna Chakra (third eye) fully.
Entry into Shivaloka dawns on the yogi when Shakti
purifies the central nerve (Sushumna) and then merges with
Shiva in the Sahasrar.

The Shiva nerve is the Sushumna Nadi, also called the
Brahma nerve. The lord of Shivaloka is nothing but Chiti
or Shakti (Shiva's energy). What is Maya (illusion) is in
Shiva, the Supreme Self. The Self is the cause of Maya.
Maya is not the cause by the Self, God. In Shiva, the entire
universe is contained in seed form. All things external are
reflections of the Supreme Subject, God, and cannot exist
without God, That - the Supreme Self.

**174. To probe into truth, requires subtle
discrimination. This subtle discrimination is Upadhi.**

The subtle is hidden in the gross. The seat of Upadhi is the heart space. When the Kundalini is raised to the heart space in the head, then, the breath is single. In this highest state, one sees the universe in one's Self.

Then one sees everything in Him. All the multitudinous changes are seen in oneself. Feeling of duality is hell. Feeling of absolute oneness is Mukti. Absolute Bhakti (love) is Mukti. Perfect peace, never perturbed peace, is the goal of man.

This is Yogananda, Paramananda. The ocean is bigger than all the rivers. The sea is almost boundless. You cannot measure the water of the ocean. It is not possible to practice Bhakti, leaving off Samsara. Being in Samsara, we must attain Mukti by being "this thing" and by doing "that thing." What is desire is Samsara. Desirelessness is Mukti. Then, one will enjoy eternal bliss, eternal wisdom Bliss. Eternal peace that is the highest Bliss, is the goal of man. When the mind is swimming in eternal Bliss, it is known as Mukti. Bhakti is the state of eternal Bliss.

Commentary: Upadhi is known as subtle discrimination. It actually refers to the seat of all discernment, THAT which has the power to discriminate because it is beyond Shiva's Maya. This is Upadhi. You have to be tuned in to this place, this Upadhi, in order to understand the Truth. That which is immanent in the world, also known as the gross, contains within it the Supreme "I" Consciousness of God. It is to this transcendental aspect of existence, residing in the heart of all living beings, that we must turn.

The heart space of a human being is in the head, the seat of Upadhi, the last of the three Shiva linghams in the subtle body, where Shiva sits eagerly awaiting his Goddess, Kundalini Shakti. When Shakti is united with Shiva in the head, then by raising the breath to the Sahasrar through internal (sushumna) breathing, you experience the highest state (Turyatita) and experience the entire Universe inside yourself. In this state, you see God everywhere and in everything. In this highest state, one realizes that the Manifestation, Sustenance and Withdrawal of this world occurs inside ones' own Self. Perfect peace is the goal of all human life.

This perfect peace is attained by merging your individual identity into the ocean of Shiva Consciousness. This merger takes place by cultivating Bhakti; complete Devotion and Surrender to God.

Bhakti cannot be cultivated by removing yourself from the world, nor your worldly responsibilities. The test of true Bhakti is attaining mad Love and Devotion for God and for the Guru, while fulfilling your worldly responsibilities. This means contact with Samsara, contact with the forms of this world without becoming of the world. It is only in this way that you can relinquish desire and merge with the eternal Bliss of the Absolute. This Bliss is the goal of your life. When you are able to dissolve the mind in this indescribable Joy on a permanent basis, that is Bhakti, that is Liberation.

175. God is in Bliss. In God, is Bliss. That is the nectar of wisdom. In that nectar, is Joy. When we approach that nectar, we experience Joy.

Commentary: God is Bliss and Bliss is God. The state of Bliss is Shiva's very nature and it is the nectar of wisdom. In that nectar is the Joy of the Self. When we approach Shiva, the Supreme Self, we experience pure Joy. This is the purpose of Sadhana.

176. The goal of humankind is Upanayanam, i.e. to be led to immortality. Dwelling in the cave of the heart is a person's goal. Living in the cave means living inside the body.

Commentary: The goal of human life is to realize God, to become Liberated from the bondage of ignorance. This is the purpose of a human birth. To become absorbed in God is the goal of humankind. Shiva Consciousness is what is referred to as the cave of the heart. It is the Paramatma (formless Absolute) that dwells in the Heart space in the head. Living in that cave means taking a human form to complete your karmas so that you can return go to God.

177. Meditate incessantly on the Paramatma who is in the Jivatma. Space is in you. It is in the head. Meditate on the heart space that is in the head.

Commentary: Meditate incessantly on Shiva-Shakti, the Absolute, who dwells inside you. Chidakasha, the great expanse of Supreme Consciousness, exists inside you in the Heart space in your head. This is the abode of Lord Shiva, the Absolute. Meditate on this Heart space that is in the head.

178. Those who are born deaf have not the least idea of sound. They have no desires. They have subtle discrimination. Those who are always in yoga sleep, have no difference between day and night, between sun and moon. To the subtle discrimination, all is one. Those who have annihilated the mind are human. Lower animals are so called, because they are in a lower stage of development. Sensual life is beastly life. The upward breath is the goal of humankind. The same is Gayatri, accomplished. The same is Yoga-Bliss.

Commentary: Just as a deaf person does not know what sound is and, therefore, has no expectation of hearing it, the yogi, having relinquished the desire for worldly pleasures, has no expectations of sense pleasures nor any desire for them. Such a Jnani has subtle discrimination and remains in the sleep of Yoga, completely absorbed in God at all times. For the Liberated, there is no difference between day and night or the sun and the moon. They see all as the one God. Those who have caused their minds to dissolve in Chit Shakti are true human beings. Those who are not absorbed in this state are in a lower stage of development. A life caught up in the pursuit of sensual desire is no better than a beast's life. It is just like that of an animal in the jungle. To obtain the Bliss of the Absolute, one must direct Prana inside the Sushumna Nadi to union with Shiva. That is the Bliss of Yoga.

179. One who has annihilated the manas is the universal teacher. One who has destroyed desire, root and branch, is the teacher of all.

Commentary: Only a person who has become completely absorbed in God Consciousness, annihilating his/her mind by merging the mind into the Supreme, only such a person is qualified to lead others. The person who has attained this state of Purnaham Vimarsha is the Universal spiritual leader. When the mind is merged completely in God, desire is destroyed and you become a Self-realized being.

180. He is a real Sanyasi who has burnt desire to ashes. He is the universal teacher. The universe is in those who have renounced desire. What is Chidakasha (space) is Sanyasa. The same is light and is Consciousness. The same is Divine light. The same is fire, internal, and external. The same is the fire of discrimination. This power of discrimination is in the universe.

Commentary: Only a person who has removed the seed of desire from his being can claim to be a Sanyasi. Taking Sanyas means renouncing the ego completely and forever. That is the only true Sanyas. A Sanyasi is one whose only desire is to serve God and humanity. A Sanyasi is one who has completely eliminated all craving and limited desire from his/her being. This person is a universal teacher.

The realization that the universe is contained inside a human being is a realization that dawns on one who has conquered craving and limiting desire by the Grace of one's chosen Guru.

Chidakasha, the Heart space in the head, is Sanyasa. This inner place is the Divine Light of Consciousness. It is the fire of Yoga that burns within and, once Liberation dawns, Chidakasha is also seen in everything and everyone, everywhere. Liberation is the power of subtle discrimination. This power or fire of discrimination is the experience of God in everything and everyone, everywhere. In this state, the Sanyasi no longer experiences a world but sees only the face of God.

181. Fire is essentially an internal thing. Fire is the supreme of all. The origin of all creation is fire. First, we must realize ourselves, and then impart it to others. This is the highest duty of man. When you feel pain, you must realize that others have pain just like you. When you feel hungry, you must realize that others have hunger just like you. We must think that what is our goal is also the goal of others.

When a physician develops a new medicine and he does not reveal it to others till his death, the medicine is lost to the world with him. One who does not know the ways and means to realize God, is not a man. The most supreme knowledge is the knowledge of God. This knowledge must be imparted to others so that they may understand it. Those who are hungry must be fed. Nobody asks you about God unless he has discriminative power.

Commentary: There is a Yajna (sacrificial fire) that burns inside you on a constant basis. This fire is the Kundalini Shakti and, once awakened by a Siddha, it burns all the impurities in your being. This internal fire is Supreme because it is the true place of all sacrifices and offerings. The first goal of human existence is to realize God through the awakening and nurturing of this inner fire. Once we are Liberated in this way, it is our duty to impart Yoga knowledge to others.

This is, in fact, the highest calling, the highest duty of a human being; to realize God and then share your knowledge and experience with others. When you feel pain, you must realize that others have pain just like you. When you feel hungry, you must realize that others have hunger just like you. Likewise, just as yourself, others also seek happiness and release from suffering. True Happiness and Bliss is the goal of all living beings. This is not just your goal, but the goal of others as well.

Just as a physician who discovers a cure to an illness but does not share it has not fulfilled his duty in life, to be blessed with the dawning of Liberation and then not to share that knowledge with others is misappropriating one's Dharma. Once the Master blesses you with the dawning of Liberation, don't keep it a secret. It is of no use that way. Share your blessing with others.

The most supreme knowledge is the knowledge of God. This knowledge must be imparted to others so that they may understand it. A person who does not have a Siddha Guru and a spiritual practice, cannot attain God. Those who are sincerely seeking the Truth are hungry for the experience of God within. They must be fed. People who seek to know God already have an understanding that there must be more to life than the mundane experience that is common to all and this is why they must be served.

182. The first requirement is faith. The second is devotion (Bhakti). Those who have no faith cannot have devotion. The judge listens to what the defendants say. Faith is just like that. When Buddhi has attained

acute discriminating power, we will experience Vivekananda. Vivekananda is Paramananda, Satchidananda. When existence (Sat) and knowledge (Chit) become one, Ananda will result. This is Brahmananda, Shivananda.

Commentary: First you must have Faith in God, Faith in the living Sadguru, and Faith in the practices. Without Faith, you cannot cultivate Devotion and, without Devotion, there is no progress on the spiritual path. The judge listens to what the defendants say. Faith is just like that.

When you have it, God comes looking for you and hears your prayers. God responds to Faith. When your individual intellect is purified in the fire of Sadhana, it will merge with the Divine and you will experience the Bliss of the Self and the complete freedom that is Sat-Chit-Ananda. When existence and awareness of the Truth become one, Bliss is the result. This Bliss is God, the Supreme Self.

183. Shiva is in you. You are in Shiva. Maya is in you. Creation and destruction are both in Maya. Those who are free from the bondage of the qualities (Trigunas) are free from Maya. He who is free from the delusion that he is the body, is nothing but Bliss incarnate. That which is free from the idea of "honor" and "dishonor" is internal.

Commentary: God dwells within you as you. You are Shiva and Shiva is you. Due to the illusion of this world appearance, the universe comes into being and is eventually destroyed. Life and death are part of the illusion of objects (people, places and things) existing separate from God. Although it may seem that you participate in this illusion, you are not this Maya. Your essence is the God-principle, the one who has created this Maya. To be free from the bondage of this Maya, one must rise above the influence of the three Gunas (Sattva, Rajas and Tamas).

If you are completely free from the notion that you are the body, if this is your constant awareness, you are free of the three Gunas and Bliss is your constant state. That which is beyond all notions of "honor" and "dishonor" can be called God within. Contemplating this is known as turning within. The goal of life is to merge with that God-principle.

184. In this world, those who are indifferent to honor and dishonor, have attained the goal. Only such people have attained peace.

Commentary: Those who have risen above pleasure and pain and have transcended both virtue and vice have attained the goal. Transcending honor and dishonor, transcending both virtue and vice means rising above praise and blame so that you have no ego, regardless of whether you have or have not attained virtue. Such people live to serve God and do not create any karmas in their actions. Such a person has become Peace itself.

185. In the infinite (indivisible), there is no finite (divisible). Those who are without a Guru, cannot attain the goal.

Commentary: Shiva-Shakti, the God-principle in its purest form, has no attributes and is without qualities. Shiva-Shakti is eternal and has no limitations in this, its transcendental aspect. Those who do not follow a Siddha and the instruction of such a Master cannot experience this.

186. Consider the physical eye. A blind man may have a light in his hand but the light is of no use to him. Those who have eaten a bellyful do not require food any more. Suppose, the cooking is over. You are not

satisfied by simply smelling the food. Your hunger is appeased only if you eat the food cooked. If you hold a piece of gold in your hand, it is of no use. It should be melted in the fire. Its dross should be removed. Then only, it shines brilliantly. Similarly, the dross of the soul is desire and anger. These should be destroyed.

Commentary: A blind person can't see a light, even if that light is starring him in the face. In the same way, those who are ignorant of the Truth cannot experience it, even though it exists right inside their own being. On the other hand, just as one who has eaten a belly full does not want any more food, a Yogi who has experienced the Master's Grace no longer wants the expectation of worldly outcomes.

Your hunger is not satisfied from simply smelling great food. It is only satisfied when you eat the food. Likewise, you cannot attain Liberation by entertaining clever intellectual discussions about God. You can only realize Shiva by devouring the Grace and instruction of a Siddha (spiritually-perfected Love being). Gold only has real value when the dross is removed from it and it is polished clean. Only then does it shine brilliantly. In the same way, in order to experience the brilliant Light of Divine Consciousness within your own being, desire and anger must be destroyed.

187. What the nest is to the bird, is the body to the soul. The body is the house of the soul. What is "that house" and what is "this house" is subtle discrimination. The gross body is the beggarly house. What to say of Brahmananda! No one can describe it. Truly, truly, realize that the eternal Atman is ONE in ALL. Hari is not the knower. Shiva is the knower. What is Hari is wandering. "Hari! Hari! I want this." "I want that." "Give me, give me," you say. This is of no use. Such a man is never happy.

Let Hari merge in Hara. Burn Hari in Hara. Saying "Hari, Hari" is nothing but mental delusion. You praise Hara, hiding this delusion in your mind!   He who has given you eternal joy is Shiva. Shiva is the giver of eternal Mukti (liberation) and eternal Bhakti. What is Hari is keeping the mind in the world. Shiva is keeping the whole universe in one's Self. Saying "Hari, Hari" is going down. But Shiva is the guide to the path of Bliss. Mukti is obtained by the upward course of Prana. Hari is like a horse without reins.

Commentary: Just as the nest is the home for a bird, the body is the home or temple that houses the Atman. And there is no difference between God inside the "house" of your body and God outside. Attachment to worldliness makes you a beggar. So, what of the Supreme state of Shiva Consciousness! To understand this requires the subtle discrimination acquired through Sadhana under the leadership of a Sadguru. Realize that the eternal Atman has taken all the forms of existence. It is only God that exists everywhere.

In many Yoga traditions, it has become common to worship Lord Vishnu (Hari) and his consort. Vishnu is the sustainer of the universe and also the one who grants boons of wealth and prosperity. Many, many students of Yoga have gotten caught up in treating the spiritual path as a business venture. They perform their worship as a means of bartering for God's blessings for money, sex, a husband, a wife, a child or a successful outcome for a business or employment endeavor. In this way, their worship becomes tainted and they become more and more attached to sense pleasures and worldly pleasures, rather than rising above these to experience God.

Spirituality is not a field to grow crops in. This is what Sri Nityananda tells us. The Self, God is the knower of the field. It is through this Ultimate Reality alone that

Liberation dawns, not through desiring to possess worldly outcomes. You can never be happy while engaging your limiting desire and cravings for this and that. You praise God superficially while, all the time, harboring desires for the fulfillment of worldly pleasures in your mind.

Give these up! Give up even the notion of the expectation of such things. Merge Hari in Hara (Shiva) in this way! Become God in this way and experience eternal joy. It is Shiva (the Universal God-principle) who bestows Liberation and eternal Love and Devotion. Hari is the focus on worldliness and the constant wish for more objects of craving and desire. Shiva Consciousness is seeing God as emanating from your own being.

In this way, you have no worries or cravings. Shiva is the guide to the path of Joy. Constant worship of Hari is the desire for worldliness. Liberation is attained by directing the upward breath into the Sushumna Nadi so that Kundalini Shakti can be carried to union with Shiva in the Sahasrar, the highest spiritual center. The desire for sense pleasures and worldly pleasures is like riding a wild horse without reigns, meaning that your life is out of control.

188. To ride a horse safely in the midst of a crowd of two thousand people, the rider must be efficient. Buddhi (intelligence) is above. Manas (mind) is below. Buddhi is the king. Manas is the prime minister. Mind must be subordinate to Buddhi.

The first is sound. The second is the impression that the sound carries. The primary Guru is the Manas. The secondary preceptor is he who initiates you. The secondary Guru is the teacher. The primary Guru is that which practices. Realization is the primary Guru. You cannot have a secondary preceptor unless you have a desire to have him. When you have the desire to possess a thing you require a secondary Guru. The

secondary Guru is he who shows you the well. The primary Guru is he who drinks water from the well. The primary preceptor banishes the darkness in you, giving you light. Darkness is ignorance. Light is knowledge. He who shows you the path to the subtle, leaving aside the gross, is the Guru. The one Guru who is in all is the Lord of the Universe. One is not the Guru to the other. One is only a secondary Guru.

Guru is the Lord of the Universe. He is the Omkar, Brahma, Vishnu, Maheshwara, the origin of Para-Brahma. Vishnu is the mental modifications (Vrittis). What is Shiva is the decoration of the body. Brahmeshwara is leaving aside of the body-idea, like the kernel of a dry coconut that is separated from the outer covering.

Commentary: Just as riding a horse through a crowd of thousands of people without trampling anyone or hurting yourself requires great proficiency; scaling the mountain of samsara, crossing the vast ocean of worldliness and ignorance requires skill through practice. Buddhi, the intellect, must be purified. It is through the purified intellect that the Light of Consciousness flows.

The mind is subordinate to the intellect. Once the intellect becomes pure, the mind follows, just as sound naturally follows vibration. The primary Guru, the primary teacher is God. The secondary Guru (the primary Guru in physical form) is the one who initiates you and instructs you, until you are set on your own path. The secondary Guru is the Siddha who leads you to the threshold of Liberation.

The primary Guru is the in-dweller, the witness of your thoughts, that Chit Shakti that gives life to your spiritual practice. Realization is complete identification with this primary Guru. When you sincerely desire to know God, the Sadguru enters your life, not otherwise. As with

anything else in life, if you have a desire to know a thing
well, you have to find a leader or mentor. It is the same in
spiritual life. The secondary Guru or preceptor is the one
who guides you to the well of your own inner essence. The
primary Guru or preceptor, the Shiva-Shakti power,
banishes the darkness within you and shows you the light,
through your own spiritual practice, as instructed by the
secondary Guru.

This requires the initiation of Shaktipat, full Kundalini
Awakening to fully realize. What is called darkness is
ignorance of your own true nature. What is called light is
your complete knowledge and awareness of your identity
with Shiva. He who shows you the path to that God-
principle inside, he who instructs you to set your ego aside,
to set your cravings for the gross world of limited desires
aside, only such a person can be called a Guru.

Such a being is one with the primary Guru. In fact, a
Siddha Guru, is God, having had his/her individual identity
erased by his own Guru. Upon the receipt of Shaktipat, the
primary Guru and the secondary Guru (the primary Guru in
physical form) become one in the Disciple. Shiva, the
Supreme Self is the Guru of all. The outer Guru is not the
guru to Shiva, but one with Shiva.

**189. All things with form are OMKAR. OMKAR is the
divine in them. What is OMKAR is the subtle Bindu.
Omkar pervades both in and out, in the form of air. It
is impossible to describe Shiva-Shakti. Only those who
have experienced it can describe what it is. Without
experience, it is impossible to describe what Shiva-
Shakti is. Men of book knowledge cannot describe it.
But those who have the knowledge of the Atman can
describe it.**

Commentary: OMKAR, the essence of Being-Awareness
and Bliss (Sat-Chit Ananda), in the form of the mantra OM,

is inherent in all forms. Om is the divine in these forms. The subtle Bindu, the seed of Unmesha (the outward unfolding of divine conscious energy) that resides in God's being as Chit Shakti, in its purest form, OM. This OM is the Shiva-Shakti power.

The Shiva-Shakti power, the energy substratum of everything, pervades everything inside and out in the form of Prana that enters and exists in living beings. It is impossible to describe with mundane words, the highest power of the Supreme Self. Only those who have experienced it can describe what it is. People who have intellectual knowledge of God cannot describe oneness with God. But those who have the inner knowledge of God can describe the direct experience of it.

190. If you see the dawn in the heart sky, it is possible to describe it. One must experience these things in one's Self. What is called Jnana is in Buddhi (intelligence). Those in whom Buddhi and Jnana have become one, can describe what this is. Those in whom intelligence and Jnana are separate, cannot describe what it is.

What is called subtle discrimination is the union of Buddhi and Jnana. The reflection of the Sun ripples in the water. So also, is mind. If mind is fickle, it is enamored of Maya. This madness (delusion) is caused by the gross. There is a madness caused by subtle discrimination. This is divine madness. The gross madness is the gross discrimination.

Whatever we may eat, the path of food to the stomach is the same. Whatever may be the contents of letters and post cards and various newspapers, the box in which they are posted is the same. The tongue distinguishes between things pungent and things sour. To the mind, there is no such difference. Just as we cage a bird

binding its legs and then teach it to speak, so also intelligence becomes one with the soul when it is caged in the cage of Manas.

Commentary: There are thousands of suns inside. These suns are called the Adityas and they are much more brilliant than the sun in our solar system. They can be seen in Chidakasha, the great expanse of the heart, the sky of Divine Consciousness. This experience is impossible to describe without having it for yourself.

Jnana is knowledge and wisdom that arises spontaneously from within when your individual intellect is merged in the Self. When this happens, the experience of the Adityas dawns. This is the dawn experienced in the Heart space reflected in the head. Subtle discrimination is the state of one whose Buddhi (individual intellect) has merged in Shiva. Such a person is a Jnani (knower of the highest Truth).

The mind is a contracted form of Supreme Consciousness. Therefore, it has great power. If the mind is not properly trained and directed back inside, it becomes enthralled and attached to the illusion of worldliness. Shiva's Maya is this illusion. It is madness caused by attachment to craving and desire for sense pleasures and worldly pleasures that are experienced in a world that is neither real or unreal, but a mere perception.

Subtle discrimination is Divine madness. It is mad love for God. This type of madness frees you from the bondage of ignorance. The gross world created by Shiva's Maya is a madness that binds. Just as all food goes to the same place to be digested, all life emanates from and returns to that ONE God. All letters and post cards are delivered to the same place, a mailbox. In the same way all thoughts, notions and ideas rise from and subside in the Self.

The mind that has not experienced God sees differences and believes itself to be separate from other objects (people, places and things). The mind that is merged in God sees no such differences. We must steady the mind in the heart of the Self and merge the individual intellect into That. The way to accomplish this is by directing the mind back inside through Meditation.

191. The Lord of Mukti is Shiva. Shiva is the Linga in the head. This Linga is nothing but Omkar. Enlightenment is the most important thing. Without nerves, there is no sound. Bhakti may be compared to the oil in a lamp. Nerves may be red to the wick. Subtle discrimination is the flame or the light. The nerves are the glass of the lantern. The various air holes of the lantern are the Brahma-Randhras. The form of discrimination is intelligence.

Commentary: The Lord of Liberation, the one who grants the state of God-realization, is Shiva. Shiva is the Lingham, the form of the Absolute in the Sahasrar. This Lingam has a vibration that makes the sound OM. Enlightenment is the goal of life. It is more important than any other effort. Just as you cannot hear properly without the nerves in your body, you can't live a joyful life free from suffering without crossing over to the other shore, the shore of God.

Bhakti, complete love and devotion for God and the Guru is the key to this journey. Having this Bhakti and performing Sadhana purifies your entire being and you become immersed in the Supreme Self. This absorption in God is what we call intelligence.

192. If you hold nose and mouth tight, you are not able to talk. Similarly, a thing that does not breathe does not emit sound. Just as water goes on diminishing in a well in summer, so also, the power of the breath goes on

diminishing in the body. When the water is moving, the air moves along with it. You can live without food or without drinking coffee for five days. But you cannot live for five minutes without breathing.

Commentary: Prana Shakti, the life force contained in the breath, is the cause of existence as we know it. Without this Prana Shakti there is no sound to be heard and no activity of any kind. Prana causes the blood to flow, the heart to pump and all the bodily functions to work. As this Prana decreases in the body through old age, the body loses its luster and starts to decline. In this way, we can clearly see that Prana Shakti is the cause, not the body. There can be life for a while without food. But life stops immediately without Prana.

193. The highest of all powers is the power of Maya. A dead body and so also a stone are unable to talk. Likewise, if air does not act, fire cannot burn. If breathing is not regular, the fire of digestion will be impaired. When the digestive fire does not act properly, the phlegm in the lungs becomes hard. Fat increases in the body. The food that is eaten remains in the stomach undigested. If there is any obstruction in the pump, water will not flow out properly. Similarly, if the breathing becomes difficult, fever, thickening of the mucus are caused. By this, all diseases are caused.

Commentary: In the realm of this world-appearance, in the activity of existence, it is Shiva's Maya (illusion of activity) that causes this Prana Shakti, this air, to flow in all living creatures. This Prana Vayu, acting on the power of Shiva's Maya, is what gives life. Without it, all things die. There is no fire without air. The fire of Yoga cannot even burn without Prana. Prana, when directed properly in the three nerves, Ida, Pingala and Sushumna, causes proper digestion and purifies all the bodily functions. If the proper

movement of Prana in the body by breathing is obstructed
in any way, the result is illness and disease.

**194. Everything comes out from within, not from
without. One becomes bad by oneself. One becomes
good by oneself. Similarly, there should be Omkar
breathing within. Then, there is purity. When evil
merges in the good, that evil is transformed into good.
The thing in your own hand has no smell. It has no
price. A thing that is got from others has smell. It has
price. A Raja yogi Mahatma is Nityananda, all
pervasive Omkar, all-pervasive Pranava. He who is the
Sri Guru is Nityananda.**

**In the beginning, before perfect peace is attained, the
power of Maya (delusion) in us will be greatly
manifested. Wherever you turn your eyes, you see
serpents. In the beginning, when you sit for practice,
the heaviness of a mountain is experienced. At times,
you feel as if you leave off the ground. You feel as if you
are sitting in the sea. You feel as if hot water is poured
on you.**

**At another time, you feel as if you are sitting in a grand
upper story. Sometime you feel like a needle. At
another time, you feel like a leaf. Sometime you do not
feel whether you are walking or sitting or talking. At
another time all feeling comes to a stand still.
Sometimes, the body becomes quite motionless, like a
coconut tree. At another time, human beings appear
like actors in a dramatic performance.**

**At one time you see black faces. In perfect peace, one
indivisible whiteness is visible. Light is in darkness.
Darkness is in light. The whole universe is in darkness.
In the universe is light. At one time, all this appears
like a bioscopic performance. At another time, like Sat
Chit Ananda. At one time, questions arise: "Why have**

**men come into this world?" "Whither are they going?"
They do not know what their main duty is.**

**Coming down is not permanent. Going up and up, is
permanent. To those who have gone step by step to the
upper story and look around, what is heard, what
appears, what is done, all is like a net that cannot be cut
through. All penetrating Omkar is the all penetrating
Pranava. Birds are like airplanes. Men are like beasts.
Beasts are like men. Dogs are like Jnanis.**

**If you feed a dog, it will never forget you till its death.
It will have constant love for the master who has fed it
but once. Men have no subtle discrimination. They
think not whence they have come and whither they are
bound. A man of perfectly ripe understanding should
be like a dog.**

Commentary: There is no outer world. What you call
"outer" and "world" is actually contained inside the body
of Supreme Shiva Consciousness. What is called
"external" is actually taking place on your own inner
screen. For this reason, you get what you meditate on.
What you think, you become. If you think impure or evil
thoughts, you become evil. If you think good, useful and
pure thoughts, you become virtuous. And if you merge
your thinking and mind in the formless Absolute inside
your own being, you become all-pervasive, you become
Omkar.

To merge your mind in God in this way requires practice
under the guidance of a Siddha. Once your Kundalini is
awakened by a Shaktipat Guru, there are many different
kinds of Kriyas that you experience before you attain the
purity of the Self. As you do your daily Sadhana, at times
you will feel heavy and at other times light. Sometimes
you will experience deep emotional upheaval and at other
times you will feel elated.

At times, you may see different kinds of lights inside or hear a variety of sounds and celestial music. Sometimes, you will view people, places and things as if watching a movie and, at other times, you will feel like you are in the movie. This is all due to the movement (kriya) of the Shakti. People everywhere have lost the real meaning and goal of life. They think they are pursuing happiness when they are actually courting misery. They think suffering is what life is about. For those who have a Guru, this is not the case.

Under the direct instruction of a Siddha you are able to gradually heighten your conscious awareness and experience of God so that you elevate yourself, step by step, to merge with the Absolute. If this is done gradually with the proper spiritual leadership, the final state is permanent and you will never again fall prey to ignorance. However, to accomplish this, you have to be loyal like a dog. Having seen the light that the Guru has shown you, you must never turn away from it. This is how you become permanently established in Omkar.

195. If you go to see a king, you have not the boldness to tell him to his face what his defects are. But behind his back, you criticize him. So also, worldly people are not bold enough to criticize a Jnani to his face. If you gaze at the brilliance of the sun and come into the house, you see nothing for a while. Similarly, if you emerge from a dark place into a light place, you cannot know whence you emerged.

Commentary: Rather than questioning the Guru face-to-face, the ignorant criticize the Master and the path behind his back. If you question a Siddha to his face, at least there is a chance for your ignorance and doubt to be removed. Such a Jnani like the Siddha Guru lives in a state that is very different and unfamiliar to those who have never tread the path to God-realization. Spending time in the company of such a saint is like gazing directly into the sun's light and then turning away from it. Your own sight is blinded for a short period.

Similarly, if you emerge from your own ignorance for the first time, you can't know much about the new space that you have encountered. If you've never built a skyscraper, you are in no place to tell the engineers that the building is not built right. In the same way, unless you have followed the instruction of a Sadguru and done spiritual practice for a while, you don't have the experience with which to criticize. Only he who first obeys can know and then command.

196. Suppose a man awakes from a sleep out of fear, and sits up. Then he is so confused that he has no clear knowledge of anything. So also, Jnanis who are always in "Yoga-Nidra" (yoga sleep) do not know anything about the external world. If you have an umbrella, your head does not become wet by rainwater. Those who take meals daily, have hunger. Those who are entirely merged in cold water do not feel cold. A perfect man is never excited to anger. A fried seed cannot sprout. Like gold, well burnished, your mind should be always pure.

Commentary: When you suddenly wake from a deep sleep out of fear, for a moment, you have no awareness of the world around you or the fact that you even exist. For a Siddha, the universe does not exist. Only God exists. A Jnani such as this experiences only God in everything and everyone, everywhere and is not conscious of an external world apart from God.

This state is called Yoga Nidra or the deep sleep of Yoga that is the state of Purnaham Vimarsha. Once in this state, you are not affected in the least by pain and pleasure and you have no expectations of sense pleasures and worldly pleasures. Just as an umbrella protects you from rainwater, absorption in the Self protects you from the bondage of this world. Just as one who eats has desire for more food, those who crave sense pleasures are always hungry for more. To become immune to Maya (the illusory aspect of this world), you must be in Maya, just as one who is entirely submerged in cold water does not feel the cold.

You have to be in this world without being of this world in order to attain God. The Jnani is ever immersed in God and does not experience the pain and pleasure of craving and desire. A perfect person is never lost in anger. Once you fry a seed, it will never sprout again. In the same way, once you merge your mind in Shiva, it will become pure and never wander in Samsara again. To perfect this you have to be fully present with the Self while in Maya (worldliness) in order to cross it.

197. A high-class cobra has internal Pranayama. A cobra is very attentive to the sweet music, arising from a musical instrument called Nagaswara. A Jnani loves ALL as a cow loves its own calf. This is what is called same-sightedness. There is no house that is without doors. There is no cooking without vessels. A dog feeds on food, cooked either in earthen vessels or in gold vessels. Birds think of today's necessities, never tomorrow's. A seed, kept in a closed box, never sprouts. Such a seed never yields fruits. If it is sowed in earth (and watered), it will sprout and yield fruits. Hence, we must practice and get experience. It is you yourself who is responsible either for happiness or misery.

Commentary: God exists even in a Cobra. Even a Cobra knows Pranayama. When it breathes internally, it can hear music and dance to its vibration. In the same way, a Jnani, having mastered internal breathing, is tuned into the Vibration of Divine Consciousness all the time. Such a

Siddha loves all people and things equally, as a cow loves its own calf. This is what is known as samesightedness.

You can't have a house without doors and you can't cook food without a pot. In the same way, you can't know God without Sadhana, without spiritual practice under the leadership of a Sadguru. Birds think of today's needs only. They live one day at a time. In the same way, people should spend a lot less time planning for a future that does not exist and much more time living in the present moment. The present moment is the only moment in which God can be known.

A seed cannot sprout if left in a box. It will only sprout if put into the earth and watered. You are the source of your own happiness and misery. If you want freedom from bondage and ignorance, you have to plant the seed of Sadhana so that you can gain direct experience and knowledge of Shiva, God.

198. Anybody can handle a lamp without distinction of caste and creed. So also, the sun gives the same light to all. Sun is visible to all alike. Fire is visible to all alike. Supreme Buddhi (intelligence) and Jnana (knowledge) are one to those who have developed in them the power of the internal eye.

Commentary: God does not discriminate. Just as the sun shines on all equally, regardless of caste, race or creed, God offers His Grace to all who will receive it. The knower, that which is to be known and the object of knowledge are all one in the same to those who have realized Shiva-Shakti, the highest power. This is Equality Consciousness.

199. Those who have no subtle discrimination are not worth the name "men." A man is not an animal. The gross is the body idea. The subtle is the thought of Atman. Jivatma is the gross. Paramatma is the subtle.

**Without the gross, the subtle cannot be realized.
Without a foundation, a house cannot be erected.
Thought power (power of discrimination) is what is
called Shiva-Shakti. The union of Jivatma and
Paramatma is called Shiva-Shakti. When this power is
intensified, man becomes "superman." A superman is a
happy man. He is a Brahmin, knower of Brahma.
Vedantic conduct or behavior is true character
formation.**

Commentary: Those who have not realized God are not
worth the name human being. Human Beings are not
animals. They have the ability to realize God while still in
the body. This is a gift that is foolish to waste. What is
called gross is the idea that the body is the doer and
experiencer of all actions. Jivatma, the individual bound
soul is of this gross nature. Shiva Consciousness is the
subtle.

You can't realize Shiva-Shakti without a body and without
being in Samsara. The power inherent in thought is really
Shiva-Shakti, God's power. The union of the Jiva with
Shiva is also called Shiva-Shakti. When this internal power
is fully realized, you become superhuman. A superhuman
being is one who lives in a state of constant Bliss and
eternal Joy. Such a person is both a Brahmin and the
knower of Brahma. The conduct and behavior put forth in
the Vedas regarding Sadhana builds true character.

**200. He who is desireless is an Acharya (great Guru).
Desireless man is the Sanyasi. He is an Avadhoota in
this world who has abandoned desire. Avadhoot is a
man of the first class. He is the most supreme of men.
There is no state higher than that of Avadhoot.
Avadhoot is he who is above all. He to whom this world
and the next have become one is an Avadhoot.
Consciousness sky, real sky, emancipation from
bondage, the Bliss of self government, the Bliss of**

Brahma, real Bliss, yoga Bliss, fulfillment of human birth, lordship of Mukti, power to teach emperors; these are the "possessions" of an Avadhoota.

Commentary: That person who has mastered dispassion, who has risen above attachment and aversion and who has no other desire than to love and serve God, such a person can be called desireless. That person is an Acharya, a Sadguru. One can only be called a Sanyasi who has risen above limiting desire by merging his/her ego with the Supreme "I" Consciousness of God. Only a person who has abandoned the limiting desire of the ego can be known as an Avadhoot.

Avadhoots relish in the constant rapture of Purnaham Vimarsha. Such a person is the best of human beings, the highest of deities. There is no state higher than the state of the Avadhoot, Shivo'ham. Such a Siddha is God and God is such a Siddha. The person who experiences this world as nothing but a Play of Divine Consciousness, the person who experiences Shiva permeating this entire Universe and sees no difference between this world and the formless Paramashiva, this person alone is an Avadhoot.

The one who experiences on a constant basis the great expanse of supreme awareness that is Chidakasha, who experiences this real sky, emancipation from bondage, the Bliss of self-government, the Bliss of Brahma, real Bliss, yoga Bliss, fulfillment of human birth, lordship of Mukti, power to teach emperors; such a person "possesses" all that is worth having. An Avadhoot is one from whom all these flow. This is the meaning of Acharya or Siddha.

201. He who meditates on God and who is desireless, is the saviour of the world. He who meditates on God is the Muni (sage). He is Shiva and Shiva is he. All that is visible is Shiva.

Commentary: The person who meditates on Shiva, on the Self within, without any other desire but to merge with his/her own Divinity; this person, with practice, does become a Siddha, a savior of the world. In time, that person who meditates on God becomes a sage of steady wisdom and then leads others. Such a person is Shiva and Shiva is that sage. When you realize the Self by the Self, you will realize that nothing exists that is not Shiva who is your very own Self.

202. One who has not realized the truth is a beggar. One who has not destroyed delusion, one who has not left off the downward (worldly) path, is a beggar.

Commentary: Without God-realization, you are subject to illusion, delusion and the suffering wrought by the pair of opposites, pain and pleasure. These are limitations that severely restrict your authorship, agency and omniscience and this limitation causes you to wander about relying on your own wits instead of God's Grace. This does make you a beggar.

203. Those who are indifferent to honor and dishonor enjoy Bliss, true Bliss that is the same as Brahmananda, i.e., at-one-ment with the Godhead. If we concentrate our intellectual powers for five minutes, we feel that Bliss. Those who have not realized the primordial cause, have not realized the goal of life. Like flies falling into the flame of a burning lamp, those who have not realized the truth, are caught, in the net of delusion. The flies repeatedly see the lamp. They repeatedly hover round the lamp and, at last, they fall into it and die.

Commentary: Those who are indifferent to honor and dishonor, enjoy Bliss, true Bliss that is the same as being one with Shiva. If we turn the mind inside, even for five minutes, we can experience that Bliss. Those who have not realized their own primordial nature as God, the Self, have not attained the goal of life.

Flies hover around a burning lamp. They watch their brother and sister flies being burned to death by the fire of the lamp. And yet, while watching other flies go to their death, these flies continue to hover around the burning lamp. Human beings are also deluded in this way. Even after observing the result of being trapped in the pair of opposites, pleasure and pain, they continue to crave pleasure and pain. To rise above this pleasure and pain, you have to make a concerted effort to realize its cause and to realize That One who is beyond the illusion of this world-appearance.

204. Those who do not practice Pranayama (control of breath) have no yoga. It is impossible to draw water from a well without a rope. Those who are not free from bondage have no peace. No one can live without drinking water. Those who have annihilated the mind, are desireless. Babies are Raja yogis till the sixth month. After the brain is developed, the same baby is Hatha yogi.

The mind in such babies is very fickle. Because the discriminating power is less in them. Babies cannot distinguish between a lump of sugar and a lump of earth. Hence, such babies regard earth and sugar as the same. The fruit is always at the top of the tree. Similarly, the fruit in man is upwards. If you plant a coconut in the earth, coconuts are eventually seen at the top of the coconut tree. For every tree, the fruit is at the top.

Commentary: It is not possible to transform human awareness into Divine awareness without learning Pranayama from one who has mastered it. It is impossible to draw water from a well without a rope attached to a bucket. In the same way, it is not possible to draw Kundalini Shakti upward into the Sahasrar without directing the breath into the Sushumna Nadi and upward, by the practice of Pranayam.

Just as there would be no life without water, no one can live without Prana. Therefore, this Prana is a very important element in Sadhana. You cannot have peace without freeing yourself from the fetters of the ego and the fickle mind. Those who have dissolved the mind completely in the Absolute are desireless. A child of less than six months old is like this, a Raja Yogi. Before six months, a child's brain is not focused on the mundane, empirical knowledge of this world-appearance and is still absorbed in the inner Truth.

After six months, as the child's brain develops, the child becomes a Hatha yogi, one who is more concerned about the body and the sublimation of the Shakti to achieve outer desires. At this stage, the mind becomes fickle. Prior to this stage, a child is in a state of wonder and does not differentiate between objects. Fruit on a tree is always at the top of the tree. In the same way, the fruit of Yoga is at the top, in the head (crown chakra) of a human being. The upward path is the path of the rising Kundalini Shakti that eventually makes its home in the Sahasrar. In Yoga, this is where you must go.

205. The umbrella does not hold the person. All is held by the mind. When the mental moods are destroyed, all differences disappear. Such a being has no desire. He is a Sanyasi. He is a yogi. A person who has Manas wants everything. A person who has no Manas, has everything in himself. Just as in a steamer, there are all sorts of commodities, so also, a being who has conquered the mind has the whole world in himself.

Commentary: Objects like an umbrella are not superior to human beings. Because you have a mind, you are the creator of those objects and the perceiver of the entire Universe. God makes a human being. A human being does not make God. This world-appearance is a mental representation created by Shiva Consciousness itself. When the mental moods of the mind are destroyed, all differences disappear and Equality Consciousness dawns.

For one who has this Equality Consciousness, there is no desire. Such a person is a Sanyasi, a Yogi. A person whose mind is not merged in God chases after desire and craving and only wants more and more. When the mind is dissolved in the Shakti of Shiva, the Absolute, the Yogi realizes that everything is contained inside him/herself. This realization dawns when the mind is conquered completely.

206. When a boat is sailing, everything around appears to move. So also, when mind is disappearing, everything appears to whirl round. What is experienced in sleep is not experienced in the waking state. What is experienced in the waking state is not experienced in sleep. If you place a vessel, without water, over fire, no sound is produced. In order to produce sound, water is necessary.

So also, those who have no subtle discrimination will not be benefitted. If you are bitten by a cobra in sleep, you will not die. In sleep, mind is quiescent. When there is Manas, there is everything. What is called creation is a mental affection. When there is thorough introspection, there is no creation.

Commentary: As the mind is purified through meditation, and as it migrates back to its primordial form as Chiti (Samanya Spanda), internal movement is experienced. A lot of this movement is part of the purification process as emotions, memories, ideas and notions are purged from the mind and the rest of the Antahkarana (psychic instrument). This purification process makes things seem, at times, like they are whirling around out of control. But this is just Shakti doing its work.

The waking state and the deep sleep state are two different realms. The waking state is the act of creation. When the mind turns outward and entertains ideas, thoughts and notions, this world-appearance comes into being. In deep sleep, you experience an absolute void because the mind is completely quiet and is resting in Chiti. This state is motionless and without sound. It is a state that is very close to the state of subtle discrimination that occurs when the mind is consciously merged in the Supreme Self.

In deep sleep, nothing affects you, not even a cobra bite. The reason for this is, in deep sleep there is no mind to experience the cobra bite or even identify it as a cobra bite. If you don't have subtle discrimination, you can't benefit from the ultimate experience of God. When the Manas (mind) is focused on anything other than Shiva Consciousness, there is creation in the form of this world-appearance. Creation is simply mental affection or mental representation. When the mind is dissolved in Chit Shakti, the entire creation dissolves.

207. In the beginning of practice, the neophyte should diminish sleep. When practicing moderation in diet, one should not bathe in cold water. If you bathe once in four or five hours in cold water, the blood circulation in the body will not be regular. An actor in a theatre first acts behind the curtain. Then he comes out. In the beginning, there must be secrecy. Afterwards, it is not necessary. If you pour water in a vessel that is already full, that water flows out. So also, when perfect peace is attained it becomes known to all. Such a person has no

desire. This peace is the supreme. Perfect peace means union with the Godhead.

Commentary: There is a discipline to Sadhana and that discipline differs for seekers in the early stages of their spiritual practice. In the beginning of Sadhana, when you are new to meditation and spiritual practice, it is good not to sleep too much so that you can practice directing your awareness consciously back inside on the Self. It is better to sleep less and meditate more. Just as bathing in cold water a lot will reduce your circulation, sleeping too much will dull your experience of the awakened Kundalini.

So, you should try to sleep less because your experience of the void (the third body) and the Turiya state (the fourth body) should be a conscious experience, not an unconscious one. An actor first rehearses a role in private for a while before performing it on stage for an audience. In the same way, in the early stages of your Sadhana you should practice vigilantly without discussing your experiences and practices with others, especially those who are not on a spiritual path and may be prone to ridiculing or criticizing your practice.

People fear what they don't understand. So, until you have become rooted in your practice and developed a firm understanding of the benefits of your Sadhana, practice in secrecy. Just as when you pour water into a vessel that is already full, the water pours out, in the very advanced stages of a yogi's Sadhana, he becomes so full of Shakti that it naturally overflows into the lives of others. Having attained the final state, such a yogi becomes a place of perfect peace for all.

208. The form of God is peace. OM and peace are His forms. He is without form. He is without change. He is above discrimination. He is Bliss, absolute. Like the lulling of children to sleep in the cradle, we must sleep

internally with the Manas for the pillow. We must be successful in each and every test. We cannot get employment unless we succeed in the tests. Knowing to speak English but not knowing how to write is not knowing English fully.

Commentary: God is eternal Peace, the primordial OM. In his transcendental aspect, He is formless and changeless. God is above distinctions. That is Bliss, absolute. Like lulling a child to sleep in a cradle, we must wean the mind into the internal sleep that is the thought-free state. In order to remove the weaknesses that are obstacles to Liberation, we first have to be completely aware of what those weaknesses are. The ego cannot be eradicated when we don't know when it is in play. To accomplish this awareness, the yogi must be tested. For this reason, the Guru tests the disciple regularly.

We must pass every test of the Guru. Don't be lazy about this. Just as, in the workplace you have to pass the tests necessary to get promoted, you must do the same in Sadhana. If you speak English but can't write in English, you don't have full command of the English language. In the same way, if you perform Sadhana but don't remain vigilant in your tests, you can't realize God and become free of your Karmas.

209. The throat place is the "Muladhara" where the serpent power (Kundalini) is originated. The heart space is the place for the throat place. The heart space is in the middle of the eyebrows. "Swadhisthana" is in the brain. Ajna is triangular. What is called "Raja Yoga" is above the neck. Ajna is the locality where man attains Mukti. What is called "this world" is Jeevatma. What is called the "next world" is Paramatma. The union of these two is the space of consciousness. Chit is the mental mood. Sat is the one, indivisible.

Commentary: Raja Yoga is that path which focuses on the union of Shakti with Shiva in the thousand-petalled lotus located in the Sahasrar. This is a chakra (spiritual center) located at a distance of twelve fingers above the head (Shiva dvadashanta). When this union occurs, the disciple is Liberated.

In Raja Yoga, the focus is on the chakras (spiritual centers) above the throat. In Hatha Yoga, the focus is on the chakras from the throat down. A Raj Yogi is concerned with the rising of Kundalini Shakti through the "command center" (which is the Ajna Chakra in the middle of the eyebrows), into the Sahasrar where the heart space of the Supreme Self is located. However, the real Ajna Chakra is Shiva-Shakti Trikona, the triadic Heart of Shiva.
This is a triangle that moves and spins at the top of the Sahasrar. It is also known in Trika Shaivism as Bhairava Bila. Once you have gained control over a particular chakra, you are no longer influenced by the chakras below it. Hence the focus in Raja Yoga on the chakras above the throat.

This world-appearance is the plane of the Jiva, the individual bound soul. Once Liberated, the yogi lives in the "next world" which is the non-dual plane of existence called Paramatma or Shiva Consciousness. This is the state of a Liberated being who continues to live in this world-appearance without being bound by it in any way. Chit is Shiva's Vimarsha aspect that creates the perception of a world. Sat is Shiva's transcendental aspect that is Prakasha (Light of Divine Consciousness) and is non-dual.

210. Pooraka is drawing the breath up. Kumbhaka is retaining the breath. Rechaka is the exhaling of breath slowly from within. Many sorts of cakes are prepared from the same rice. So also, by breath, everything is accomplished. The functions are different. What is called Pranayama is all internal working. The same is

Shiva-Shakti in a person. When this Shakti is guided to Brahmarandhra, it is communion with God-head.

Commentary: Apana (pooraka) and Prana (rechaka) are inhalation and exhalation. Kumbhaka is the retention of the breath after both Apana (inhalation) and Prana (exhalation). Just as the same rice is used in many different recipes, the breath takes on different forms to accomplish purification inside a living being. The functions are different. There is Prana and then there is breath. True Pranayama is internal. Prana is the life force, the indweller that travels on the breath. Prana is the transcendental aspect of the breathing apparatus and breath is the immanent aspect. Prana works internally to purify the subtle spiritual energy centers. The breath nurtures the cells, tissues and organs of the physical form.

Pranayam is the practice of directing the breath inside the Sushumna Nadi without taking any air in from the outside. In this way, breathing is internalized and dissolves in the space between the breaths. This gives rise to the experience of the Shiva-Shakti power. When Kundalini Shakti is directed to the Sahasrar in this way, communion with God is achieved.

211. Shiva-Shakti is one, indivisible. Shiva-Shakti is salvation. Shiva-Shakti is the upward breath. Shiva-Shakti is Prana Vayu. It is the Omkar. It is the Pranava. From Pranava is creation. Pranava is awareness of the body. Omkar is soul consciousness. Omkar is like the kernel in a dry coconut. The finite becomes one with the infinite. River becomes one with the sea. The mental moods are the rivers. The indivisible Shiva-Shakti is the sea. Just as paper when burnt in fire loses its individuality, the mind loses its individuality in the Atman. Five or six roads may have only one junction. We may travel by these roads either

by walking or by train. The body is the train by which we come and go.

Commentary: Shiva and Shakti are the same, one God, indivisible. Shiva is a reference to Shakti. Shakti is a reference to Shiva. They are contained in each other. Shiva-Shakti is salvation. Shiva-Shakti is Prana Vayu, the movement of the breath inside the Sushumna Nadi. When the breath moves inside the Sushumna without taking any breath in from the outside, this is Omkar.

When the Prana moves outside the Sushumna Nadi in the physical body, this is the Pranava Mantra Om expressing itself as the creation, sustenance and withdrawal of the Universe. Just as the kernel is the cause or the source of the coconut, just as all rivers originate and return to the sea, this finite Universe is contained in the infinite Shiva-Shakti principle.

Just as paper, when burnt, merges into the fire and loses its separate existence as paper, in Meditation, the mind loses its individuality and distinctions by merging in the Absolute. Just as several roads may intersect at one point, all spiritual paths lead to that one God, Shiva-Shakti, the all-pervasive Consciousness. We may travel by these roads either by walking or by train. The body is the train by which we come and go.

212. Firm posture of the body is like the station. This posture should be an easy posture. This is Raja yoga. What is Asana is seat.

Commentary: A steady posture is necessary for Meditation. A steady posture is any posture that is easy for you to hold while meditating. If you are able to sit cross-legged in an easy pose, this is best. If not, a steady posture seated in a chair or lying on your back is just as good. Asana (posture for meditation) is very important. But this

posture should not be confused with expertise in Hatha
Yoga. The real Asana is causing your mind to become
absorbed in the seat of the Absolute. This occurs when
there are no thoughts in your mind. That is true Asana.
When meditating, take whatever posture will easily allow
you to free your mind of all thoughts. This is Raja Yoga.

**213. Samadhi means controlling one's energy.
Samadhi is the upward breath. The upward breath is
what is called the Taraka Brahma. When the upward
breath has become perfect, the whole world is within
you. This upward breath is the same in all creatures. A
Raja yogi is one who has realized the one, indivisible.
He is one with God when he is talking or sitting or
walking.**

**Raja yoga is like sitting in an upper story and looking
around below. Raja Yoga is so called because it is the
king of all Yogas. When our intellect becomes one with
God, the same is known as Raja yoga. It is all peace; it
is formless, qualityless. Bliss has no characteristics
whatsoever. This is known as Jeevan Mukti.**

Commentary: Samadhi means directing one's energy back
inside to the Sahasrar where the experience of the
Nirvikalpa state is automatic. This is accomplished by way
of Prana, the upward breath that, upon exhalation, is
directed into the Sushumna Nadi and sent to the head. This
is known as Taraka Brahma or Shiva Dvadasanta. When
you have mastered this upward breath, the entire universe
unfolds inside you. It is the same for all creatures.

A Raja yogi is one who has realized God. He experiences
the state of Liberation, known as Purnaham Vimarsha, at
all times, even when he is walking, talking or just sitting.
Raja Yoga, the yoga path that focuses on the upper chakras,
is like sitting in a plane that is beyond this physical
universe and looking around below. It is the king of

Yogas. When the individual intellect merges in Shiva-Shakti, this is Raja Yoga. It is complete peace, formless and without any qualities. The Bliss of Samadhi has no characteristics whatsoever. This state is known as Jivanmukti.

214. Creation disappears in the primordial nature. Coming out from this primordial nature is called creation. Entering into it again is called destruction. When you are conscious of the body, and of nothing else, it is creation. For Raja Yoga, there is no particular action prescribed. There is no Shiva worship. There is no particular place. All this takes place to a Raja yogi in the brain center. Salutation takes place in the brain center. If one salutes in the brain center, it reaches all.

Commentary: When you direct your focus towards objects of sense, the mind comes into being and creation occurs. When you remove all objects, thoughts and notions from your mind, it dissolves back into the primordial Shiva-Shakti principle. For one who is aware of this at all times, no specific practice or ritual is required. Worship of God takes place in the Heart space in the head. This is Raja Yoga. From this God is reached and all are reached.

215. Brahmahood means realization of oneness within oneself. Pindanda (microcosm) is that which is visible outside. Brahmanda (macrocosm) is seen inwards. This macrocosm is beyond creation. Creation is a mental condition. Atma is uncreate. Mind has fears of all sorts. All creation appears to exist only to the embodied. When the external is internalized, there is an end of all fear.

If you have gold ornaments on your body, you have fear of thieves. Those who have not such ornaments, have no cause for sorrow. They have one sightedness. Desire is in those who see with the physical eye. They see

differences. Desire causes a man to work. Desirelessness is Mukti. Desirelessness for fruit is JivanMukti. This is the state of an Avadhoota.

This state is a subtle one. Jnanis have the internal sight. They have annihilated the Manas. They experience one spirit everywhere. They have no idea of differences. They have realized the one, indivisible. In the gross state, there are differences. The internal breath is not divisible. It is indivisible. It is one.

Commentary: Brahmahood is the realization that you are God. Pindanda is the visible world of manifestation that is the product of Shiva's Maya. Brahmananda is the inner realm of Shiva. This Shivalokha is beyond all creation and is your primordial dwelling place. Creation is a mental condition. Atma is the absence of this mental condition, the absence of creation.

It is the impure mind that has fears, based on desires and cravings for objects that it strives compulsively to possess. This world-appearance only exists for those who have not realized God. When God is realized, only God exists in everything and everyone, everywhere and all fear dissolves. Just as if you wear precious gold you fear that it will be stolen by thieves, if you have desire for worldliness, you fear losing the people places and things that you falsely believe belong to you. So, the root of all fear is desire for sense pleasures and worldly pleasures.

Desires are cultivated due to the belief that what you see with the physical eye is all that exists. This kind of sight causes distinctions and differences to arise in your mind. Yogis who have banished craving and desire do not have this fear. Limiting desire is a characteristic of those who see differences among others and who believe they are separate from God and imperfect. These conditions are called Anava Mala and Mayiya Mala. The existence of

these two Malas in the bound soul (Jiva) causes one to act
compulsively out of fear of lose and with a fear of death
that causes one to cling to objects of sense.

This limiting desire causes you to believe that you have to
struggle to make your life work. This is due to the third
Mala, Karma Mala. Desirelessness is the state of
absorption in Shiva. It is a state in which there is no world
or universe, but only God everywhere. In this state, your
only desire is to follow God's Will and to remain absorbed
in God. This is the state of Liberation (Mukti). This is the
state of an Avadhoota. It is internal sight. This is the
experience of the Jnani. The mind is dissolved in Shiva-
Shakti and becomes pure Chiti, once again.

In the gross state of the Jiva (individual bound soul), one
experiences differences in objects (people, places and
things). The state reached by way of the internal breath,
the upward breath, is indivisible. This state is that of
Equality Consciousness, the experience that only God
exists in everyone and everything, everywhere.

**216. The idea of grossness is all mental. The subtle
state is Atmaic. Jnanis always enjoy Yoga Nidra. They
are in this state whether they are sitting or walking.
Jnanis may be compared to a tortoise. These animals
project their limbs outside only when necessary. At all
other times, they keep themselves inside the shell.**

Commentary: This world is a mental representation in
Consciousness. It is a Superimposition in Shiva's Maya,
borne of ideation. The thought-free state is the Atman.
Jnanis enjoy this state always. It is the state of being
absorbed in one's own perfect Bliss. Jnanis are in this state
even when going about their mundane activities in this
world. They may be compared to a Tortoise that projects
its limbs outward only when necessary and remains in its
shell at all other times. These Jnanis only turn their focus

outward when it is absolutely necessary. At all other times, they remain indrawn.

217. To the mail train and to the local train, the energy is the same. Time only differs. The Sanyasi is like the mail train. Sanyasi is one who sees the whole external world within himself. One who concentrates his power in the external world, is like the local train. It is difficult to get into the train. After getting into the train, there is no difficulty. One does not then think of the luggage.

When we purchase a thing, sitting in the train, our attention is directed towards the train. So also, the first is discrimination. The second is sound. Whatever one may be doing, the attention should be fixed in the head. Seeing, hearing, talking are not actions in themselves. Breathing through the nose is an action in reality. What is called good action is the downward path.

Commentary: The express train and the local train function on the same energy. It is the same engine that drives them both. This is the same with respect to the world-appearance and That which is beyond this world-appearance. The only difference in the two is the sense of time. One train arrives faster than the other. For one who is absorbed in Shiva Consciousness, it is like riding the express train. Such a Sanyasi sees the external world within himself and continues to direct his attention back inside where he quickly becomes reabsorbed in Shiva Consciousness.

A person whose focus is only on the external world is like someone riding the local train that is making many stops before arriving at the person's true destination, the Atman. At first, it is difficult for one to switch trains. It is difficult for one, at first, to change old habits of attachment to this world-appearance with its many objects. Once we have entered into the Self, our own primordial nature, then this difficulty ceases. Just as when you ride a train, you don't worry about your luggage that is stowed away on the train, in the same way, once you enter the Self, you no longer have to worry about this world-appearance and your existence in it.

The first step is to orient your will towards God. The second step is to absorb your individual awareness in the Bindu-Nada that is heard resonating in Shiva-Shakti Trikona, the Heart space in the head. Then, whatever you may be doing, fix your attention on this Bindu-Nada in the head. Seeing, hearing and talking are not actions in and of themselves. Action is the inward and outward breath.

When the mind, by the movement of breath taken in from outside, is engaged in thoughts and desires, even if they be good thoughts and desires, this is the downward path of creation. When, by the same breath directed into the Sushumna Nadi or subtle body, all thoughts and desires are removed, this is the upward path of withdrawal into Shiva. When this upward path is your primary focus at all times, this is known as living in a state of Grace.

218. What is called "silence" refers to the mind, not the tongue. What is done when the Buddhi and Jnana are in communion with the Atman, is not Karma. Silence is the real locality of the mind, not of the tongue. It is by silence, yoga is accomplished. He is a yogi who has united into one both Buddhi and Jnana. One who subjects the Manas to Buddhi and makes Buddhi control Manas, is a yogi. What is called "the vow of silence" is another name for the Sushumna that is the junction of the Ida and Pingala. The three important nerves of the body are the Ida and the Pingala and the Sushumna. Sushumna is the seat of the Kundalini.

Commentary: In Sadhana, to be silent means to have no thoughts in the mind. Silence is not a reference to speaking or not speaking. Whatever actions or words are undertaken when the individual will and individual knowledge are fully invested in God, do not create any new Karma because they emanate from this place of silence. It is by silence that one attains Liberation. The yogi is that person who has merged her individual will and awareness into Shiva Consciousness. This is the union of Buddhi and Jnana in the body of Supreme God Consciousness.

The person who merges his mind in the purified intellect and places the mind under the control of Buddhi, under the control of God's Will, is a yogi. In Raja Yoga, what is known as taking a vow of silence is really the practice of directing Kundalini Shakti into the Sushumna Nadi and up into the Sahasrar. The Sushumna is the junction point of Ida and Pingala, the other two important nerves in the body. The Sushumna is the most important nerve, since it is through the Sushumna that Kundalini Shakti rises to union with Shiva in the Sahasrar.

219. All Tatwas have one root Tatwa called Parabrahma. When this is realized, it is called Jivanmukti. You must see the river at its source and not after it merges into the sea. You should see the mother root of a tree. All the trees have one mother root. So also, all have one and only one God. When you have realized all as one homogeneous, this realization is Mukti.

Commentary: On the Siddha Path, there are 36 main principles or realms of manifestation. These are known as Tattvas. All Tattvas have, as their source, Shiva-Shakti Tattva that is Parabrahma or Paramashiva. In Sadhana, one must go to this source. This source is the root cause of everything created and uncreated in this world. When you have realized this for yourself, you are Liberated.

220. The actors in a drama, first of all, perform a trial behind the curtain and then perform it on the stage. So also, is the performance of Yoga. First of all, it is secretly practiced and when it is accomplished, it gets publicity of its own accord. When you begin to learn an art, you do not have experience of it all at once. The more you practice, the better will be your experience of it.

Commentary: Sadhana is daily spiritual practice. To attain the fruits of such practice takes time, patience and vigilance in practice. Sadhana is not something you do like a television reality show. It is your personal walk to God. Keep it to yourself in the beginning. As you become more and more absorbed in Shiva Consciousness or the God-principle, people will start to notice your Light and they will want to know more about what has caused a change in you. That will be a perfect time to share what you've been up to.

221. One's hunger is not appeased by simply smelling the food cooked. One must take the food himself to satisfy his hunger. So also, the experience is the only accomplishment. There is nobody to oppose you when you have experienced the Truth. By simply holding sugar in your hand, you cannot experience its sweetness. Sugar must be placed in the mouth to taste its sweetness. This is experience.

Book knowledge gives room for doubts and discussion. But self-experience does not. Experience for oneself is like the command of the king to the subjects. Experience is like the king's command. Book knowledge is the subjects. W hat is called Jivanmukti is one's true home, the aim and end of yoga. This is the thing to be attained.

The dwelling in the cave is the thing to be accomplished in life. The cave is the Buddhi. When Jivatma learns to dwell in the Buddhi, the aim of life is realized. The heart space, which is the place of dwelling (cave) of the Atman, is the place of the third eye. The heart space is discrimination. Buddhi and Jnana have become one, a screw is turned by male or a female. Male and female are distinctions only.

Commentary: Just as you have to eat food (not just smell it) to satisfy your hunger, to know God you have to go inside to have your own direct experience of God. Intellectualizing about God is not enough. Experience is the only true accomplishment. When you have experienced Shiva-Shakti in complete fullness, no one can question your experience. You know it because you live it. No one can oppose that.

Knowledge of the scriptures alone will only create doubts in your mind, and the necessity for debate and discussion. Once you have verified what is in the scriptures by your own experience, there is no doubt and no need for discussion and debate. And if you have direct experience of the Self and no real scriptural knowledge, still you have everything. Personal experience of God is like the command of the King to the subjects. It is from personal experience that all scriptures and sacred texts are written. Therefore, this experience alone is what is worth following.

The aim of Yoga is Liberation, the God-realized state known as Jivanmukti. This is the goal of all Sadhana. Remaining absorbed in God is what is to be accomplished. When you merge your individual intellect into the Divine Buddhi, Shiva's independent Will, the aim of all life is realized. The Heart space or dwelling place of the Self is reached through the Ajna Chakra, the third eye. This Heart space is the place of Supreme discrimination or discernment. When Buddhi and Jnana have become one, the goal is realized, whether you be male or female. Male and female are only perceptions in Shiva's Maya. They are distinctions in language only. The doer of a thing is that One Absolute God.

222. Gold does not make a man great.

Commentary: Money, fame and connections do not make you great. They are indications of your Karma only. You can only become great through direct contact with the Divine.

223. Through science the bondage of Karma is not cut through.

Commentary: Karma cannot be absolved through scientific knowledge or application. Even though some karmas can be removed by the Master, the Master cannot remove all your karmas. Karma, whether good or bad, must be suffered to be absolved. Shiva gives you final Liberation. But even He will not remove all your karmas.
Remembering this, the yogi becomes very aware and very careful about the thoughts and actions he/she engages in.

224. O Beggar! Burn the delusion of the mind in the fire of Yoga! Those who have not realized the Brahman do not know the truth. They do not experience real joy. Egotistic tendencies are not destroyed. Be always immersed in Ananda. Bury your desire in the depth of your Manas. Desire is fruitless. Destroy it internally.

Commentary: The mind is purified in the fire of Sadhana, the fire of daily spiritual practice. Do this practice and, by the instruction of a Siddha Guru, you will become the Truth. There is no other way to know the Truth but to become absorbed in it. This is the only path to Joy and the only way to destroy the destructive tendencies of the ego. Immerse yourself in the eternal Bliss that is Shiva

Consciousness. Bury your desire in this God
Consciousness. Any desire other than the desire to know
God and become one with Him is fruitless. Destroy limited
desire by depositing it inside at the feet of your living Guru.

**225. When Jiva leads the Shiva-Shakti in man
internally to the center of the brain (Brahma Randhra)
and there becomes one with Shiva, the indivisible,
Mukti is realized. Brahmananda is for him who has
attained this Mukti. Always concentrate on Shiva. In
the beginning, was Shiva. In the beginning, there was
Shiva-Shakti alone. The Great Protector is the eternal
Ananda. The great desirelessness is the eternal Ananda.**

**He who is without desire, is without the three qualities
(Gunas). That is real virtue. You are the king of
yourself. You are the lord of Mukti. Look within
yourself. The real form is the human form. Man stands
at the head of the animal kingdom. In this world, there
is nothing higher than man. It is man that has created
all the countries.**

Commentary: When you lead Kundalini Shakti along the
central channel (Sushumna) into the Sahasrar, and when
this Shakti merges there with Shiva, Liberation is attained.
Once Liberated, you experience Shiva at all times and in all
things, everywhere. Always concentrate on Shiva. In the
beginning, there was only Shiva and there is only this
Shiva-Shakti, this God Consciousness, now.

Eternal Bliss of Shiva is the Great Protector. Remaining
absorbed in this state is what is known as desirelessness
and this desirelessness is eternal Bliss. Remaining in this
state, you rise above the three Gunas. This is real virtue.
In fact, you are God. You are the Lord of this Liberation.
Look inside yourself. God is this human form. Only by
taking this human form can you realize God. For this
reason, a human birth is the highest birth and the most

sacred. It is from inside a human form that this world-appearance is perceived.

226. He is a Brahmin who has experienced Brahmananda. Your Maya (delusion) is transient. O Hari! Burn the ego! One who has destroyed the Manas has destroyed Maya. Hari (Maya) is not the lord. Shiva is the Lord. All know that butter is latent in milk. When we boil milk, butter must be obtained. Those who take butter are very few. Milk is Bhakti. Heating milk on fire is the power of discrimination. The vessel for discrimination is Buddhi. The fire of discrimination is the fire of yoga. By this Viveka fire, the six enemies of the body: anger, desire, envy, passion, greed and delusion are destroyed and the butter obtained.

Commentary: One who has experienced the Bliss of the Self is a Brahmin. Shiva's Maya is transient. This world of forms is transient. O Hari! Let the ego be burned and purified in the fire of Sadhana. Once the mind is merged in Shiva, Maya dissolves. Hari (Lord Vishnu) is Maya. Hari is not the Supreme attainment that Liberates you. Shiva is the Lord. Shiva is the Supreme attainment who Liberates you. Just as butter is latent in milk, Shiva is contained inside every living being. And yet, few seek Him out in earnest.

Most become hopelessly attached to the body and to sense pleasures and worldly pleasures. Bhakti is Devotion to the Guru and to God. When this Bhakti is heated in the fire of Sadhana, Viveka, subtle discrimination, which leads one to God, is the result. The vessel for this Viveka to shine through is the purified Buddhi, the purified intellect. As you develop Viveka (the ability to discriminate between what is real and what is not) the six enemies of anger, desire, envy, passion, greed and delusion are destroyed. Then Shiva is obtained.

227. Without oil, a lamp cannot burn. So also, without breath, the body cannot move. Without a helm, a boat cannot be steered to its destination. A steamer is steered by steam energy and by the intelligence of the captain. A boat cannot go like a steamer. Similarly, a Sanyasi is like a steamer. He who has the whole world, in himself, is like a steamer. He who is in the world, is like the boat.

The guiding light of a steamer is on the top. Similarly is the Brahmarandra to a Sanyasi. Mind in a Sanyasi is merged in the heart space. What is light is Sanyasi. A cow cannot run like a horse. He whose mind is merged in the Self is like the horse. He whose mind is in the world is like the cow. All cannot become kings at the same time. All cannot be traders at the same time. Customers are also required.

Commentary: Without oil, a lamp cannot burn and without the breath, the body cannot survive. Without a helm, a boat cannot be steered to its destination. A steamer is a more efficient type of boat. It runs better because it relies on a better energy source. In the same way, a Sanyasi, one who has experienced Shiva, leads life in a more sublime manner. One who has not experienced Shiva is like the inferior boat and does not lead life in a sublime fashion.

The guiding light of a steamer is on top of the ship. In the same way, the guiding light for a Sanyasi is the Sahasrar. A Sanyasi is one who has merged his mind in this heart space in the head. Such a person sees the Divine Light of Consciousness all the time. A cow cannot run like a horse. One whose mind is sunk in worldliness and craving for this and that is like the cow. One who has merged her intellect and ego in Shiva is like the horse.

All do not rise to the consciousness of Shiva in the same way, nor at the same time. Only he who first obeys can

command. Likewise, only the person who has become a
disciple of a Siddha and follows that Guru's instruction can
realize God. That disciple does become a Siddha in time
and is then worthy of leading others.

**228. When you walk in darkness, you have fear. But in
light, there is no fear. Ignorance is darkness.
Knowledge is the light. Guru is such a light. Light is
Guru.**

Commentary: Ignorance of the Truth is like walking in
darkness. One of the afflictions that comes along with
cravings and desires for sense pleasures and worldly
pleasures is Fear. When you don't know your own true
nature, when you are not aware that you are God, you also
fear death, believing yourself to be imperfect and finite.
When your mind is absorbed in Shiva Consciousness and
you see God in everything and everyone, everywhere, you
have no fear. Ignorance of the Truth about your real
identity as Shiva is darkness. Direct knowledge of your
true nature as Shiva-Shakti is the Light. The Siddha Guru
who teaches you is also this Light of Divine Consciousness.
This Light is the Guru.

**229. In perfect sleep, men forget everything. Suppose
you walk ten miles and then sleep. You are quite
unaware of your existence in this world. So also, when
you are hungry, you must satisfy your hunger by taking
food yourself.**

Commentary: When you fall into deep sleep, you forget
everything and this world does not exist. Also, you are
completely unaware of even your body when you are in
deep sleep. Just as, when you are hungry, you take food to
satisfy your hunger; in the same way, if you want to know
the real Truth of your existence, you have to go inside
yourself and experience God there for yourself.

230. Just as there are the gutters (storm drains) on both sides of the road for the water to flow freely, so also, you must allow the breath to take an upward course freely. It requires great effort to carry a stone upwards. But without the least effort on our part, it suddenly comes down. Similarly is concentration. It is easy to take birth. But it is very difficult to leave this body. We must discover the source of a river. After it joins the sea, there is no use in seeing the river.

To a tree, its mother root is the most important. All other roots are subsidiary. When we raise a chair, our breath goes upwards. That is the seat of Prana. When we are cooking, flames of fire have an upward course. So also, the smoke takes an upward course. In the lighted chimney, the course of the heated air is upwards.

Similarly, in the heart space, the course of breath is upwards. Our joy is caused by the motion of the air (Vayu). Without this air motion, there is no blood circulation. When a water canal is dammed, the motion of water has come to an end. So also, in this body, such a dam is Vatha, Pitha, and Kapha (three humors of Tridishas).

Commentary: Just as there are gutters on both sides of a road for water to flow freely, in the human body there are three channels or nerves for the breath to flow freely in the body and psychic apparatus. It is important to direct the breath into the Sushumna Nadi so that it can maintain an upward course, carrying Shakti into the Sahasrar in the head. In the beginning, this requires proper instruction and a good deal of concentration in practice. It is easy, in the beginning, to get lazy with this practice. Therefore, you have to be vigilant.

It is easy to become attached to the body and remain ignorant of the Truth. In this way, you continue to get caught up in the vortex of Samsara, in the cycle of birth and death. More difficult is the Sadhana required to break the chains of this ignorance so that you can become Liberated from the cycle of birth and death. However, with the Grace of the Master and your own self-effort, Sadhana becomes a Joyful event that you constantly look forward to.

If you want to find the source of a river, you don't go looking for it in the sea. In the same way, to experience God and merge with the source of all existence, you can't go looking for this source in sense pleasures and worldly, mundane existence. You will not find the source there. You have to perform Sadhana (spiritual practice) to experience God within and this Sadhana needs to be done before you approach your death.

The root cause of this world-appearance is the most important root. All other "roots" are secondary. To find the source of your existence, Prana must be directed upward into the Sahasrar. When Kundalini Shakti is caused to rise in this way, Joy is experienced. This Joy is the Bliss that you experience when Shakti merges with Shiva in the Sahasrar.

Without the breath, the heart will not pump and the blood will not circulate. In the same way, the three humors (vatha, pitha, kapha) that create obstacles to the free movement of Prana in the body (owing to your Karmas) cannot be transcended unless you learn Sushumna breathing.

231. Head is the seat where the smell of musk, sandal-paste, camphor and concentrated camphor is experienced. Ants swarm at the place where there is sugar. Where the sound of Omkar is experienced, there is no ignorance. That which is seen by the spiritual eye

is the real heart. That which is seen by the physical eye is not the real heart. The greatest is the head. The origin of breath is true Ananda. The real Ananda is in the cavity of the heart.

The house of breath is the dwelling of Kundalini. This is the house of Shiva. This is our real happy home of peace. This is the home of Satwa guna. One who lives in this house, does not care for honor and dishonor. This is the home of a yogi who has renounced everything. This is the home of those who have the power of subtle discrimination. This is the home of Kundalini. This home is the heart home.

Commentary: The heart of all existence, the heart of Yoga is in the head in the chakra known as Brahmarandhra or the crown chakra. It is here that incredible scents can be experienced and sounds heard as Shakti merges in union with Shiva. It is here that the golden nectar, spoken about by so many Saints, falls from, lighting up one's entire being. Just as ants swarm to the place where there is sugar, Shakti swarms to the place where Shiva dwells.

It is in the Sahasrar that the eternal sound OM is experienced without interruption. There is no ignorance in this state. Once established in the Sahasrar, you see with the spiritual eye of knowledge that is Shiva Dhristi, the outlook of Shiva. The origin of the breath is Shiva's eternal Bliss. It is out of this Bliss, this pure Joy, that the entire universe comes into being.

This Bliss exists in the Heart space in the head. Kundalini and Prana are one in the same. The home of peace is experienced when Kundalini merges in the Sahasrar. This is the House of Shiva. When this merger occurs, your actions become taintless and you want only to be pure and to operate from that place of purity (Sattwa). Remaining in Shiva Consciousness, in this uninterrupted state of

Purnaham Vimarsha, you rise above both honor and
dishonor. You attain subtle discrimination and the vision
and outlook of God.

**232. Those who do not concentrate on breath have no
aim, no state, no intelligence and no fulfillment. So,
concentrate and think. Concentrate on indrawing and
outgoing breath. Draw the breath in properly.
Breathe, concentrating on the sound the breath
produces. Concentrate on the sound that is produced
internally.**

**Have faith in the internal sound and breathe. Breathe
in. Breathe deeper and deeper. Breathe in so that the
internal sound may be audible to the ears. Do not think
of anything else. Eating and drinking, coming and
standing and eating, these do not elevate the soul. Cook
for yourself. Do not desire to eat what others have
cooked. O Mind! Do what you do with faith.**

Commentary: Those who do not concentrate on breath
have no aim, no state, no intelligence and no fulfillment.
The science of Hamsa, of So'ham, is the greatest yoga
science, the greatest spiritual practice. So, concentrate and
think. Concentrate on the indrawing and outgoing breath.
Focus on the space between the breaths. Draw the breath in
properly. Breathe, concentrating on the sound the breath
produces. This sound is the mantra Hamsa, otherwise
known as So'ham. It is the only natural mantra. It repeats
itself, resonating within you 21,600 times each day.

Breathe deeper and deeper. Breathe in so that the internal
sound of Hamsa may be audible to the ears. Do not think
of anything else. Focus on Hamsa and the space between
the breaths. Eating and drinking, coming and standing,
these do not elevate the soul. Experience this for yourself.
Do not simply take the word of others. Practice it! Have
your own experience of God within and seek knowledge of

the Self, by the Self and not from others! O Mind! Do this
with unwavering faith!

**233. Round a leafless tree, wind blows in vain (there is
no response). In a dead body, there is no air (Prana), no
sound. Without air, an animal can never live in this
world.**

Commentary: Prana is life itself. The body has no power
and no life separate from Prana. Without Prana the body is
a mere lump of useless flesh. Where does this Prana come
from? You should seek to learn the mystery of this before
you draw near your death.

**234. The engine does not move without steam. A
coconut tree does not yield jackfruits. What one talks
without experience, is in vain. The judge and the
magistrate hear what the plaintiff and the defendant say
and form an idea of the case. But they do not know the
truth of the case. It is not enough if you have sugar in
your hand. You must taste it to know its sweetness.**

**Although there is water in the bowels of the earth, we
must dig a well in order to get the water. The main
thing is the internal practice and the union of Prana
with Parabrahma in the center of the brain. This is
seeing God face to face. This is the fulfillment of yoga.
This is the eternal peace.**

Commentary: An engine does not function without a
power source. In the same way, the body cannot function
without God. A coconut tree does not yield jackfruits. To
seek out the Truth, you don't go to a financial advisor or
someone who seems to have intelligence. To experience
God you need the Grace and instruction of a Siddha. Only
such a person is competent to instruct you.

It is not enough to intellectualize about God. And forming opinions about Divine Consciousness based on hearsay and debate is useless. To know God, you have to go where God exists as the source of the Universe. That place is inside your very own being. Through the practice of Meditation and Pranayama as instructed by the Master, you can see God face to face in the Sahasrar. This is the fulfillment of Yoga that brings eternal Peace.

235. There is no prescribed food for a neophyte. Peace is the food for the practicer. The highest of all arts is the Brahma Vidya (art by which God is realized). Such an art cannot be bought for money. It isn't obtained by honor or dishonor. It is not obtained by the outer fame. It is acquired only by unwavering devotion (Bhakti). Without Bhakti, there is no liberation from bondage. Mukti is attained by a man only by the subtle Bhakti. Brahmananda is not empty talk but solid experience. This is the same as Satchidananda. This is acquired by the unceasing practice. All is Brahmananda to one who has realized.

Commentary: The right path for you to follow is the one that brings you unwavering peace and the one that will guide you to the realization of God. Liberation or God-realization cannot be bought and it is not obtained simply by engaging in honorable behavior and avoiding dishonorable behavior. Liberation is acquired through unswerving Devotion/Love for God and the Guru. Without this Bhakti, there can be no Liberation.

The key element that draws God's Grace to you through the Guru is your Devotion and your complete surrender to the practices and instruction of the Guru. It is this Bhakti that causes God to come looking for you. This is known as Disciple's Grace. It is the element that enables the Guru to teach you and guide you across.

If Bhakti is not present, no matter how powerful a being, the Guru cannot serve you. For the Siddha's power to work, your Grace, your Bhakti, has to be present also. God is realized through the solid experience that comes from unceasing practice. This unceasing practice causes you to merge with Shiva. Then you see only God in everything and everyone, everywhere.

236. O Mind! Banish the idea of duality. Have subtle discrimination. Having abandoned the idea of duality, think that the visible universe is all Shiva, the spotless. There is no disguise. Have everything within you. That which is permanent is faith. O Mind! Control the breath. Have internal life. Discover the truth by means of subtle discrimination. That which is related to subtle discrimination is eternal.

The essence of every creature is eternal joy. Acquire eternal joy. What is eternal Ananda is eternal Mukti. The mental seats (posture) are the thrones of kings. The eternal seat is the eternal joy. When Sat and Chit are united, the same is Paramananda. The same is called Chaitanyananda.

Commentary: O Mind! Only Shiva exists. Nothing exists anywhere that is not Shiva. Have this subtle discrimination and banish from your mind all sense of duality and differences. When you encounter an object, say, "Hello, my Shiva!" When you see a place, say, "Ah, my Shiva." When you interact with a person, think that you are interacting with the Lord himself. Have this attitude.

In truth, Shiva is not concealed. It is only your limited perception, your limited vision that makes Him seem so. Have Faith in the one Reality. Control the inward and outward breath to remove all thoughts from the mind and experience Him there. Discover this truth by means of this subtle practice and discrimination.

Practice, practice, practice this and make Him reveal himself in your very own being. The essence of every creature is pure Joy. Acquire this Joy by going inside yourself. This Bliss is the Bliss of Liberation (Nityananda). This mental posture of seeing God in everything and everyone is the throne, the eternal seat of Joy. When Sat (pure Being) unites with Chit (awareness or Sat), Shiva is realized.

237. All creation is mental. The body is nothing but a means to an end. Shakti is of the Atman. The highest tower is in the head. This is the seat of the Atman. This is the sky of Consciousness. This is the greatest support. The Ajna (the sixth chakra of the body) is the support. The seat of Kundalini is the heart sky. What is traveling in a train is the thought of the Atman. The mail train is the Raja yogi. The local train is the Hatha yogi. The difference is only in time. Although the velocity is the same, time differs. This difference is the delusion of the mind.

Commentary: This creation is a mental representation of Divine Consciousness. It is a superimposition in Shiva's Maya, an illusion created by perceptions that are the mental moods. I n truth, this is all the one Shakti and this world appears out of the glory of Chit Shakti. The body is simply a means to an end, a means to revealing God and basking in His eternal Joy.

The highest tower is the seat of Shiva-Shakti in the Sahasrar. The Sahasrar is the sky of Consciousness. It is the seat of Shiva and is the greatest support one can have. It is also the seat of Kundalini Shakti in Her expanded form. It is reached by way of the Ajna Chakra. When Ajna is pierced permanently, Shiva comes looking for you and Liberation is at hand.

Raja Yoga, the yoga that includes the chakras above the neck as its focus, is the express train or the quickest means. Hatha Yoga, the yoga that has as its focus on the chakras from the neck down, is the local train. It is a slower means. When you realize God, time disappears. You experience timelessness and the delusion of the mind vanishes, as a result.

238. A man's birth is from his parents. He is first a child. He grows to manhood and himself becomes the parent of children. The difference is due to time. The nature of the child is according to the thought entertained by the parents when they are in union. If the parents entertain devotion, mischief, wrath, activity, desire, etc. at the time of union, the child born to them will imbibe the same qualities.

Creation is caused by Vayu's entrance in the womb. If the parents at the time of union have worldly or celestial inclination, the child born will have the same inclination. When the child has the latter inclination, it will soon be enlightened. The first essential is desirelessness, after birth. The destruction of the seed of birth and death comes next. When a man is subjected to repeated sorrows, he must see the light after the exercise of subtle discrimination.

What is called Prana Vayu is the destruction of creation. Prana Vayu and the Apana Vayu must be merged in the Atman. When these two are united, all conditions are annihilated. Before the expiration of Prana, one must attain Mukti. Then it becomes one, indivisible, losing its duality.

Commentary: Your birth is due to your past karmas. Karma also causes you to choose your parents. The qualities you grow up with are, in part, derived from your parents' mental state at the time of your conception, and while you are being carried in the womb. If, at the time you are conceived in sexual union, your parents are thinking only on God and Devotion for God, you will be born with those qualities and will soon become enlightened. If not, if your parents are thinking on simple sexual satisfaction or if they have anger, greed, desire or any of the lower qualities in their mind at the time of your conception, you will be born with those qualities. In this way, the parents are the first Guru.

For one to become Liberated in the present life, the first essential step is to remove limited desire and craving from one's being. The next step is to destroy the seed of birth and death by performing Sadhana under the direct guidance of a Siddha, until God is realized. This is the aim of life. When a person is subjected to the pain and pleasure of this world-appearance, both of which bring sorrow, that person must strive to know God. This is the only way to rise above misery.

Prana Vayu, the upward breath that is directed into the Sushumna Nadi, is the withdrawal of creation. Both exhalation and inhalation must be merged in Shiva in the Sahasrar. When the breath is directed into the Sushumna and inhalation and exhalation are internal, all mental conditions are annihilated. Before your death approaches, you must attain Liberation (Mukti). Then you will destroy all sense of duality and experience only Equality Consciousness.

239. Upanayana is the goal of life. Jivatma must be merged in the Paramatma. Upanayana is internal. Upanayana is the subtle. What is called Upadhi is the third eye. The object to be attained is to be near God. What is Upanayana is not the body idea. It is the thought of the Atman. In this world, he who has performed such Upadhi is a Brahmin. Upadhi is the

Sushumna nerve. It is the Brahma Nadi where gods and goddesses dwell.

Commentary: Upanayana is the practice of remembering God until you have merged in God. When you merge your individual identity into Shiva, this is Upanayana. This remembrance of God is internal. It is subtle. It is the practice of Meditation and Contemplation that brings Upadhi, the crossing of Ajna Chakra (the third eye) into Sahasrar.

Upanayana has nothing to do with body consciousness. It is supreme detachment from the body. It is Dispassion. It is the understanding and experience that nothing exists that is not Shiva. It is the constant, uninterrupted vision and recognition of God. A person who has mastered this Upadhi is Shiva. Such a person is a Brahmin and is Liberated while still in the body.

240. Shabda (sound) is generated in Akash (space). That which is generated in space is life energy. What is called Akash (a space) is in the head. Akash is heart space. Life energy is one only. Just as there is difference between a river and the sea, so also, there is difference between Jivatman and Paramatman. It is one of degree, not of kind. One must not think as "I" and "mine."

This is the cause of next birth. That man is of little intelligence who thinks in terms of "I" and "mine." By so thinking, he descends into lower birth. The energy in the sun appears as light. Likewise, there is an energy in the form of light in a gas light. To those who have lost the difference between day and night, the light of the sun and that of the gas light are the same. There is no difference between the two.

One's faith is the greatest thing. Above faith, there is no God. In this world there is nothing higher than faith. A Man with faith cannot be deceived by the wicked tricks of others. Man enjoys that in which he has his faith. The internal faith should be concentrated upon breath. Those who have no faith have no thoughts of anything. Those who have no faith have no regard for Sadhus and Sanyasis. They think (wrongly) that thousands of Sadhus are merged in them.

Commentary: Shabda is the primordial sound that is generated in Akash (space). This Akash that appears outside is a reflection of Chidakasha, the inner expanse or Heart space of Supreme Consciousness. Life energy emanates from Chidakasha. This space is in the Sahasrar. The life energy that flows from Chidakasha is Chiti or Shakti. This Shakti contracts to take all the forms of existence. This Shakti becomes Shiva's reflection in this world-appearance.

The difference between the river and the sea is a matter of degree. The river actually manifests from the sea and, eventually, returns to it. In the same way, the Jiva (individual bound soul) is a manifestation of God and returns to God in time. Therefore, everything and everyone is God. The yogi should strive to have this outlook. He must not think that there is any difference between God and these objects, nor between himself and all other things.

Harboring the notion of differences is what causes Karma and rebirth, again and again. To those who have become immersed in Shiva Consciousness, to those Siddhas, there is no difference between the light of the Sun, the light in a lamp and the Light of Divine Consciousness. These are one in the same to a Siddha. Faith is the greatest attainment. By Faith, God is found. Without Faith, you cannot realize God. Therefore, there is nothing greater than this Faith in God. Armed with Faith, no one can fool you or sway you from the Lord. The greatest Faith is Faith in the instruction of a Siddha. The greatest practice of Faith is directing the breath inside the Sushumna Nadi.

This is known as internal Faith. One who has this kind of Faith has no thoughts and no worries. Those who do not have this kind of Faith, have no discrimination. They are not able to tell the difference between a criminal and a Siddha. They disrespect Saints and they wrongly believe that they are greater than the enlightened.

241. To a blind man there is no difference between day and night. To him, external light is of no use. In him, the light of Jnana is strong. To the blind, their bodily form is of no use. As their physical eyes do not see, their spiritual eye must be very effective. Blind men cannot describe the form of a carriage by feeling it with touch.

Commentary: The blind are not able to see differences in anything. However, the fact that they are blind means that their other senses are heightened. Blind people also have a more developed intuition. Because they have no sight, they have not developed the vanity that would cause them to be attached to the body. Because they can't see forms, they have no attachment to this world-appearance.

Jnana is stronger in those who are blind. Their spiritual eye is more developed. A blind person may not be able to describe the form of a carriage by touching it, but his/her intuition will still tell him what the carriage looks like. Just as a blind person has no use for the bodily form, seekers of the Truth should become blind to sense pleasures and worldly pleasures to destroy their use for them. Blind to craving and desire, you become one-pointed on attaining God.

242. Is the sound generated from the world or is the world generated from the sound? Is the effect from the cause or the cause from the effect? The world is generated from the sound. From the sound is generated the form, and the world which has form. From the cause is the effect. Whence is the cause? The cause and the effect are from the Self. Cause and effect must be the slaves of oneself. Both these are from the Self.

This Self absorbs the cause and the effect and they become one (indivisible). The Maya that the Self creates is annihilated by the Self. A lie is a lie. If you believe the lie, you will have to tell the lie. If you believe the truth, you must tell the truth. Those who utter falsehood have no truth about them. There is no falsehood separate from them, but it is one with them.

What is the cause of falsehood? Their mind becomes habituated to falsehood and they do not feel it to be false. They do not feel falsehood as a separate thing. If they knew it (falsehood) to be evil, their mind will not be inclined to falsehood. Then they will feel that there is a separate thing called truth. Then they will attain the good. Then they will know the correct path.

Commentary: Which came first, the chicken or the egg? The answer is, neither came first. Shiva-Shakti is and always was. From Shiva-Shakti came Light and then Sound. Actually, Light and Sound are first in an indistinguishable unity. Then they separate as Chit Shakti contracts. Then there is only sound and then comes the world of forms (including the chicken and the egg). Shiva is both the cause and the effect. This is very important to realize.

Shiva has two aspects, transcendental and immanent (expanded and contracted). Shiva is both these aspects. All the forms of this Universe emanate from Shiva-Shakti

and are reabsorbed back into Shiva-Shakti. Chit Shakti is
the cause of Shiva's Maya. This Maya is the illusion that
the Universe actually exists. It is this same Shakti that
Maya dissolves into when the Self is realized by the Self.
Just as a liar has convinced herself that her lie is actually
the truth, people have convinced themselves that this
world-appearance is real and exists separate from God.

When the mind develops the habit of lying, it causes the
belief that the lie is not a lie at all. People are so used to
justifying their bad behavior with false notions that they
convince themselves that they are actually telling the truth.
In this way, the lie becomes their "truth." There is your
truth and there is the Truth. Once a liar decides to seek the
actual Truth, that person has the realization that he/she has
been lying.

In a good person, this realization causes one to attempt a
change in behavior. It is the same for one who seeks God.
Once you have the realization that there is a force greater
than you that has caused the existence of this Universe, you
develop the desire to want to know God. Then, in time, the
illusion, the lie that there is a world separate and apart from
God, vanishes.

**243. Just as all rivers enter the ocean, both the good
and the evil enter the Atman. Both are sacrificed to the
Atman. Both the good and the evil are from the Atman.
They enter in that from which they came. Mind is the
cause of good and evil acts. Mind is Atman's power
(instrument). No one can increase or diminish it (the
soul force). What will happen will happen. It will
happen only in one way according to the eternal law.**

Commentary: Good and evil are concepts that exist in
Shiva's Maya only. It is only in this Play of Divine
Consciousness that takes the form of this world-appearance
that good and evil are played out. Both are reflections in

Shiva, in God, that exist for his sport. They are perceived
to be real because of the existence of the mind.

In Shiva Consciousness there is no good or evil, only the
Bliss of the Self. The mind is the cause of good and evil
acts and these acts dissolve in Shiva when one attains Shiva
Consciousness. A Siddha, a God-realized being, has risen
above both virtue and vice in this way. The mind is the
instrument of Shiva-Shakti and functions by the sacred law
and will of the Divine. No one can diminish its power nor
change its function. The mind is a contracted form of Chit
Shakti and exists through Shakti's power.

**244. The seed is not from the tree. The seed is the
beginning. A seed falls down from a tree and that seed
grows into a small plant that grows into a tree. Again
and again, trees grow from seeds. Similarly is creation.
In the seed is the beginning but there is no ending.
Wherever you may see, you see the same seed.**

Commentary: It is God who takes the form of a tiny seed
from which a great tree grows. This seed is God's creation
and God's reflection. It comes from God. Therefore, we
don't have to argue about which came first, the seed or the
tree, because neither existed first. First and always is Shiva
and His Shakti that creates all the objects of our perception.
This Shiva-Shakti power or God-principle has no beginning
and no end. It is timeless, eternal.

The concept of time is one that only exists in limitation, in
Shiva's Maya that is the illusion of this world-appearance.
In Shiva Consciousness there is no concept of time. This is
why it is said that Siddhas, the saints, are timeless beings.
Whatever you can observe in this world is a reflection of
Supreme Consciousness. This reflection has, as its seed,
the Shiva-Shakti power.

245. Those who have no doubt, find that this doubtlessness is the path to one-pointedness of mind. A doubting person's intellect is small (limited). Wherever they may see, they see nothing but doubt. Everybody is subject to his own nature. There is no cause for finding that quality which one has not. In the shaking water, a man cannot see his shadow. In the still water, a man can see his shadow quite properly.

Similarly, to a fickle-minded man, his real nature is not visible. To a steady-minded man wherever he may see, he sees the ONE, indivisible. He sees himself in others. If you put on red spectacles you see everything red. You cannot see green color. Everyone sees according as he thinks.

Commentary: The world is as you see it. One who has doubt and fear experiences these everywhere. A person who has Faith and has removed doubts about God and spiritual practice does become one-pointed on God and becomes God. Each of us is subject to how we think. Whatever we think on we become. Gurudev Muktananda always said, "Change the prescription of your glasses." If you want to attain your true nature, if you want to rise above your mundane experience of life and realize your true identity, you have to absorb your mind in Shiva, in God. Then you will become Shiva. Of this there is no doubt.

246. Why do you hold an umbrella? To prevent the rain from falling on you. Rain is the Maya. Truth is the umbrella. Chitta is the handle. In everything, there is truth. But there are very few men who have realized that truth. Maya is from Atman. But Atman is not from Maya. The prime minister is of the king. The prime minister is not the king. Mind is not Atman. Mind is the reflection of the Atman. Mind is two ranks below Atman. Mind is subject to destruction. Atman is

indestructible. Mind is deluded by the various objects of the senses.

Atman is not subject to the delusion caused by the three fold qualities, Trigunas. Mind is subject to the three fold qualities. When we say that mind is a fragment of the Atman, we mean mind is to Atman what the river is to the ocean. Atman is the ocean. Its water is measureless and endless. Similarly, Atman has neither a beginning nor an ending. Atman has not come from anywhere nor does He go anywhere. Atman is everywhere. There is nothing existing but Atman. Interior to you and exterior to you is all creation which fact is unknown to you.

Commentary: Just as you hold an umbrella to keep from getting wet, you perform spiritual practice under the instruction of a Siddha Guru to keep from being devoured by delusion and ignorance. The Chitta, the individual mind, is the means by which you experience God within. Therefore, the mind needs to be trained to turn within to become absorbed in God. God exists in everything and everyone, everywhere. Yet, relatively few have realized who they carry inside their own being.

The Truth is inside you, yet you continue to search for it outside yourself. This world-appearance is an illusion supported by Shiva's Maya. Shiva is the Atman. Maya is from Shiva. Just as the prime minister serves and reports to the King, Maya does not create Shiva but is the servant of Shiva. The mind is also a product of this Maya Shakti. The mind is transient and subject to the control exerted by the senses and the three Gunas (sattva, rajas and tamas). These Gunas cause one to become deluded. Shiva is not subject to these. Shiva is eternal.

The mind is to Shiva what the river is to the ocean. Shiva is the ocean and is timeless and without any measurement.

Lord Shiva and His Shakti have no beginning and no end. Shiva-Shakti is everywhere and nothing exists but this Shiva-Shakti power, the One, unifying God-principle. The entire creation exists inside you and is reflected outside of you. But you are ignorant of this fact. The removal of this ignorance requires study and practice under the guidance of a Sadguru.

247. When the life energy moves in an outward direction, desire is generated for the sense objects. It manifests as mind and it is divided and subdivided into two, three, and six. Thus what is called "world" comes into being. From this world all qualities (good and bad) come into being. Five organs of action are related to the earth. Five chief senses are related to space. Organs of action are said to belong to Sat-guna. He who conquers the senses is the free man. To such a man, fulfillment comes from himself.

Commentary: When you focus your Shakti outside yourself, this Chit Shakti becomes the mind and desire for sense objects is created. This outward flow is the first of The 5-Fold Act of Divine Consciousness, known as the act of manifestation. In this way, Chiti manifests as the mind (Chitta), the intellect, the ego, the five senses and their offspring. It is by this manifestation that what we call "world" comes into being.

All qualities, both good and bad, are manifestations of Shiva's Maya, as is this world-appearance. The five organs of action (Karmendriyas) are a part of your physical body and the five senses and their offspring are the powers that function through those organs. They are aspects of Chiti that take the form of all these. When you conquer your senses, you become truly free. This freedom is an inner attainment.

248. Think and think about Brahman. Mind, though seemingly different, is one and one only. Mind when it is one pointed is great indeed. This mind is the eternal mind. This eternal mind is supreme joy. This eternal mind is called Chidakasha. A clean mind is a clean space. A clean space is Siddhi. This clean space is yoga (union with God). This clean space is the heart. When you move in this clean space, it is the fulfillment.

When you move in this clean space, the difference between "you" and "I" will vanish. In this clean space is Mukti, Bhakti, Shakti and the path suitable. This clean space is Buddhi. When the Jiva dwells in this clean space, the attachments to sense objects will be burnt away. This clean space is Brahmarandhra. What is called Raja Yoga is above the neck. What is called the "Color cavity" is above the neck.

Commentary: Keep your mind absorbed in the Absolute. Though the mind may seem to be different, it is not different from God. The mind, when turned inside and absorbed in God, becomes God. Then it is the eternal mind. When you merge your individual identity and your mind in Shiva Consciousness, you experience Supreme Joy, Supreme Peace and all that is worth knowing. This space of Shiva Consciousness is known as Chidakasha.

This Heart space is completely pure. It is the place of complete fulfillment in God (Siddhi). When you dwell in this space of Chidakasha, the notion of "you" and "I" vanishes. All is the one Shiva there. In Chidakasha one is Liberated and experiences uninterrupted Devotion and Love for God. Chidakasha is full of Shakti and is the spiritual path. It is Divine Intelligence of the Will of God (Buddhi).

This clean space is the Sahasrar. The teachings and practices of the Siddha path are practiced to arrive in that space. The Siddha path is any path that focuses on the chakras above the neck, arrived at by the upward movement of Prana Shakti (the awakened Kundalini) inside the Sushumna Nadi. What is known as the Blue Pearl (color cavity) is above the neck.

249. Mantra is this Brahmarandhra. Mantra is the minister to Prana. This prime minister of Prana is Atma Bindu. In the midst of this is eternal Mantra, in the midst of this is Chidakasha. This Chidakasha is Chit. This is supreme joy. This is the supreme medicine. This supreme medicine is the supreme guru whose Mantra is Tatwamasi: That art Thou, Thou art That.

Commentary: The primordial mantra sounds in the Sahasrar and reverberates downward into the Heart space in the head. This primordial mantra is contained in this Heart space known as Chidakasha. It emanates from a point known as Bindu, Vindu or Visarga and is also called Bindu Nada. It travels on Prana, on the breath, and is sounded with every breath you take.

Chidakasha is Chit Shakti in its transcendental form (also called Chiti). This Chiti is Supreme Joy and is the Supreme medicine. This Shakti of Shiva is the Guru whose mantra is this primordial mantra Tatwamasi (Hamsa), which means I Am That.

250. Why is man called man? The true man is he who ruminates. If you do not know the path leading to Brahman, you will be born again and again. If you do not know the path, you will have no contentment. This contentment consists in doing your duty without attachment to results. This non-attachment to results of action is called Mukti. It is also called the supreme joy. Desire is hell. Desirelessness is supreme joy. The

supreme position is Shiva-Shakti. The Shiva-Shakti is the knower of both the visible and the invisible.

Commentary: A true human being is called so because he/she directs his/her attention to God through Meditation and Contemplation. Here "ruminates" means full awareness of the Self, of God, at all times, even while engaged in action. If you do not know the path leading to Brahman, you will be born again and again. If you do not know the path, you will have no contentment.

This contentment consists in performing your duty, engaging in your daily mundane activities, without attachment to results. This non-attachment to results of action is called Mukti. It is also called the Supreme Joy. Selfless Service (Seva) is the act of going about your mundane activities with the knowledge that it is God who is acting through you. When the prime minister is told to deliver a gift for the King, does he tell the receiver that he himself is offering the gift? No. He tells the receiver that he is acting on behalf of the King who the gift is from.

In the same way, take action with this understanding and without appropriating the glory to yourself. Do your absolute best without being concerned over the result and while offering the result to God. In this way, you remain desireless and absorbed in God at all times. This is the way to experience Supreme Joy and Liberation. The Supreme position is Shiva-Shakti. Shiva-Shakti is the knower of all things created and uncreated. Merge with That.

251. Atma is not perceived by the senses. Atma is quite different from the senses. It is perceptible to Jnana. It is free from the body idea. Those are yogis who know the true nature of the senses and behave according to that knowledge. Those are called the Mahatmas. What they utter is Veda word. They are like the seeds of the tamarind fruit. The tamarind matter is sticky to the touch. But the seed is perfectly pure. The heart of a

**Mahatma is like the tamarind seed perfectly pure.
These Mahatmas are ever young. For a Jnani, there is
no age idea.**

Commentary: Atma, the Self or God, cannot be realized
through the senses. The Shiva-Shakti principle, dwelling in
its purest form as the Supreme I-Consciousness of God, is
beyond the senses. In order to merge with this Shiva
Consciousness, you have to go beyond the senses. God is
perceived through Jnana that is direct knowledge and
experience of the Self and the wisdom that arises
spontaneously as a result.

To attain this Jnana, you have to Meditate on God in order
to become God. Through Meditation, Chanting, Selfless
Service and Prayer/Contemplation, Jnana is attained by
going beyond the senses to the pure Bliss of Shiva. Those
who have gone beyond the senses and become one with the
Absolute are the Mahatmas, the Siddhas. Even though they
live in the world, they are not of the world. They are
perfectly pure. Because they have no age idea, they remain
forever young.

**252. Fill a lamp with oil and light the wick. When the
oil becomes less, the wick comes lower and lower and
the light becomes less and less. If you again supply the
lamp with oil and light the wick, the light shines as
before. Similar is the internal life of a Jnani. Their
mental life is like butter placed in water. The butter
does not sink in water. It floats above water. The body
is like the water and the butter, the soul.**

**Subtle intelligence should be concentrated in the head.
The intelligence should be concentrated at the top of the
Sushumna. Both the mind and Buddhi should be in the
head. The mind must be in the Buddhi and Buddhi in
the mind. Discrimination is from Buddhi and from**

**discrimination is effected the union of Jivatman and
Paramatman.**

Commentary: The light in an oil lamp does not shine by
the power of the wick, but by the power of the oil in the
lamp. In the same way, a Jnani, one who has merged
his/her identity in Shiva, operates from that Shiva
Consciousness at all times. Such a Jnani relies on the will
of God and the intuition that comes from absorption in God
for all his/her needs.

Like the wick in an oil lamp, the Jnani understands that his
individual intelligence has no power of its own, but rather
should be merged in the pure Shakti that is the sole agent of
this world-appearance. A Jnani knows that he is not the
body, but that which transcends the body, and he acts
accordingly.

You should direct your individual intellect to the Sahasrar
through Meditation. Allow your limited intellect (buddhi)
to merge with the Divine Intellect and Will of God that can
be experienced at the top of the central nerve (sushumna) in
the Sahasrar. Concentrate both your mind and intellect
there and allow them to merge into the Buddhi of Shiva.
Through Meditation, direct your mind to that place until it
dissolves. Then you will attain the subtle discrimination of
the Self and become God by merging your individual
identity in Shiva, the Paramatman.

**253. From one coconut, many coconuts are produced.
If you cut the trunk of the coconut tree at the bottom,
the production of coconuts ceases. Vasana
(attachment), which is like the trunk, should be cut at
the root by the ax of discrimination. Then comes peace.
The characteristics of Sadhuguna, Satwaguna, and
peace and all such qualities, come from non-attachment.
When Buddhi becomes steady, it is called Satwaguna.**

Sat (truth) is like letters engraved in stone. The talk of the worldly is like letters engraved on a chalk slab.

Commentary: Just as from the seed of one coconut many other coconuts are produced, from one thought, notion, craving or desire many others are produced. The root of this problem is the expectation of sense pleasures and worldly pleasures that come from attachment to craving and desire. These are like the trunk of a tree. To remove them you have to uproot this tree of ignorance and destroy its roots.

You can only accomplish this through the subtle discrimination that allows you to tell the difference between what is limiting and binding and what is the true Reality, the Absolute. Then peace is attained. When you merge your will into the Absolute One God, it is purified and becomes steady. This is the real Sattva Guna. This Truth is permanent. Worldliness is transient.

254. Once the well should be emptied of its water. All the mud should be removed. The water that then comes is the purest. Jnana is like this pure water. Once you burn away the thought of "I" and "mine," then non-attachment to the objects of the senses will result of its own accord.

Commentary: To clean a water well, you have to remove all the mud and dirt in the well. Then you get pure water. In the same way, to become Liberated, you have to empty yourself of the impurities of the ego, the mind and the intellect. Once you have purified these three through spiritual practice as instructed by a Siddha Guru, then you experience the "pure water" of Jnana. Once your sense of difference and separateness has been destroyed, dispassion results naturally as your attachment to objects of sense dissolves.

255. When a man has learnt to write on paper, he need not practice writing on sand spread on the ground. Similarly, when a man has attained Brahman that is qualityless, he does not descend to Brahman with qualities. When the milk has been changed into buttermilk, can the latter be again converted into milk?

Commentary: Once buttermilk is churned from milk, it cannot be converted back to milk. Having learned to write on paper, humankind has never reverted back to writing in dirt or sand. In the same way, when a person is Liberated, when a person attains the state of God-realization known as Purnaham Vimarsha, she becomes God, he becomes Shiva-Shakti and does not fall back into ignorance of the Truth. Such a person remains in the uninterrupted state of Shiva Consciousness, even while going about her mundane activities.

256. Those who have come to buy the milk, should not ask what the price of the cow is. Similarly, those who hanker after Atma should not bother themselves about the body. The man who has attained the Atman is like the dry kernel within the coconut, i.e. he has no attachment to the body. When the rope is burnt to ashes, it cannot be made into a rope again. No man can do evil to another man. Atman will be good or evil according to his own thinking.

When we say some other man is the cause, it has a subtle meaning. The boat must be pushed off with the hand that it may move. Similarly, there must be some one as Guru for Atma knowledge. When the boat has reached the opposite bank, the boatman's help is no longer needed. How is the boat in the water? So is the Atman in the body. Suppose the feet are dirty with mud. In order to wash off the mud, we must go to a place where there is water. If you fear to touch the water, how can the mud be washed away?

You cannot produce sound with one hand only. When both hands strike against each other, then you are conscious of an energy (sound is produced). Although all fingers are not of the same size, when you take your meals, they come to one size. So, when your experience ripens, you see the one, indivisible.

Faith in the guru is like the cry of a jackal. Just as the cry of all jackals is similar, so also are the hearts of all Sadhus similar. The water in the well is the same at all levels. There are not two waters in the same well. So also, the life energy is the same in all mobile and immobile beings. Likewise, the energy in the sun and the moon is the same. Atma is in space and space is in Atma. Those who have realized this will sing with joy.

They know the Ananda Kundalini. They will try to discover where this Kundalini is. They will join it by Pranayama after finding it out. They must join it by repeatedly performing Pranayama. They must realize Bhakti. They must realize Mukti. They must conquer both birth and death and must forget all. One must conquer death and things allied to it. One must understand the true nature of Maya. One should realize Nityananda (eternal joy).

O Mind! Become one with this eternal joy. Enjoy such a mind which has become one with this eternal joy. Become one with the Supreme Being. O Mind! The external world must melt and become one with the Supreme Being. One who has become one with the Supreme has accomplished the object of his birth. One must concentrate his mind on the Supreme. One must become one with the Supreme.

Wakefulness, dream state, and sleep state must melt in the Supreme and become one. The power of discrimination (Buddhi) is the key to self-knowledge,

and that key must always be in the hand. Just as a man, possessing a treasure box, must be very careful about the key of the box, so also, Buddhi must be concentrated in the brain.

The water is hot only so long as it is kept on the fire. But when the vessel is kept on the ground, the water becomes cooler and cooler. Our Buddhi must be like the water placed over a fire. Similarly, faith should be constant. Jiva is like a calf tied in a room. The calf is always very eager to go out of the room. So also, Jiva is very eager to drink Jnana that is like Amrita (ambrosia).

Commentary: Those who seek the Truth of their own true nature will find it by breaking their attachment to the body and merging with what is inside the body. For one who has become Liberated there is no attachment to the body. When the rope is burnt to ashes, it cannot be made into rope again. In the same way, once the yogi has gone across and merged her individual identity in Shiva-Shakti, he does not become attached to the body again. Breaking this attachment to the body and the senses requires that you follow the instruction of a Siddha Guru until you are set on your own path.

Just as a boat needs an agent to leave its port (to push it off into the water), a seeker needs the guiding hand of a Siddha to cross the ocean of worldliness. When the feet are dirty, we need water to wash them clean. We don't fear the water. If we did, we would walk around with dirty feet all the time. In the same way, to experience God and to merge with God, we have to wash the dirt of countless lifetimes of ignorance from our being. To do this, we need a Guru, a Siddha.

If we fear taking such a Guru for spiritual leadership, our ignorance can never be removed. Just as you have to put two hands together in order to get a sound from clapping, Guru and Disciple must come together and become one being if Liberation is to be attained. (In India, during Sri Bhagawan's time, many people ate with their hands. This is still the practice in some places today. To take food in one hand, you have to clump the fingers together with the food in your fingertips.)

Just as bringing the fingers together makes it possible for you to hold and eat food, when your spiritual practice ripens under the instruction of a Siddha, you are able to grasp and hold the constant rapture of Shiva that is indivisible. All yogis engaged in spiritual practice require Faith in the Guru to go across. This faith is essential. Without Faith in the Guru, you will falter. God exists equally in all sentient and insentient beings. The yogi's role is to verify this Truth for himself by going inside. Atma, the Absolute Paramashiva, is contained in all space, time and ether. And this space, time and ether is also contained in Paramashiva.

Those who have realized this bask in the joy of the Self at all times. When you discover the awakened Kundalini through Shaktipat Diksha, then you must nurture it through repeated Pranayama (yogic breathing). In this way, you must realize Bhakti (devotion/love) and Mukti (Liberation) in this very life. You must conquer the cycle of birth and death by realizing God. You must come to realize the true nature of Shiva's Maya that is an illusion of a world that does not really exist separate from God.

Realize eternal Joy! O Mind! Become one with this eternal Joy (Nityananda) that is the Bliss of the Absolute. Enjoy such a mind that has been purified by dissolving into Shiva Consciousness. In this way, melt the notion of an external world and remain absorbed in your own Bliss. One who has become one with Shiva-Shakti has fulfilled the goal of all life. Concentrate your mind on the Supreme.

Become one with the Supreme. Merge your states of waking, dreaming and deep sleep with your own Shiva Consciousness.

Viveka (discrimination) is the key to attaining knowledge of the Self. This subtle discrimination becomes ripe when your intellect is purified. You must guard this Buddhi (intellect) carefully to make sure that it remains free of the ignorance of sense pleasures and worldly pleasures. The water is hot only as long as it is kept on the fire. The Buddhi remains pure only as long as it is kept focused on God. This focus requires Faith. Every human being longs for true happiness and the experience of peace and ultimate Joy. Everyone wants this Jnana. It's just that most look for it in all the wrong places.

257. Dharana is the means by which Buddhi's power of discrimination is increased. Dharana is the path to Mukti. Dharana is the path leading to the highest. Prana (life energy) to become steady, Dharana is a means. When life energy becomes steady, the mind becomes steady. When Prana is given an "upward" direction, then Jnana enters every nerve and peace is the result. Then nature and the subtle become separated. Then powers resulting from yoga peace of mind, forgiveness, patience -- these are experienced in Buddhi.

Those who practice constant Dharana feel that the whole external world is existing in themselves. One should, being quite steady in mind, be enjoying eternal joy (Nityananda). Atma is beyond all karmas and formality. Karma is that which is done without attachment. A man is free from sin if he performs karmas disinterestedly. Karma is that which is done by the knowledge of Atma who is actionless and passionless.

Commentary: The constant, steady contemplation or rumination over God (Dharana) is how the individual intellect is purified. It is how you develop the subtle discrimination that allows you to see God at all times. This steady contemplation, this constant remembrance of God is the path to Liberation. Through Dharana, the breath becomes slow and steady. When Prana, the life force, becomes steady, the mind becomes quiet. When this Prana is directed upward into the Sushumna to Sahasrar, Jnana (true knowledge/wisdom) enters every nerve of your being and a steady peace is the result.

When this steady peace dawns, you are able to discriminate between what is real and what is unreal. You are able to observe God's immanent and transcendental aspects at play and you are able to choose the transcendental over the ignorance of worldliness. Then the qualities of peace, compassion, patience and forgiveness come looking for you.

When you practice the constant Dharana that quiets the mind, your experience is that the entire universe exists inside you and is reflected on your own internal screen. In this way, you come to enjoy eternal Bliss (Nityananda). This state of Bliss is the Atman. It is beyond all activity and formality.

Selfless Service (Seva or Karma Yoga) is that which is done without attachment to the result. A person is freed from the bondage of ignorance when she performs actions with complete dispassion. When you perform karma (action) in this way, you do not create any new karmas for yourself.

258. Atma is not perceptible to the senses. It is perceived by intelligence (Buddhi). It is not perceptible as a thing with form and qualities. To those whose attention is fixed on the body, it is very difficult to attain

peace. It is also very difficult for them to see the Atma. The attention towards the visible should be lessened. The love towards the invisible should be increased. So long as the attention is directed towards the visible, pain and pleasure may appear to be dual. But when the attention is directed towards the invisible, the sense of duality will disappear.

Commentary: God cannot be perceived or experienced through the senses. God is experienced when the senses and the mind are completely quiet so that the individual intelligence (Buddhi) can be easily directed to Shiva. You cannot attain peace by attachment to the body. The job of the body and the senses is to conceal God. It is their very nature to cause delusion and to limit your awareness of your true nature. For this reason, your attention should always be on God, even as you go about your daily, mundane activities. This is the goal of Yoga, to destroy all sense of duality.

259. The sacred syllable OM is like a storm in the sky. OM is without beginning or ending. Omkar is like a stage manager in a drama. As it works through the bodies of men, those bodies are pervaded by Omkar. This syllable is inside us, outside us and everywhere. It is the cause of everything that exists. We need not bring it up to consciousness anywhere. That sound exists in everything.

We need not recall it separately to memory. This energy is not divisible but indivisible. This sound exists in every animal. Whatever sound is produced by animals, it is nothing but Omkar. What is called Pranava is another name for Omkar. When it is united with Prana and moves in the body it is called Pranava.

When nature and the subtle (i.e. physical and non-physical) Sthoola and Sookshma are separate, it is

Pranava. When we feel both to be one, then it is called the feeling of oneness. This is identical with Omkar. At that time, one sees the ONE everywhere. That which you worship with faith, becomes ALL.

Commentary: The sacred mantra Om (Aum) is like the power of creation and destruction. Om is in everything and everything is in Om. This sound pervades everything and everyone, everywhere. The mantra Om is contained inside every living being and creature. It is who we are and, therefore, requires no concept or idea to understand and experience.

The sound Om is the indivisible energy of Shiva-Shakti. Even animals produce the sound Om. When this sound mixes with Prana, it becomes all of the vital constituents of the body. It is known as Pranava in this way. When this Pranava merges with our experience of the Absolute, we experience Shiva Consciousness. To worship this inner experience with Faith is to absorb the entire universe into yourself.

260. That energy called Omkar pervades the universe and is formless. It is the light in ALL and light of ALL. Ignorance and knowledge are mere phantoms, not realities. Happiness and misery will never touch a man who has realized the oneness.

Commentary: Omkar is Chit Shakti. It emanates as sound from this one unifying Spanda principle that is the formless Absolute, Shiva. What we refer to as ignorance and knowledge are concepts created by the use of language. And language is a limitation in Shiva's Maya that is responsible for illusion. Concepts like happiness and misery are only words used to educate the unenlightened. A Siddha, a God-realized being is not tainted by these concepts and lives beyond their limitation.

261. If you have Manas, you want everything. If you have no Manas, you do not want anything. If you have Manas, God becomes a separate being for you. When you have merged Manas in Buddhi, you have no separate God. All appears as one. If you have desire, you want a separate God, because God's help is necessary to accomplish your desire. Then the Manas goes after the various objects of the senses and causes doubt about various matters. Then one feels the necessity of an idol or image. Cause and effect appear to be two separate categories. The image worship is due to Maya or ignorance.

Commentary: When you focus your inner energy outside of yourself, the Manas (mind) is formed. The nature of the mind is to think and to become active with concepts, notions and desires for this and that. So, once the mind is formed in this outward flow, you start to desire objects and that desire leads to cravings and your want for everything. When the mind is thought-free, it dissolves in Chiti. This is the state of Samadhi. In this state, your experience is that of complete Bliss and, because there are no thoughts, you have no desires and do not want anything.

When the Manas is formed, you experience God as being separate from yourself. When engaged in thoughts, concepts and notions in this way, you begin to see spirituality as a field to grow crops in. The notion of a separate God serves your idea of the fulfillment of sense pleasures and worldly pleasures because you want something or someone to turn to help you acquire objects. This pursuit of limiting desire and craving leads to the experience of pain and pleasure.

Pain and Pleasure create doubt in the mind, and this doubt causes you to have fears. Then you feel the necessity to worship an idol or statue, something that will listen to your problems and grant your desires without questioning your

motives. Although cause and effect seem to be two
separate things, one who has merged his conscious
awareness in the Absolute knows that these are one in the
same. They are experienced inside the body of Supreme
Consciousness on one's own internal screen.

**262. What is called Akash is in the upward direction.
What is called "male" is a subtle state. What is called
"female" is nature.**

Commentary: Akash means space. The upward direction
is a reference to directing Prana upwards through the
Sushumna into the Heart space in the head in order to
experience Chidakasha. In Yoga science, references to
"male" are references to the transcendental aspect of God's
nature and references to "female" are indications of God's
immanent aspect or his representation to himself of this
world-appearance, which he manifests inside His own
being. To a Siddha, the physical body is not real. Only
Divine Consciousness is real. So, the words "male" and
"female" cannot be references to the body or the gender of
that body.

**263. Men who have no desire need not have a separate
God. They need not strive for anything. When the
mind runs after various objects of the senses, to bring
the mind to one-pointedness, what is called the practice
is necessary. Man should concentrate on Buddhi as
long as there is the beating of the pulse in man, and as
many times as the pulse beats. The Manas should not
be united with the senses. Whatever you may do, your
mind should be concentrated inwards upon Buddhi.**

**In order that a man may not be drowned in water, he
must learn how to swim. Maya should be conquered by
the Supreme Maya. What is Maya? When the Manas
runs after sense objects a variety of desires is created.
It is you that clings to the coconut tree. The coconut**

**tree does not cling to you. Similarly, has Maya hands
and legs to catch hold of you?**

Commentary: Once you remove limiting desire from your
being, once you desire only to remain absorbed in God and
to follow God's will, then you realize that you are God and
God is you. It is the nature of the mind to be fickle. It is
the nature of the mind to chase after and crave objects of
sense. So, the mind must be trained to break this habit.
This training occurs through daily spiritual practice under
the instruction of a Siddha Guru. It is only through this
practice that the mind can be taught to seek God and to
become absorbed in God.

This world-appearance is like an ocean of craving and
desire. When you eliminate craving and desire, then you
are able to swim in this ocean without drowning. Shiva's
Maya is this ocean of worldliness. Conquer this Maya by
merging with the creator of it, Shiva. You are greater than
your cravings and desires for pleasure and pain. You are
above these. It is not that they come looking to subdue
you. It is that you chase after them.

So, stop chasing after pleasure and pain. Stop clinging to
craving and desire. Shiva's Maya cannot keep you in
bondage unless you choose to remain ignorant by turning
away from God. So, follow the Guru and do your practices
daily for as long as your heart is beating.

**264. Purposelessness is felt only in the subtle.
Discrimination is becoming one of Manas with Buddhi.
What is called Samadhi is seeing the one in all. By
practice, one must conquer the six enemies of the
Atman in the body; desire, anger, etc. A Sadhaka, a
beginner in God-realization, should not talk ill of
others. If he does so, his progress will be retarded.
Like that of a sprout on which a heavy stone is placed.
A Sadhaka must not relax his practice even for a**

ghatica (24 minutes). The mind should be ceaselessly engaged in the practice.

Commentary: Freedom from attachment and aversion is known as the state of purposelessness or dispassion. This state can only be experienced by going inside. Perfect Discrimination is what happens when the intellect and the mind are merged in God. What is called Samadhi is seeing God in everything and everyone, everywhere.

By practice, one must conquer the six enemies of the Atman in the body that are limiting desire, anger, greed, lust, illusion and envy. In the early stages of your spiritual practice it is very important that you don't gossip about other people and find fault with them. This is a mistake that many seekers and yogis make.

Fault-finding and gossip destroy the Shakti that you are seeking to build inside you through your practice, like that of a sprout on which a heavy stone is placed. A Sadhaka, a practicing yogi, must not relax his practice even for a ghatica (24 minutes). The mind should be ceaselessly engaged in spiritual practice through cultivating the constant awareness of God.

265. The Prana must be firmly fixed in an upward direction with great faith. That is the path to Liberation. This body is like a cave to the Atman, and in this cave, dwells the eternal Atman. Yoga means becoming one. When the two become one, that is Yoga. When the mind and Buddhi become one, it is called Yoga.

When Jiva travels by the path of Buddhi and enters Brahmarandhra, it is called Yoga. Devotion, reasoning and power, these three become one and become Omkar. Egotism becomes merged in Omkar. Just as camphor is lost in fire, mind and Buddhi become one with each

other. Like little children rocked to sleep, Chitta, being placed in Buddhi, must know who the "I" is.

Commentary: The path to Liberation is inside yourself. That path is, literally, the central nerve or Sushumna Nadi and that is the Siddha Path. When the awakened Kundalini Shakti blazes upward through this central path, your entire being is purified and the ego, individual intellect and mind, along with the senses, become absorbed in Shiva Consciousness. This is the only true spiritual path.

In order to cause Kundalini to rise, you first need to receive Shakipat from a Siddha. After Shaktipat, once instructed in the right use of Pranayama, Kundalini rises on the back of Prana Shakti. When this Prana (riding on the breath) is properly directed into the Sushumna Nadi and remains there, Liberation is attained. This is the path of Yoga that causes the intellect, ego, mind and the senses to merge in the Absolute.

Only that which causes your identity to become one the Absolute can be called Yoga. When this occurs, your limited power of reasoning merges with Chit Shakti and you become one with the power of the mantra Om. You become one with the deity of the mantra, Shiva. Just as camphor dissolves in fire, when the mind becomes absorbed in God it dissolves in Chiti, the Universal Buddhi.

Just as a child can be rocked gently to sleep, you can gently wean your mind (chitta) off of the limitation of sense objects and cause it to dissolve in Shiva Consciousness. In this way, you come to know who you really are, that Supreme I-Consciousness of God.

266. O Mind! Enter the house of Ananda! When the whole area is flooded, we cannot distinguish the wells and tanks in that area. Because there is darkness, we must infer there is light. When you taste sweet things,

remember there are pungent things to be swallowed. What is the state of Jiva when Jiva has realized that the Atman is not the body? Such souls have attained their pristine condition. "I" and "mine" are not visible to the physical eyes. "I" and "mine" are not to be found above the tip of the nose.

That which is above these, has neither beginning nor ending. A visible object has a beginning and an ending. Since Atma is invisible to the physical eye, Atma is without beginning and ending. It is impossible to lessen the power of Atman because Atman is always constant. Just as space is homogeneous everywhere, so is the Atman the same everywhere. The head of man is the abode of the light, of millions of suns. Which is bigger, the eye or the sun?

If the eye is spoiled, is it possible to see the sun? So the eye is more important. The form of gold images is the creation of the mind. When a man is photographed, the picture is according to the posture of the sitter. The virtues and the opposites in the photographer are not seen in the picture.

Commentary: O Mind! Merge into the eternal Bliss of Shiva. Just as, when an area is flooded, you cannot find the separate streams, wells and tanks; in the same way, flood your being with Shiva Consciousness so that you can no longer see any difference between yourself, the other objects of this world, and God.

Shiva has two aspects, the transcendental and the immanent. If you are only conscious of this world-appearance as a mere world, then you have to remember that pain always follows pleasure and pleasure always follows pain. If your knowledge is limited to the mundane activity of this world-appearance, you will be hopelessly bound by this pair of opposites, pleasure and pain. Once you realize God, all duality ceases and you realize that you are not the body and that there is only unity in this world.

Freedom is seeing only the ONE Shiva-Shakti where others see difference and diversity. This freedom is the Absolute. It has no beginning and no end. What is visible in this world-appearance is transient. It takes birth and dies. But the Atman neither takes birth nor dies. It is, eternally. Shiva's power cannot be lessened, for it is the power behind every power you experience in this world. Shiva is constant.

Just as space is one and the same everywhere, Shiva is the same everywhere. His nature is unchanged, even though he takes the form of all the objects of this world. In the Sahasrar is the light of millions of suns. But without the ability to see those suns, to experience them in the Sahasrar, without this ability, those suns do not exist for you. So, which is more important? Those suns or your ability to see and experience them?

This is why the Siddhas say practice, practice, practice. Everything that can be experienced in this world is an illusion created by the mind. When a photographer takes a picture, often it is the case that you see in the picture what the photographer wants you to see, and not all that is really there. In the same way, the impure mind, the impure ego and intellect, show you the taint of your craving and desire, not your true nature. This is why they must be purified in the fire of Yoga, in the fire of your spiritual practice.

267. The fruit is according to the internal faith of a man. Good and evil are not of the Atman. Atman, like the reflection of an object, takes that form which the mind wants Him to take. The Jiva is like a bird in a cage. When the nest is spoiled, the bird is not affected. The bird flies away. The bird may build a new nest and enter it in six months, in a year, or in five minutes. That

**depends on the birds' efforts. From this place to the
railway station, you can go in 24 minutes or in a month.**

Commentary: Your inner state is your fate. Your direct
experience of God, along with the degree to which you
have that experience, will be determined first by your Faith.
Shiva-Shakti, the Atman, is above good and evil. Good
and evil are notions that exist only in Shiva's Maya, only in
this illusion of a world-appearance. This is so because the
Shakti of Shiva, like the reflection in an object, takes
whatever form your mind desires. This is His Play of
Divine Consciousness.

The individual bound soul (Jiva) is like a bird in a cage. If
the nest gets spoiled, the bird is not affected. It will simply
fly away and make another nest somewhere else. In the
same way, the Jiva does not die when the body rots. It
simply drops the body and takes another form after death.
Depending on your Karmas, you can be reborn in several
minutes or several months. In this way, you continue to
wander about in the cycle of birth and death until
Liberated.

**268. Sadhana (practice) is necessary for Vairagya
(desirelessness) to be steady. For Vairagya to be
permanent we must have practice. Vairagya is not
related to the body. When the mind is unwavering in
all the external and internal causes and effects, then the
one sees the Atman. When the idea of Jnana and
Ajnana is absent, then one sees the Atman.**

**When one knows but he is not aware that he knows,
then one sees the Atman. Men who have realized the
Atman, are like blind men, are like deaf men. Although
they hear, they do but they are unaware of what they
do. When the senses are acting, they are disunited with
them. So their action is inaction to them. In them, the
idea of creation is less and the idea of nihility is more.**

**Since their power of forgetfulness is great, their actions
are inactions. Their attention is concentrated not on the
coconut shell but on the kernel (on Atman, not on the
body). They are beyond both sin and merit. They are
like a boat in water. Just as water and boat are quite
distinct, they feel the gross and the subtle to be separate.
They are indifferent to bodily functions but
concentrated in Jnana. They drink the juice of the
sugarcane and throw away the outer skin.**

**When the sugar is manufactured, it does not become the
cane again. When by practice, one has realized that he
is Atman, the idea that he is the body never returns.
Like an old vessel, after the necessary repairs, shining
with the lustre of the new, Buddhi, when the Vasanas
are annihilated, can be transformed into the pure Satva
quality. Then we will have contentment.**

Commentary: Dispassion or non-attachment (Vairagya) to
objects (people, places and things) is necessary on the
spiritual path. To go across, to become Liberated, your
Vairagya has to become steady. For this to happen, you
have to perform Sadhana (spiritual practice after Shaktipat),
under the leadership of a Siddha. This dispassion has
nothing to do with the body. It dawns when your mind
becomes completely absorbed in God and remains that
way, even as you experience internal and external
movement in the cause and effect of this world-appearance.

When the mind dissolves, there are no concepts or ideas.
Therefore, the notions of Jnana and Ajnana (wisdom and
ignorance) are also absent in the highest state of Shiva
Consciousness. When these are absent, you experience
only the pure scintillating Spanda of the Absolute, Shiva.
Then your state is one of knowing all without being
impressed by the fact that you know. Pain and pleasure
become the same to you and you become immune to
compliments and insults, you become immune to happiness

and sorrow and you remain completely detached from the activity of your own senses.

You commit actions only as necessary, and with no expectation of the result, which you know is directed by God and belongs to God. When you are able to live in this manner, what is known as the creation, or this universe, pales in comparison to the experience of your own inner state. You realize that this world-appearance is like a city in a mirror and the only Reality is the ONE Shiva who masquerades as the objects of sense that are really reflected only in your imagination.

In a Siddha (perfected being), the experience of memory is weakened. One who is Liberated begins each day as a brand new adventure without perpetuating anything from the past. Her constant state of samadhi ensures that her memory is purged on a constant basis. This is what is meant by forgetfulness. A Liberated being is no longer attached to the body. Having burned this attachment completely, along with the seed of this attachment, a Siddha never becomes attached to the body again.

When you acquire this state, your intellect becomes so pure that you merge your individual identity into Shiva. And you are then dwelling in this world without being of this world. To attain this constant state of Shivo'ham, the vasanas (latent impressions) in your being must be destroyed. Once they are destroyed, you become the Pure Perceiving Awareness, the Supreme I-Consciousness of God. Then you will be eternally content.

269. Unless the intellect is purified, contentment does not spring. Unless the intellect is purified, Chitta does not become steady. Unless Chitta is purified, a man cannot free himself from verbal delusion. W hen ice is placed in water, both become one. Similarly, man who has realized the Atman, merges in the Atman. Just as

the rivers enter the sea, all Vasanas are merged in Atman.

Atman is not a thing. Karma is a thing. The steamer is in the sea. To the looker on, it appears to touch the sea water, but the steamer is quite different from the sea water. There is no relation between the two. So must a man be in the affairs of the world. He must not have any attachment to worldly things. Just as Brahmins wait eagerly for plantain leaves to be spread and meals served, so must a man wait for mental purification and Mukti.

Commentary: Your individual intellect must be purified by your own Sadhana in order for you to experience contentment. Without this steady experience of contentment, your mind cannot become quiet. If your mind is not quiet, you become a slave to the delusion brought about by Matrika Shakti, the power of sound inherent in language. When the mind is bounced about by constant thoughts and notions, words have complete power over you and you are easily swayed by them.

Ice, when placed in water, dissolves into that same water. In the same way, when you realize your true nature as Shiva, you merge with Shiva. Just as a ship can travel in the sea without losing its properties as a ship, so too, Shakti travels through this world-appearance becoming all the various forms, but without losing her essential nature as Divine Consciousness.

One who has realized God knows this from experience and behaves the same way as this Shakti when engaging in worldly affairs. A yogi must not become attached to worldly things, even when he finds himself in situations where he experiences and enjoys them. To acquire this state, you have to be eager to perform Sadhana under the

direct leadership of a Siddha and you have to want
Liberation.

**270. No one wants to look at a fruitless tree. Why is
man called man? Because he has Manas (thinking
power), he is called man. Manas should get knowledge
of various sorts and, being united with peace, must
become one with Omkar. He who desires Mukti
(eternal life) should at once give up the idea "I am the
body." Such people alone can realize the Atman. To
those who think "I am this body," it is very difficult to
see the Atman. Those who hold fast to the idea "I" and
"mine" may practice for a thousand years. Yet they
will not attain even the slightest fraction of Shanti.**

**If one bathes in a river, his body becomes clean, let him
be a pariah or a brahmin or a child. Likewise, the
internal state of man is the same, though the exterior of
every man may appear to be different. Chilis,
watermelons, etc., may grow in the same field. The
nature of the one is different from that of the other.
The heat of fire is only felt by those who sit near the fire
but never by those who sit in water.**

**Peace is cool like water. Before you are hungry, the
food must be prepared. So also, before you become a
householder, you must know the duty of a householder.
A householder should have his exterior and interior
equally pure. He should distinguish clearly between
cause and effect.**

Commentary: Just as no one values a barren tree, you
should not place any value on the body. It is barren, just
like a fruitless tree. A human being is called such and
valued as such due to the existence of the energy known as
the mind. It is due to thinking power, that human beings
are recognized as such. For this reason, you should seek to
know the very nature and substance of the mind.

Acquire the knowledge you need to interact in this world-appearance and then train your mind to become one with its source, the Shakti of Shiva. This is Omkar. If you want eternal peace, if you want true happiness, if you want to be Liberated from the bondage of ignorance, you have to completely surrender the notion that you are the body. Only then can you realize God. If you continue to believe that you are the body, and if you continue to engage the notions of difference and the notions of "I" and "mine," you will never have peace.

All, regardless of social status, race and behavior, become clean when they wash in water. And all bath in the same substance called water. In the same way, all are purified when they turn their attention to God. Although appearing to be different on the outside, by way of looks, color, language and behavior, all are that ONE God. And all must go to the same place inside to realize this fact.

Different crops will grow in the same field of dirt. Although being different in qualities, these crops owe their existence to that same field of soil. If you remain absorbed in the peace of the inner Self, you cannot be burned by the fire of illusion that is this world-appearance, even though you may walk through that fire.

Before you can eat, you have to prepare the food. In the same way, before you can merge with God, you have to perform Sadhana. Know your place in this life. Know your Dharma. Assume the role dictated by your Karma, by your past superimposition, and play that role gleefully, while remaining absorbed in the Truth.

271. A man may run after a horse in vain for any length of time. Let him ride the horse. Let him bind the legs of a horse and get on its back, quickly. So also, worldly men must keep their mind free from attachment to sense objects. Just as water slips off from

an umbrella of palmyra leaves, so also, a man must be free from the idea "I am the doer."

A householder must be like a calf offered to a temple. All should be offered to the Brahman. But one cannot say that a man who does like this is nearer God and a man who does not like this is far away from him. If you keep a light before a thousand people, it reaches all without making any distinction. Anyone may take it.

Where there is light, there is no darkness. In the darkness there is no light. There can only be one thing (either light or darkness), not two at the same time. One's nature should be like the sun. One's Chitta must be cool like the moon.

Commentary: You can't ride a horse by running after it, chasing it from behind. In order to ride a horse, you have to subdue the horse, bind it with reigns and ride it from on top. In the same way, you can't subdue the mind by chasing after sense pleasures and worldly objects. In order to bring the mind under your control, you have to free it from the expectations of sense pleasures and worldly pleasures.

In this way, allow the results of your actions to "slide" off you like water rolls off an umbrella. Don't allow your ego to claim the results of your actions. In this way, the yogi must become free of the notion "I am the doer." One who maintains a career, a home and a family should offer all these to God, just as a calf is offered in a sacrifice. Take responsibility for your life and the role you play, remembering that you are a tool of God and that your life belongs to God. In this way, remain in this world, loving it as your very own Self.

Do not criticize or condemn those who do not have your same outlook. Do not condemn those or judge those who you perceive not to have your same experience of God. God exists in those people also and to the same degree that God exists in you. The Light of Divine Consciousness is always shining and anyone can embrace that Light, regardless of his/her past actions.

The Light of God does not coexist with ignorance. There is either ignorance or the Light of God. Where this Light shines, ignorance is dissolved. Purify your nature and align it with this Light, while keeping your mind absorbed in the cool, moon center of the Sahasrar.

272. Vairagya should be like fire burning a cloth. When Vairagya is highly developed, the interior (Atma) splendor will be visible. The body may sit firm but it is the mind that should sit firm. Those whose minds are not purified, seldom have equal sightedness. Those who do not practice, will have great difficulty in possessing the Satwa quality in them. The subtle intelligence is developed by practice. Unless you practice, the desire for worldly things cannot be destroyed.

Hankering after landed property, after woman, and after gold, is difficult to be extinguished. What is the thing to be attained by man? When the chitta is free from the three forces, Satwa, Rajas, and Tamas, it is called Purushartha. Just as dirty linen becomes clean when washed in soap water, so also, Chitta should be purified by washing it in the soap water of Buddhi and it must be made as pure as space.

When you learn sewing on a machine, in the beginning your attention must be fixed not on the legs but on the hands. When we fix our attention on Buddhi and make the mind merge into the heart space, then we will attain that eternal peace which is called NITYANANDA.

Commentary: Burn the ignorance of duality in the fire of Vairagya (detachment/dispassion). When this dispassion is highly developed, the complete splendor of God becomes visible. What is most important is the posture of your mind. The mind should be firmly rooted in the Self. If your mind has not been purified in the fire of Sadhana, it will be very difficult for you to attain Equality Consciousness.

It is only through Sadhana (spiritual practice under the leadership of a Siddha) that your desires and cravings for sense objects can be destroyed. The habit of chasing after sense pleasures is difficult to destroy on your own. You need the Grace-bestowing power of God to accomplish this. When you free yourself from the effects of the Three Gunas, when you rise above these, you become Shiva. Attain eternal Bliss by merging your individual identity into Shiva Consciousness. When you wash your being in this Chit Shakti, you will attain the eternal Bliss called Nityananda.

273. Those whose minds are pure may call God by any name they please. Prakriti is like a railway carriage. Those who are in it are like Jnana. The stations are like chakra. Within the chakras is the subtle. The subtle is within the tube. Within the subtle tube is the energy of the Kundalini. Kundalini, in the form of Omkar, is in the subtle tubes. Let this subtle be known by experience.

Commentary: Those whose minds are pure may call God by any name they please. Prakriti (nature) is like a shell. Within this shell is pure Shiva Consciousness or Jnana. Just as a railroad train stops at different stations, this Shiva Consciousness, in the form of Chiti or Spanda Shakti, runs through and makes stops at each of the Chakras and Nadis in your being.

This Shakti is very subtle in its movement. Shakti moves through the tube called Sushumna and all the 72,000 Nadis (subtle energy points) in the body. Moving in this way, She is known as Kundalini. It is this Kundalini, this Omkar that is what we call the subtle in the gross. It is Shakti who moves, Shakti who pulsates through the Sushumna and the other Nadis. Let this subtle be known through personal experience.

274. A certain man is a lord of scores of money. All cannot be millionaires at the same time. It depends on their past karmas. Everyone is rewarded according to his due. There is plenty of water in the sea. But the quantity of water one fetches depends on the size of the vessel one takes to fetch water. The fruit depends upon the vasanas of one's karmas.

It is because of the vasanas of former births that a man has a hankering after hearing the teachings of a Sadhu. It is because of these vasanas that one feels no happiness in worldly pleasures. Those who are guided by the vasanas of former births do not require separate vasanas. Vairagya itself is the result of the vasanas of former births. For such people, it is the time to tread the path to Mukti.

Commentary: Financial wealth is a direct result of past karmas from past lifetimes. Not everyone can become a millionaire. Acquiring vast sums of money is a direct result of the skill and relationships developed over several lifetimes of desire. Everyone reaps their desires based on the cycle of their karmas. Just as gathering a large amount of seawater will depend on the size of the vessel, the fulfillment of your desires will depend on the intensity of your desire and the level of your skill.

For some, the skill required to fulfill the desire may take more than one lifetime to attain. All desires are, eventually, fulfilled by the Lord who takes the form of the objects of desire and the skill required to fulfill that desire, based on your karmas. Karma is this limited desire for objects. This desire creates a ripple effect in your being called vasanas. When your desire becomes a desire to know God, when this kind of vasana ripples through your being for an extended period of time, God sends you a Guru and you begin to take an interest in spiritual instruction.

Once the quality of your desire changes in this way, you become less interested in worldly pleasures and more interested in a personal relationship with God. When this type of vasana, the desire for true knowledge, develops in your being over several lifetimes, Vairagya becomes stronger in you. When Vairagya becomes strong in you, it is time to tread the path to Liberation.

275. For attaining Jnana and Mukti, age is no consideration. This very moment is the time for the attainment of Jnana and Mukti. As soon as a man is hungry, it is the time for taking his meals. Those who are not hungry should wait for meals until they are hungry. One should have a keen hunger after Bhakti. The greater the heat of fire, the greater the boiling of water.

Shradha is the heat. Peace is like the ice in the brain. It fills the inside and manifests outside. Such a man becomes content in all respects and his mind becomes pure. Peace of mind, for attainment, does not cost us anything, like charity and dharma. When one is filled with peace, those who are near him are also infected with peace. It is enough if one person is filled with peace. Out of a thousand, if one has peace, a fraction of peace is enjoyed by all those who are around him.

A Sadhu, when he enters a crowd of worldly people, should have that peace which a hunter has when he approaches a tiger. A sadhu, to be in the world, should have immense peace and patience. Peace is very useful to move among thousands of worldly people.

Commentary: The only requirement for attaining the Wisdom of Liberation is Bhakti. Bhakti is complete surrender to and devotion for the practices as instructed by the Guru. This Bhakti is Love for and Devotion to the Guru and to God. This is all that is necessary. Age, race, brainpower, physical appearance and status are not considerations.

Just as it is time for food at the moment you are hungry, when a person has this Bhakti, that is the very moment to begin on the path to Liberation (Mukti). Water boils based on the intensity of the fire. The greater the fire, the quicker the water boils and the more intense the boiling. In the same way, the greater the Bhakti, the greater the spiritual attainment. Inner peace is attained through Bhakti. This inner peace then fills a person inside and then manifests outside, as a result.

Once this peace dawns, you become content and your mind is purified. This peace does not cost you anything. It's not like having to go into your pocket for money to pay a bill or to give to charity. When you are filled with this peace, everyone around you becomes infected with this peace. It only takes one person filled with this peace, to cause a transformation in others. It only takes a handful of people to spread this peace to the rest of the world.

A yogi should approach a crowd of people with the same steady courage and peace that a hunter uses to approach a crouching tiger. The yogi should go about her mundane activities with immense patience, while remaining absorbed in her own inner peace. To live in this world, inner peace is very useful and very necessary.

276. Various kinds of articles are brought to a fair. Similarly, peace should be practiced in various ways. When we are in the midst of thousands of people, we should have a firm will. When you think (wrongly) that you are in the midst of thousands, the idea of duality arises in you. Just as an airplane moves without the help of the earth, so also, one must learn to act without the help of the body.

The crown of firm belief "I am not this body" should be firmly planted in the heart. A traveler after being in the sun for a long time, becomes tired and goes for shelter to the shade of a tree on a hillside. There he forgets his fatigue. So too, those whose minds are absorbed in the search for God, forget all their worldly anxieties. Just as in the shade, the sun's heat is forgotten, "mineness" is forgotten by the absorption in God.

When we are inside a house, we do not want an umbrella. We are in need of an umbrella only when we go outside the house. Just as you do not want an umbrella inside the house, so also, when you are in the Great House called God, you feel no necessity of worldly enjoyment. When a man shuts the door of a house, he sees only things that are inside the house. Let him open the doors and come out. Then he will see what is outside.

Similarly, you must learn how to shut the doors of the five senses and how to open them. When the doors of a warehouse are locked, buying and selling ceases. When doors of the senses are shut, the difference between the external world and the "I" will vanish.

You must always be careful about the senses. Like a horse being controlled by the help of reins, you must control your senses by the help of discrimination. Your attention on the senses should be fixed like a nail in a wall. Buddhi (intelligence) should be concentrated in the head. Your attention should always be above the neck, never below the neck.

Commentary: When you go to a fair, you have choices on what to buy. Similarly, you have a number of choices in how you practice Peace. The experience of Inner Peace should be cultivated, not just in Meditation, but when you are going about your day, as well. When engaged in your daily mundane activities, even if those activities require you to be out of your home amongst a crowd of people, do not have the attitude that you are in a crowd of many. Understand that, no matter where you go and how many people there are, there is really only the ONE Shiva everywhere.

No matter where you are, God is the only one there. Just as an airplane moves about the earth without needing the help of the earth, you should move in this world, engaging in activity, without relying on the senses to guide you. The senses should be trained to rely on you, on your purified awareness, and you should not rely on the senses. Perform Sadhana every day so that you come to the understanding and experience that you are not the body or the senses. Plant the understanding firmly in your heart that you are Shiva. Like a traveler seeking shade from the sun under a tree, take refuge in God inside and place your anxieties at the feet of the Lord. Leave your worries there and do not take them up again.

The notion of "I" and "Mine" is forgotten completely when you dissolve your mind in Shiva-Shakti. This is the means of rising above Pleasure and Pain. When you become completely absorbed in your primordial nature, in your own

Shakti, you do not have to worry that you will again succumb to craving and desire. Once you have taken complete refuge in God and learned to trust in God's Divine Will, you will no longer have any expectations of sense pleasures or worldly pleasures.

Learning to be in this world without being of this world is essential. The way to accomplish this is to become absorbed in God through Sadhana. Once you have purified your senses in the fire of Yoga, you learn to use them as tools for the Divine. You learn to only engage them as is necessary to carry out only those mundane activities that are essential for your daily living. You don't require any additional stimulation because your only desire is to rest in your own Joy.

In this state, you see only God in everything and everyone, everywhere and it is only God that you want. Until you attain this state, you must be cautious about how you engage your senses. The senses have to be monitored constantly like a nail is fixed to a wall. Direct your individual intellect into the heart space in the Sahasrar and learn to keep your focus there so that you can keep the senses under your control. In this way, keep Kundalini focused in the heart space, in the Sahasrar, and not in the Chakras below the neck. If you leave Kundalini to rest in those Chakras below the neck, you will only fuel the craving and desire for more sense pleasures.

277. Just as gold is burnished after repeatedly being put into fire, so by repeated exercise of discrimination, the subtle should be enlightened. You must see the world in you. Our intelligence is only a means of Moksha. What is called Dharana is nothing but clear understanding of the subject. By this clear understanding, we come nearer to the Atman. We do not get experience from books. First experience, and from that experience, books are written.

The tree is in the seed. The seed is not in the tree. Man is not in the world. The world is in man. The world is subject to man. We express in words what we think in our minds. The heart should be free from hypocrisy. The heart of man should be perfectly pure. What the heart thinks, the tongue should talk. What one thinks, one must talk. Nobody you should deceive. Nobody you should hate.

You must not mix with others. Your mind must always be one-pointed. When you have a deceptive heart, it is like the sun in the mid-summer, a star comes out of the clouds and shines with glory. After a few seconds, it is hidden again by the clouds. So also is the mind of man. Sometimes, it appears to be pure but again in five minutes, it is over clouded by passions.

The egotistic mind melts in the Atman like a star that falls down from the sky. Akash (space) is not visible to the physical eye. Akash is that which is visible to the divine eye. By discrimination, we can experience discrimination. Sound is known by sound. Mind is perceptible to mind only.

Commentary: You get gold by purifying ore in fire. You get God by purifying your intellect in the fire of Sadhana. Individual intelligence exists only to see God inside and to become Liberated by that very sight. The entire universe is contained inside you. Experience it there by the outlook of Shiva. What is known as Dharana or contemplation is nothing other than the constant, uninterrupted vision of the Supreme Subject, Shiva-Shakti. Understanding this, you know and understand everything.

This experience cannot be found in books. It can only be found by going inside yourself through Sadhana. Great books have been written by those who have done so, and not the other way around. Just as a tree is innate in the seed, so too, the entire universe is contained inside a human being. The entire world-appearance is subject to humankind and not the other way around.

Free yourself from duality and hypocrisy. Only in this way can you attain Equality Consciousness. Equality Consciousness means the experience that nothing exists that is not Shiva. Having attained this state, keep your mind absorbed in Shiva so that you do not become prone to deception, greed or hatred. Keep good company and do not mix with others who believe that they are separate from God.

If you engage in deception, you will conceal God from yourself and, thereby, forget your Natural, Free state of being. The mind of the unenlightened is just like clouds that reveal the Sun for a few seconds, only to cover it up again. It is bounced back and forth between pleasure and pain, between deception and hatred and greed. People remember God in one moment and are overcome with passion for objects the next moment.

You can't have both. To become Liberated, you have to rise above both virtue and vice. Once your ego melts in the constant presence of the Divine you will realize this. Just as space is not visible to the eye, Shiva is not visible to the limited ego. So, purify the mind by the mind, purify the ego by having the ego that says, "I am God." Use discrimination itself to discern the source of that discrimination.

278. He is Paramatman (supreme being) who is in Jivatman (Atman). Paramatman is the witness to the qualities of the Atman. When Jiva realizes that he is not different from Paramatman, he is called Nityatma (the eternal spirit). When the tender mango is on the tree, it is united with the tree. So also are Jiva and Paramatman united. When Sat (Being or Existence),

Chit (pure perceiving awareness), and Ananda (bliss) are in union and when the three gunas are merged in Sat-Chit-Ananda, then only do we say that it is Yoga (union).

Commentary: The Supreme Being is in you and you are in the Supreme Being. The Absolute is the witness to the Creation, Sustenance and Withdrawal of this entire universe. When you realize that you are no different than God, then you become the eternal Subject. Jiva and Paramatman are one just like a tree and its fruit. Yoga is the transformation of human consciousness into Divine Consciousness. This transformation occurs when the activity of the three Gunas is absorbed in your primordial nature, which is Sat-Chit-Ananda.

279. The energy called Kundalini should be roused by Pranayama. By rousing Kundalini, a man must attain liberation. Faith is like a rope. Vayu (air) is the rope. You must hold the rope of Vayu tight. Faith must be tied by the rope of Dharana. What is faith is nothing but Dharana. Our attention must always be concentrated on Dharana. That concentration must always be coupled with faith. Faith should be filled in every nerve of the body.

To such people, there is no existence of Maya as a separate thing. Mind itself is Maya. It is the mind that creates (mental) images or ideas. All sorts of relations, all creation, cause and effect, light and universe, universal light and the Supreme Light; all these differences are caused by one's own ignorance (Maya). When this is realized, there is no fear of Maya. "All these forms are MY OWN FORMS." Thus should a wise man meditate.

When the mind becomes firm in meditation, and when the Supreme Oneness is realized in the sky of

Consciousness, it is called Moksha. The path of Moksha
is not far from one's Self. Like the distance between the
eye and ears, the distance between sin and merit is very
slight. Moksha is not beyond Buddhi. Pleasure and
pain are things to be merged in Buddhi. By the help of
Buddhi, one must attain Moksha. When the mind is
merged in the Self and when the oneness is realized, one
attains Moksha.

Jnana is internal. At the beginning, Jnana can be
known. As one progresses, this Jnana is also forgotten,
then there is nothing to be said or nothing to be listened
to. All is Brahman and Brahman is all. This state may
be called the state of "nothingness." Prana is like a
rope. When exhaling and inhaling it moves
harmoniously. Prana is indivisible. It has no difference
of time. Prana feels this difference when it is coupled
with the gross.

Jiva, because he is engrossed in the various qualities of
the world, has forgotten his real Self and has occupied a
lower rank. Let him take a higher (upward) direction
by the help of Buddhi. Prana should be tied down by
the rope of faith. Let Prana attain Moksha by its
upward direction. Liberation from the sensual ties is
Moksha. Then comes peace. O Prana! Enter the abode
of Peace. Have under control both this world and the
next! Such souls will attain Sat-Chit-Ananda.

They have no attachment to the results of karma. They
are eternally liberated from bondage. They are
eternally one minded. They have conquered the
qualities of the Jiva. Until the consciousness "I am the
body" is wiped off, Mukti is a thing far off. Unless the
idea of "twoness" is annihilated, there is no yoga, no
Mukti. In a sense, everyone is a yogi. But everyone of
such yogas has a certain object in view.

When a substance becomes one with the original substance, when the dualities of lives is wiped off, it is called union or oneness. When this is realized, we see oneness in all. The real Yoga is that which is detached from everything. That Yoga by which a man becomes free from desires is the path to Moksha. Doubt will not disappear until Jiva unites with Shiva and becomes one. When one does a thing that is not palatable to the other, one takes the other to be a mad man.

When both are interested in doing the same thing, one does not take the other to be a mad man. When both are equally interested in doing the same thing, there is nothing strange in doing that thing. The mind is like the cotton placed in the wind. Devotion to God is like water poured on the cotton. Similar is the destruction of the mind. The mind that is like cotton should be wetted by the water of Jnana and the Chitta should be freed from desires. That is Moksha.

In the manner of the cotton, let man attain Mukti. A man may meditate on the Atman although he is engaged in various actions. The various objects of the senses are outside us, not inside us. Even when we are performing various actions, it is not possible to keep the Buddhi separate from them. If a car driver, when he steers the car, takes his hands off of the wheel, the car runs in whatsoever direction and is endangered. Mind should be in Buddhi. We must not let the mind wander. Mind should be fixed on internal Dhyana.

Mind should be developed by the power of introspection. O Mind! Enter the sky of Consciousness by developing the subtle Buddhi and filling every nerve of the body with this Buddhi! O Mind! Be always content! O Mind! Do not be deluded by shadowy appearances!

Commentary: Kundalini Shakti lays dormant in three-and-a-half folds at the base of the spine. When awakened through Shaktipat, it begins its journey upward, through the Sushumna, into the Sahasrar, where it rests in union with Shiva. This journey is the path to Liberation known as the Siddha path or the easy path. Once awakened, the rising Kundalini should be supported by Pranayama. Performing this Pranayama as instructed by your chosen Guru causes Kundalini to rise in the central nerve, the Sushumna Nadi.

This specific breathing technique is its own Dharana, its own supreme contemplation. If you have Faith in this practice of Pranayama, you can, with practice, direct Kundalini to rest in the Sahasrar. This is the way to Liberate yourself from the effects of Shiva's Maya. This Maya is not separate from you, nor is it separate from God. It is contained within you. When you believe it to be different and separate from you, that is called ignorance.

Shiva's Maya is really none other than Shiva himself. Once you have purified your mind by causing it to turn within on a constant basis, you realize this fact. The mind is the tool Shiva uses to perpetuate Maya through the creation of thoughts, notions, ideas, concepts and language. These are perpetuated in your own imagination, where God becomes all those objects that you want him to become. Once you have dissolved the notion of duality in your own mind, Shiva's Maya, the veil that conceals His true nature, is destroyed.

This veil is destroyed through making your mind firm in Meditation. Then you realize that "All the forms in Shiva's Maya are my very own forms. It is I, the Supreme Subject, Shiva that exists everywhere I look." The dawning of this realization is not far from you. It is a short distance, just across the threshold of your own heart. The difference between the state of ignorance and the state of Liberation is very small. Illusion is the shadow of Truth. Knowing the

Truth is a matter of merging your individual intellect into the Buddhi, the Divine Will and Intelligence of Shiva-Shakti.

Once this is accomplished, the next step is to deposit all your notions of pleasure and pain into that Buddhi. When the mind is merged in the Self, this Supreme Buddhi becomes active in you and by this Buddhi, you attain Liberation. Jnana, the concept of Wisdom or true Knowledge, is known as such in the early stages of your Sadhana. Once you have attained Liberation, the notion of Jnana disappears and all that remains is Paramashiva, the Absolute or one Brahman that is like a burning flame where there is no wind.

In the state of the Absolute, there is no ignorance and, therefore, there is no Liberation either. These concepts don't exist in Shiva. They only exist in His Maya. Prana, the life breath, is like a rope tied to a bucket that you are using to raise water from a well. Prana is God. It is indivisible and timeless. Prana only senses difference and the measurement of time and space when it comes into contact with thinking, as it moves in the other channels outside of the Sushumna Nadi.

It is through attachment to this thinking that you have forgotten your essential nature as Shiva-Shakti. It is through craving for sense pleasures and worldly pleasures that you have concealed your true nature from yourself. In this way, you occupy a lower rank, a limiting and binding position. Take the upward direction with the help of the wisdom of the Self. Direct Prana into the Sushumna with complete Faith in Sadhana and the goal of Liberation.

When you break the ties of sense pleasures that bind you, this is Liberation. Eternal Peace follows. O Prana! Be into the Sushumna Nadi and up, up where the abode of peace awaits you in the Sahasrar. O Prana! Take refuge there.

Those who have mastered internal Kumbhaka by breathing internally in the Sushumna have no attachment to the results of their actions. In this way, they offer every deed to God and do not create any new karmas.

As a result, they are eternally Liberated from the bondage of ignorance and remain eternally absorbed in the Self (Sat-Chit Ananda). They have conquered their own limitations by wiping off the idea that they are the body. You cannot attain Liberation unless the notion that you are the body is completely destroyed. Unless the notion of duality is removed, there cannot be Mukti (liberation). In a sense, everyone is that Yogi, Shiva. However, you don't know that you are Shiva until the notions of "I" and "Mine" have been destroyed.

To be a real Yogi, you have to see God in everything and everyone, everywhere, without the slightest sense of difference between yourself and other objects (people, places and things). Yoga is that path by which you become free of craving and desire. Fear and doubt will remain in you until you merge your individual identity in Shiva Consciousness. People fear what they don't understand or have not been exposed to. Those who don't have a Siddha Guru, those who don't follow a Guru and who don't perform Sadhana, consider those who do to be mad.

However, they don't consider others with the same values and behavior to be mad. So, if they were to experience the Master and perform spiritual practice, they would no longer consider those who do the same to be mad. Therefore, there is nothing strange about performing Sadhana under the leadership of a Siddha. Trust your own experience of this and keep the company of those people who are like-minded on the spiritual path. KEEP GOOD COMPANY. This is everything.

If you put a piece of cotton in the wind when the wind is blowing, the cotton will blow away. But if you pour water on the cotton, it will not blow away. The mind is fickle and, like the piece of cotton, when allowed to experience worldly pleasures and sense pleasures, it will blow back and forth aimlessly, completely lost. But if you pour the water of direct knowledge of God on to the mind, the mind becomes steady and cannot be "blown" about by craving and desire.

Once the mind is completely absorbed in Shiva, you attain Mukti. The key is in training the mind. This is accomplished through Meditation on the Self. Even while engaging in the mundane activities of daily life, you can keep your mind centered in God. In this life, you have to act. You cannot avoid action. So, the goal is not to become inactive. The goal is to remain absorbed in God, even while taking action. This is Liberation.

Allow your mind to engage in the thoughts necessary to carry out the activity of your daily life, while remembering God at all times. This is what is called internal Dhyana or Meditation. My Gurudev used to say that anyone can sit in a corner with eyes closed in Meditation. The real accomplishment is to carry on this Meditation with your eyes open while engaging in action.

280. Those whose minds are merged in Samadhi, are not deluded by the external jugglery. They are quite fearless. Siddhas (God-realized Beings) are not afraid of the world. A tiger or a cobra, when they see such a person, becomes calm, forgetting its ferocity. Similarly, all animals become calm at their sight. Even enemies forget their enmity and become friendly. As soon as they see a Siddha, they become stone-still. What is the cause of this? It is because of their doubting nature. At the sight of a Siddha, there is no darkness. Mind gets purified, realizing the Satwa quality.

Commentary: When your mind remains absorbed in Shiva even as you go about your daily activities, this is known as Samadhi. When this is your state, you become fearless and cannot be deluded by the illusion of Shiva's Maya that is this world-appearance. You become a Siddha and Siddhas are not afraid of this world.

They have no anxiety and no doubt. In this state, you no longer have to cling to life out of fear of death. At the very sight of a Siddha, even evil people become still. This is because their own essential nature of Divinity is reflected back to them through the Siddha's being. At the sight of such a Sadhu, there is no darkness and the mind becomes calm. This is why we say keep the company of the saints, the Siddhas, if you want to go across.

281. All do not feel hungry at the same time and to the same degree. Similarly, all do not attain Mukti at the same time. There is only a difference of time. Men dispute among themselves because of the difference of language. In Hindu-Thani, sugar is called mittha. In other languages it is called sakkare, etc. The use of sugar is the same to all. Although the sugar may be put to different uses, the places where it reaches is only one (mouth).

Instead of believing in thousands of gods, if a man believes only in one God, he can realize what bliss is. Then only is a man content. Those who believe in thousands of gods are never content. So long as you think of two, there is no happiness. So feel happy only in ONE. God is only ONE, never two. Those whose faith is such, see God in themselves. They see all as Self. This is the path to Moksha.

For such a man, there is no enemy. All are his friends. A man should not spoil himself by believing in two. He should attain by believing in one. A man must return

from whence he has come. Knowing the cause and
effect, playing on the external matter, reach the place
from whence you started. This is Moksha. Moksha
does not come in search of us. We should search for
Moksha and enter therein.

What is Moksha? Moksha is freedom of the mind from
actions and standing apart from the internal state.
Moksha is not to be attained by a different outward
path. What is Moksha is not different from one's Self.
We have not striven for Moksha. So, we feel that it is
far off from us. Moksha is not a thing to be attained by
going "here" and by going "there." One should search
within oneself.

The mind should be merged in Buddhi and, by the path
of discrimination, one should enter Mukti. God is the
Indivisible One. Man, because of his doubts, has made
images and called it god, due to ignorance. This doubt
should be removed by the path of discrimination. By
doing so, he must attain Jivanmukti. Bhakti (devotion)
is nothing but love a man manifests towards an object.
A man should believe that thing as great, by which,
because of his faith, he has been much benefited.
This belief should not be relaxed.

There is not a single thing without Bhakti. All animals
have Bhakti. Just as water flows in different directions,
so also, is Bhakti of different types. All animals have a
right for Bhakti. Bhakti is in all objects. Bhakti should
be absolutely pure. Bhakti should be realized in the sky
of Consciousness. Bhakti should be internal and it
should realize the subtle. Then, a man becomes
desireless and sorrowless. This state is eternal Mukti.
Let Mukti be entered into by the path of Sushumna.

Commentary: All beings must, eventually, retrace their
steps back to God. This is inevitable. If you don't perform

Sadhana to become God-realized in this life, you will continue to return, you will continue to take birth and die, until you choose to tread the path back to God. The goal of life is Moksha (Liberation or Deliverance). Some attain it sooner and some later. The difference is only in the time it takes. All will, eventually, be Liberated.

To experience the Bliss of the Absolute, you have to believe in that one God-principle, Shiva-Shakti. Regardless of which "label" you use, whether it is Shiva, Shakti, God, Mohammed, Jesus Christ, Mary Magdalene, Ram, Vishnu, Krishna; believe in the ONE unifying principle of Divine Consciousness. This is the only way to see God inside yourself and in others. This is the only way to attain Moksha. Moksha means returning to the place that you started. It means returning to your primordial state of being. It is the freedom that results from dissolving your mind in the Absolute.

Moksha is attained only by going inside, with self-effort and the Grace of the Guru. If this state of Liberation seems far off for you, it is only because you have not made the effort to attain Moksha in earnest. Moksha cannot be attained by investing yourself in sense pleasures and worldly pleasures. It cannot be attained by gathering possessions. There is only one path to Moksha. That path is an inner path. It is the path where the mind is merged in the purified Buddhi.

This path is not contained in objects of worship or statues of deities. It is not contained in mere rituals or ceremonies. This path to Liberation can be tread inside yourself when you remove all doubt from your mind and cultivate Bhakti (devotion) for the Master and for God. With this Bhakti you make Shiva visible within yourself. Then you become a Jivanmukti, one who is completely Liberated while still alive in the body.

Every living creature has this Bhakti within them. From
animals to insects to human beings, all have Bhakti
internally. It just needs to be cultivated and focused on.
When Bhakti is completely pure, when you love God and
are devoted to the Guru for your own sake, then you
become free from limiting desire and craving and you
attain a state where there is no suffering or sorrow.

This state is the eternal Mukti (complete recognition of the
Absolute). Mukti (moksha) is attained by way of the
Sushumna. When we say believe in one path, in one God,
this is what we mean. The one path to God is the
Sushumna Nadi. When Kundalini rises in this nerve, all
vasanas and samskaras are destroyed. Through this
Sushumna path, the Siddha path, Shakti then merges with
Shiva in the Sahasrar.

**282. The subtle power of Kundalini must be
comprehended by the path of Buddhi. By
discrimination and Shradha, the Prana should be
heated in the Sushumna like boiling milk, and led
towards the Sahasrar in the head. When the Kundalini
crosses the various chakras in the body, our bodily
qualities change. The change of one quality means the
change of one birth.**

**When the Prana is led upwards through the chakras,
peace of mind and forgiveness are acquired. Five
chakras and five houses (Pancha Bhutas) should be
crossed and the sixth chakra should be reached. After
conquering the six qualities, Sat-Chit-Ananda should be
entered into. After enlightening the Ajna Chakra,
Akash (internal) and Agni Mandala should be attained.
Shakti and Shiva should be one, present, past and the
future. The place of these is Bindu. In Bindu is Jnana
fire.**

This should be meditated upon and Prana Linga should be entered into. Let Prana become one with Shiva. Conquer both Yantra and Mantra. Let Buddhi, proceeding through Akash (internal), go to the center of the sky of Consciousness and there be one with the dawn of the Atman. Let the qualities of karma be sacrificed and let Jiva, by the path of pure Akash, become one with Paramatman. Let Jiva take his stand on the top of the Sushumna that is his real home.

Let the feeling of "mine" and "yours" disappear. Let all the qualities of Jiva be unified, and man become a Siddha and be fearless. Knowing the path of the Atman, O Mind, distribute spiritual food to others! Knowing the path of the Atman, O Mind, conquer both birth and death! O Mind! Be free from birth and death! O Mind! Enjoy eternal peace!

When the Buddhi is enlightened, every man comes to know his own defects and merits. Like one's reflection in the mirror, the various desires of the mind will be visible to Buddhi. The gross and the subtle will seem to be separate like the reflection of the sky in clear water. These experiences will be had by those who have realized the Atman. The internal state of man will be like an object sunk in water. In all forms, the One is seen. So be sunk in the water of Jnana.

Let the desires of the mind be washed in the Ganges of the Atman. Thus realize Ananda. Enter Mukti. O Mind! While sitting, lying, sleeping, and walking, be on the path of Mukti and enter it. For Mukti to be attained, no particular time is prescribed. When you are walking in the company of others, let your mind be in the sky of Consciousness. Let the mind with Shraddha drink the nectar of Mukti. Realizing Bhakti and Mukti to be one, become one with Omkar.

Let the ten Indriyas become slaves of Buddhi, like a bird deprived of its wings. Let Prana that is moving in ten directions be made to move in one direction only. Let this be done internally. Let Prana enter Chidakash. Let internal peace be attained. Let Mukti be attained in same-sightedness. Having attained Mukti let them see the whole universe as freed from bondage.

The body is the engine. Knowledge (Jnana) is the steam. Discrimination is the movement. Shraddha is the line. Knowing this, let the train be driven. The driver is the intellect (Buddhi). The digestive system is the boiler. The nerves are the screw. Knowing this, enter the Atman by the subtle path of Buddhi. Attain thou peace. Just as the train moves on rails, so also, discrimination should move on the path of subtle Buddhi.

Commentary: You should become constantly aware of the movement of mother Kundalini as she purifies your being. Cause Kundalini to rise by allowing your individual intellect to become absorbed in the Buddhi, the Divine Intelligence of God. By the recognition of Shiva, and by unwavering Faith, direct your Prana into the Sushumna Nadi and cause it to rise to the Sahasrar. In this way, support the rising Kundalini as she pierces and purifies each of your Chakras (spiritual centers).

On the journey of the Siddha path, all of the 36 Tattvas, from the Pancha Mahabhutas, beginning with Earth up to Shiva, must be crossed. As Kundalini purifies each chakra, the qualities, leanings and tendencies (vasanas and samskaras) are destroyed. With the death of each quality, a future lifetime of birth and death is changed or completely destroyed.

As Kundalini rises on her journey to Sahasrar, peace of mind and the Sattvic qualities of compassion and honor are cultivated. After the rising Kundalini pierces the Ajna Chakra, the Sahasrar should be reached and the experience of the Heart space attained. One should attribute everything to Shiva-Shakti, including the past, present and future. This is the experience of the Vibration of Divine Consciousness called Visarga or Bindu. It is the fire of all Yoga.

One's Meditation should consist of the complete awareness of Prana Shakti (Prana Linga) as it moves in the Sushumna Nadi without taking in any breath from outside. In this way, the Prana becomes one with the Absolute and one rises above the need for ritual and mantra repetition. The mind becomes completely absorbed in Bindu-Nada. This is pure Akash, the experience of Chidakasha.

Let your intellect travel in the Heart space in the head to become one with Shiva. Sacrifice your attachment to objects and sense pleasures in the pure space of Chidakasha and become one with Paramatman. Take your position at the top of the Sushumna Nadi in the Sahasrar. Surrender the false notion of difference and the false notion of "I" and "Mine" and unite your qualities with the Absolute to become a Siddha. Once you have become this fearless saint, teach others and lead them to the same state. Become free of birth and death in this way.

As your individual intellect is purified through Sadhana, you will start to see all of your defects, all of your weaknesses. These become glaringly obvious with spiritual practice. You also begin to see all your strengths and your own purity. In this way, you learn to choose the transcendental aspect of God over His immanent aspect. You learn to choose expansion over contraction and you avoid limitation in order to constantly experience your limitless nature.

In this way, you are able to get better at observing this Play of Divine Consciousness from the "director's seat' and you will start to observe your Divine nature as being separate from and untouched by the illusion of this world-appearance. This will become your strength. Realize the eternal Bliss of the Self in this way. There is no time that is better than another for realizing God. So, do it now. By the instruction of the Master, attain Mukti right now where you are, in whatever activity you find yourself engaged in.

See God everywhere, in everything and everyone and remain absorbed in Shiva-Shakti, even as you go about your mundane activities. With complete Faith let the mind drink the nectar of Self-awareness at all times. If you can realize that Devotion to the Guru and the instruction of the Guru is the path to Liberation, you will merge with God. Of this there is no doubt.

Let the Pithas, the seat of the senses (powers behind the senses) become slaves to your own purified intellect. Make them tools for God's use. Let Prana, which is moving through all the subtle channels that fuel the senses, be redirected into the Sushumna Nadi. Cause Prana to move in this one direction, to the Sahasrar. Do this kind of internal work. In this way, cause Prana to roam in the inner expanse of Divine Consciousness (Chidakasha) where eternal peace and Bliss can be experienced constantly.

The body is the engine. Wisdom (Jnana) is the steam that fuels that engine. Viveka (discrimination), the willingness to choose the transcendental over the immanent, is the movement of the engine. Faith (Shraddha) is the motivation and the purified Buddhi (intellect) is the driver. Let this "train" make its way through the Sushumna to its final destination in the Sahasrar. Attain eternal Peace in this way.

**283. If we look at the rails and the carriages, both
appear to be closely connected. But really the rails and
the wheels are separate. The rails are the gross passage.
The train's motion is caused by the energy of steam.
Similar is the connection between the body and the soul.
It should be shaken by the subtle intelligence and the
eternal peace should be attained. Just as the carriages
of the train are connected by chains, so also, let Jiva and
Paramatma be united. The bodily qualities should be
cut asunder by equal sightedness. Let Jiva attain
Mukti, his eternal home.**

Commentary: Just as the cars of a train are separate from
the rails that the train rides on, so also Spanda Shakti is of a
very different nature than this world-appearance. Her
nature as Shiva Consciousness is unchanged and untainted,
even though she becomes all the objects in this universe.
Just as the train's motion is caused by steam, the activity of
this world-appearance is caused by Chit Shakti.

Shakti should be realized as the energy that gives this
world-appearance life. Attain eternal Peace by purifying
your being with the subtle intelligence (Buddhi) of this
Divine Shakti. Unite your awareness with the
Consciousness of God by taking complete and total refuge
in Shiva. Make all the qualities in your being serve God by
attaining Equality Consciousness. Go and dwell in your
eternal home that is the state of Liberation (Mukti).

**284. Let Meditation, Manas, and Faith be merged into
one. Let the subtle point of light be kindled between the
eyebrows and the union be established. In the Omkar,
let the pure Chitta be firmly fixed, following the path of
subtle Buddhi. Let the Manas become steady being
firmly fixed in Dharana and Samadhi. Let the mind be
one-pointed. To establish Chitta in Akash, there is no
other means than Samadhi. O Jiva! Enter thou Akash!**

To the Jiva who has entered the Akash, there is no separate existence for this world. O Mind! Be quite free from the body idea! To make Chitta firm is very difficult without Sadhana. To those who are ever merged in Samadhi, the body's existence is quite foreign.

To such, the gross and the subtle become separated like the kernel and the shell of the mango seed. To those who always think, "I am not the body," there is no separate Samadhi. They enjoy eternal Samadhi, absolute Samadhi, Shivanatha Samadhi, Manolaya (mind annihilation) Samadhi. To those who are always sunk in the sugar of Jnana, sugar does not exist as a separate thing. Such men are quiet, regardless of the external acts and the external world.

Commentary: With complete Faith in the Guru and in your own spiritual practice, dissolve your mind in Meditation. Meditate and practice the instruction of the Guru so that you can direct Kundalini through Ajna Chakra into the Sahasrar. In this way, merge your individual intellect into Buddhi, the Supreme Intelligence of Shiva-Shakti. Attain Samadhi by dissolving your mind in the Absolute.

Samadhi, the thought-free state, is the only way to enter into Chidakasha. It is the only way to experience Shiva. When you have this experience, sunk in the sweetness of Chidakasha, the world does not exist separate from you. When you maintain this experience, you realize that the entire Universe is contained within your own being. To hold this experience, you have to eliminate the notion that you are the body.

285. The energy of Omkar is like a mine of water. It moves in all directions. It pervades both inside us and outside us in the form of reason. It becomes vibrationless, creating, maintaining, and destroying all.

The vibrationlessness becomes one with reason. Reason becomes merged in Omkar. Omkar becomes one with reason. Omkar becomes one with the world. The world becomes one with Omkar.

The Omkar and the world become one with Akash. Akash becomes one with reason. Reason becomes one with Akash. Reason and Akash become one with Omkar. The imperishable becomes one with reason. The imperishable and Jnana become one with reason. Reason becomes one with Atman. Atman becomes one with reason. Form discrimination becomes one with Atman through the path of Buddhi. The cause and effect juice of Yoga. The juice of Yoga transforms every quality of the body, directing it upwards.

O Mind! By the upward path, pervade all those qualities of the body. Shake off all doubts from all parts of the body by bathing in the Ganges of Shiva. Let Shiva and Shakti be one with Omkar. See, with the third eye, the forms and qualities of the world. Let the doubts of the mind be reduced to ashes. Let the six enemies of the body be burnt to ashes. Let the body be smeared with these ashes. Thus enter thou Shiva by the help of the third eye.

Be thou Shiva and Shiva, thou. Let the difference between thee and Shiva be sacrificed in the midst of the five fires of the five senses. Let all doubts be heartily sacrificed in these fires, O Jiva! Perform penance by sacrificing all thy qualities Satwa, Rajas, and Tamas. By the disinterested path, drink the nectar every moment. Drink that nectar without doubts. When thou hast realized the truth, thou hast no fear of death.

After realizing the truth, "I" and "mine" are as if they are dead. The fear of death is dead forever. What is called the feeling of "I" and "mine" is nothing but the fear of death. This is an obstruction to the path of God-realization. When the truth is realized, death becomes an external condition just as thou sleepest, forgetting the external world. This is not different from what is called the internal life. Then the senses are turned inward and, when they move internally, "I" and "mine" become atomic and become merged in the highest.

When the Jiva suddenly awakens from sleep and becomes aware of the external, then only he realizes the nature of sleep. This is the state of Jnana. The cause of birth and death is desire. By this desire, the shadow appears as reality. This desire is under man's control. Those who have the power of discrimination, have no fear of birth and death. Since mind is controlled by desire, you give room to enjoyment and difficulties. If the desire is subdued by man, he is no longer under the sway of Pleasure and Pain.

Because mind is subdued by desire, man requires external help to satisfy his desires. When a man becomes a slave to certain habits, this is the cause of lower birth. All habits must be under the control of man. A man must be indifferent to habits. For this you want a firm will. The work depending on fancy is not permanent. The work done by the power of discrimination lasts till the body lasts.

Sankalpa is not always permanent. Sankalpa is far inferior to Buddhi. Sankalpa is like the little finger. Buddhi is like the middle finger. Vasana is the great love for a certain thing. This Vasana is the cause of birth. Vasanas, which are related to the body, come and go now and then. Like bubbles which appear and disappear in water. Body is all nature. Because of the great love for a special thing, which is called Vasana, we have to take another birth.

Juice of Yoga. The juice of Yoga transforms every quality of the body, directing it upwards. O Mind! By the upward path, pervade all those qualities of the body. The Vasana has a special form. That form reflects the internal. It appears in the form of a body in a special family. The man having such a Vasana, whatever work he may be engaged in, his body only is working. His Vasana stands apart and there a body is created according to the Vasana. It is impossible for the body to satisfy the Vasana.

Hence, the body suffers from some disease, and the outgoing Prana, after death, assumes a particular body. This body is gone and a fresh body is generated. The birth is for the fulfillment of that special Vasana. The birth is of the same nature as the Vasana. For instance, when one is walking, can he lift up both feet at the same time from the earth? Lifting up the feet alternately, one must walk. Similarly is the Vasana of former birth.

Commentary: The energy of Omkar is the Chiti of the Absolute that pervades the entire Universe of forms and all other realms seen and unseen. This Shakti of Shiva is contained inside each of us and outside everywhere. Although completely still and pure, Shakti is responsible for all the vibrations of the Universe; creating, sustaining and withdrawing the Universe at will. It is this Chiti that takes the very form of the individual intellect known as reason.

When Omkar becomes one with the individual intellect, you realize that you yourself pervade this world-appearance and are one with it. When the individual intellect is purified, this reason merges in Buddhi, the Divine Will and Supreme Intelligence of Shiva that is the Heart space of Chidakasha. This Buddhi is Shakti in its' purest form. Once enlightened, a Siddha experiences that all the forms and experiences of this Universe merge inside his own being and become one with this Chiti. Then he realizes that this entire world-appearance exists in his own imagination and that the only Reality is Shiva-Shakti.

Liberation comes to those who perform Sadhana. The practice of Yoga, under the leadership of a living Master, is this Sadhana. Sadhana, which begins with Shaktipat, transforms every quality of one's being and makes those qualities tools of God's Will. O Mind! By the upward path to Shiva, purify all the qualities that exist in the body. Destroy all fears and doubts by resting in the abode of Shiva in the Sahasrar, O mind. By spiritual practice, reduce craving, desire, doubts, fears and worries to ashes. Let the six enemies be burnt to ashes in the fire of your Sadhana.

Let your sense of separateness from Shiva be destroyed by depositing all expectations of sense pleasures at the feet of Shiva, where they will be burned to ashes. Let the body be smeared with these ashes, just as the body of Shiva is smeared with the ashes of the impurities of all His disciples. In this way, enter into Shiva by crossing the Ajna Chakra with the Blessing of the Guru. Sacrifice the three Gunas to Shiva and become free from attachment to this world-appearance.

When you realize God, you will have no fear of death. After becoming Liberated, you will have no sense of difference or diversity. You will not get caught up in the notions of "I" and "Mine" and "You" and "Yours." These notions are the act of clinging to life out of fear of death. They are an obstruction to God-realization and must be removed. When you realize Shiva, you will experience that death is only the death of the illusion that a world and a universe actually exist. You will realize that Shiva is this world, this world is Shiva and you are Shiva also.

You will understand, in this way, that you have no beginning and no end. Once you realize that the world does not exist separate from you, you will experience your own death in Meditation, and then you will realize that death does not exist either. The notion of death only exists because you have woken from the sleep of the Atman, which is your own deep sleep. Because you rise from deep sleep each day, you have come to believe that there is such a thing called death. In truth, "death" is nothing but the deep sleep of Yoga (yoga nidra).

This "death" is merely your withdrawal from this illusory world-appearance. The cause of the belief of birth and death is attachment to and desire for the illusion of this world-appearance. Just as, when you let go of your desire for an object, that object no longer exists for you, yet you continue to exist; in the same way, when you let go of the object known as "world," it no longer exists for you, yet you continue to be.

The truth is you create your own heaven and hell by entertaining desire for this and that. Therefore, desire is under your full control. But you are deluded by your own powers because you have forgotten your true nature as Shiva. In this way, you place yourself under the sway of pleasure and pain and become a slave to this pair of opposites. This becomes the cause of your death and rebirth.

The only means to break this vicious cycle is by the power of Grace and that Grace comes from a Master. It is the power of Viveka (discrimination) that allows you to be aware of what is real and what is not. Individual will (sankalpa) is inferior to Divine Will (Buddhi). What is manifested by sankalpa is not always permanent. Therefore, it is best to direct your sankalpa to Shiva and merge it in Shiva-Shakti. Not to do so is to create more Vasanas for yourself.

Vasanas are latent impressions caused by attachment to objects (people, places and things). A single Vasana can cause another birth. These Vasanas are the reason you are caught up in the cycle of birth and death and the cycle of pain and pleasure. Only through Sadhana can they be destroyed. O Mind! By the upward path, through the Sushumna Nadi, merge with Shiva and destroy these Vasanas! Now. The thing to remember about Vasanas is that they create the Prarabdha Karma, the karma that cannot be destroyed and must be suffered. This is why the body does not have the capacity to completely fulfill all Vasanas in one lifetime. It is not possible. The Prarabdha is the reason you take another birth.

So, for a particular Vasana, there is another cycle of birth and death. These Vasanas can only be fulfilled one at a time, just like you can only put one foot in front of the other when walking. So, in this way, many karmas are created by way of these Vasanas. This is why you continue to be trapped in the vortex of Samsara. The way out is to burn these Vasanas in the inner fire of Yoga. There is no other way.

A great general who commands the King's armies can choose to leave the kingdom to start his own army. But, because all the soldiers in the kingdom belong to the King and are loyal to that King, it would be difficult for that general to convince those soldiers to join him, especially when all that he has to offer them belongs to the King. Now, this general, with great difficulty, may succeed in convincing some of those soldiers to join him outside the kingdom. But he will never command the powerful army he commanded when he served the King.

So, align yourself with That King known as Shiva-Shakti. Align your comings and goings with His Divine Will so that you can command the army, The Wheel of Energies that is His and that is the power of His Kingdom. Return to the Kingdom from whence you came and remain there in His power, in His glory.

286. Desireless Bhakti is not for the enjoyment of worldly happiness. This Bhakti is not related to nature. This Bhakti is not for getting rid of any difficulties. There is no relation whatsoever between this Bhakti and difficulty. No one should shrink back from the path of this Bhakti. He should proceed on the path of this Bhakti. Just as the big lizard (in a fort) embraces the fort wall very firmly and never leaves it, so also, desireless Bhakti should firmly embrace the heart lotus with steadfast faith.

Bhakti by the path of skill (Yukti) should be one with Shakti. Let, by such a Bhakti, the heart be purified of all its Upadhis (latent tendencies). Let such a Bhakti become absolutely free from desire. Let this desirelessness become the strongest. Let the senses become quiet. Let his Bhakti become unwavering in that Giver of Peace. This is real Bhakti. This is eternal peace. This is the Self-luminous. This is what is called Sat.

This Bhakti is beyond both this world and the next. This is nothing but the mind filled with eternal Ananda. The mind filled with eternal Ananda is the seed of all things. The mind filled with eternal Ananda is the subtle seed of all things. Let this be developed with discrimination. The mind filled with eternal Ananda is that without qualities. It is the diseaseless. It is the Universal reason. It is called the Creator. It is the witness of all. It is the one Sat for this world and the next.

It is the One, pervading in and out. It is the Knowledge, higher and lower, (Jnana and Vijnana). It is the one Cause and Effect. It is the Universal Witness. It is the

Sinless Atman. Witness of All, it is the Universal Guru. It is the Universal Light. It is the Universal Father and Mother. It is the Bindu in Omkar. It is MA, A, E, OM the Great. Movable and the Seen, OM the Essence. It is what is declared by the sages as The Truth. OM. OM.

RECOMMENDED FURTHER READING

The Verses On Witness Consciousness by Sadguru Kedarji
https://www.nityanandashaktipatyoga.org/books-on-meditation-the-verses-on-witness-consciousness/

Vibration of Divine Consciousness. A Spiritual Autobiography – by Sadguru Kedarji
https://www.nityanandashaktipatyoga.org/books-on-self-realization-vibration-of-divine-consciousness/

Websites

BhagawanNityananda.org
NityanandaShaktipatYoga.org

For more information about Shaktipat Blessing Retreats and mini courses in the U.S.A., or to buy books and meditation aides:

NityanandaShaktipatYoga.org
info@nityanandashaktipatyoga.org
330-623-7388 Ext. 10

GLOSSARY

Āchārya – Literally means "great teacher." An Āchārya is a Siddha Guru. Āchārya is also a reference to the line of Sanyāsīns (monks) in the lineage of Śrī Śankarachārya.

Ānava Mala – The first taint or impurity. Ānava Mala is that which causes you to feel separate from God and to feel impure and a sinner.

Āshram – Place of rest; Gurukula or school of the Guru; the place where a Guru and his/her disciples live.

Bhagawān – Lord; also one who is Divine, venerable, glorious.

Bhajans – Devotional songs; hymns.

Bhaktī Yoga – The Yoga based on intense Love and Devotion for God and the Guru; Surrender to God's will; The burning longing to be free.

Bhandara – Blessed food usually served during a major spiritual celebration and given away for free.

Ganeshpurī – The village in Mahārastra India in which Bhagawān Nityānanda lived for many years doing his work, and where he later took Mahāsamādhī; This is a place where many Siddhas have lived and performed their spiritual practice.

Guru – Literally means from darkness into the light; spiritual preceptor or Master; God-realized being.

Jñāna – Direct inner knowledge of the Absolute that rises spontaneously from within by the Grace of the Guru.

Jñānī - One who is filled with Jñāna.

Karma – Action or activity; Action or work that is
associated with the limitation of the ego; Doership;
attachment to objects of sense that creates pain, pleasure,
suffering and future lifetimes.

Karma Mala – The taint or impurity that causes you to
believe that you are just the body, the mind, the senses and
the ego, and that you have the right to appropriate people,
places and things to yourself; The ego sense; doership of
action.

Karma Yoga – The spiritual path in which all work and all
action is undertaken as selfless service to others and to
God; The path in which all thoughts and works are offered
as a blessed sacrament to the Lord; Guruseva.

Kurukṣetra – The land adjoining Samantapanchaka where
the great battle of the Mahābhārata between the Pandavā
and the Kauravā took place.

Lord Ananta – The Endless One; Another name for
Nityānanda, the eternal Bliss of the Absolute.

Lord Rāma – The hero of the great epic Ramāyana;
Disciple of the sage Vāśiṣtha; A saint of the Siddha path
who slew the demon King Rāvana.

Lord Kriṣṇa – A great saint of the Siddha path and one of
the incarnations of Lord Viṣṇū; The Guru of the Pandavā;
Arjuna's Guru and the author of the Bhagavad Gītā.

Māyā – Illusion; to measure out; the illusory power of
Lord Śiva that contracts to become the objects of this world
appearance; that which creates an appearance of duality
and diversity.

Māyīya Mala – The taint or impurity that causes you to feel
separate from other people, places and things; That which
causes you to feel different, greater or poorer than others;

the cause of the perception of diversity or uniqueness.

Mīra (also Mīrabai) – The princess of Chitore born into a family of Kśatrias who worshiped Durgā; Lover and worshipper of Lord Krisna who was severely punished by her family for worshipping Krisna.

Muktī – Liberation from the ignorance that causes death and rebirth; God-realization.

Mutt – A small Āshram or center where people go to perform Sādhanā under the guidance of a Siddha Guru.

Navarātrī – The spiritual celebration that precedes Diwalī (the Indian New Year) in which the Goddess Durgā is celebrated; The celebration of the warrior aspect or the aspect of courage in the human spirit.

Paramātma – The formless Absolute.

Prāṇāyāma – The retention of Prāṇā inside the Suśumnā Nadi.

Rājas – The second of the three Gunas; That which causes compulsion and doership; Action or the achievement of goals that is attributed to the mind, body, senses and the ego.

Sat Cit Ananda – Existence (Being), Consciousness (Awareness) and Bliss; The Absolute and the qualities reflected in it.

Siddha – A perfected being or liberated sage who experiences God in everything and everyone, everywhere at all times; A God-realized being.

Siddhāchārya – A Siddha who teaches and leads others to the attainment of his/her own state of Liberation; A great teacher of Mahā Yoga or Siddha Yoga.

Sāttva – The first of the three Gunas; The tendency or leaning to righteousness, moral and ethical conduct, justice and the longing to know God.

Tāmas – The third of the three Gunas; The tendency to dullness, darkness, evil and unethical behavior, procrastination and the sabotage of Grace.

Vajreṣwarī – A village next to Ganeshpurī near the river Tejas where the renown Devī temple (temple to the Goddesses Lakshmi, Durgā and Saraswati) is located; The village in which Sītarām Shenoy built his hotel and maintained a gymnasium in which he also housed traveling monks and youth looking for work.